THE
Baseball ◇30◇ Research
JOURNAL

This is my last project as SABR's Publications Director. I want to take this opportunity to thank SABR for entrusting me for nearly a decade with a position that many of my friends felt was the best in the world. (I never agreed—shortstop for the Red Sox is the best position in the world.) Being SABR's PD gave me a chance to meet hundreds of wonderful people who are part of the great SABR network, and to make many good friends. Thank you. Thank you all. I look forward to hearing greater and greater things about SABR and SABR publications.

—*Mark Alvarez*

Editor: Mark Alvarez
Designated Reader: Dick Thompson
Copy Editor: A.D. Suehsdorf

THE BASEBALL RESEARCH JOURNAL (ISSN 0734-6891, ISBN 0-910137-87-0), Number 30. Published by The Society for American Baseball Research, Inc. P.O. Box 93183, Cleveland, OH, 44101. Postage paid at Birmingham, AL. Copyright 2001 by The Society for American Baseball Research, Inc. All rights reserved. Reproduction in whole or in part without written permission is prohibited. Printed by EBSCO Media, Birmingham, AL.

The Society for American Baseball Research

History

The Society for American Baseball Research (SABR) was founded on August 10, 1971, by L. Robert "Bob" Davids and fifteen other baseball researchers at Cooperstown, New York, and now boasts more than 6,900 members worldwide. Among the Society's objectives are:

- to foster the study of baseball as a significant American institution,
- to establish an accurate historical account of baseball through the years,
- to facilitate the dissemination of baseball research information,
- to stimulate the best interest of baseball as our national pastime

Baseball Research Journal

The Society published its first annual *Baseball Research Journal* in January 1972. The present volume is the twenty-ninth. Most of the previous volumes are still available for purchase (see inside back cover). The editorial policy is to publish a cross section of research articles by our members which reflect their interest in history, biography, statistics and other aspects of baseball not previously published.

Interested in Joining the Society?

SABR membership is open to all those interested in baseball research, statistics or history. The 2002 membership dues are $50 US, $60 Canada & Mexico and $65 overseas (US funds only) and are based on the calendar year. Members receive the *Baseball Research Journal*, *The National Pastime*, *The SABR Bulletin*, and other special publications. Senior, Student and family options are available. To join SABR, mail the form (or a photocopy) below to SABR, 812 Huron Rd E #719, Cleveland OH 44115 or visit www.sabr.org.

SABR Membership Form: 2002

Name: _____

Address: _____

_____

Home Phone: _____

E-Mail/Fax: _____

Birthdate: _____ Application Date: _____

__ How I Found Out About SABR
__ SABR member who referred me
__ Gift from:

_____
Mail to: SABR, 812 Huron Rd E #719, Cleveland OH 44114
Photocopies Acceptable

2002 Annual Dues:	US	Canada/Mexico	Overseas
	$50	$60 US$	$65 US$
Three-Year	$140	$170 US$	$185 US$
Students	$30	$40 US$	$45 US$
Seniors	$30	$40 US$	$45 US$

Family Membership: Additional family members living at the same address may join SABR for $15 per year per person. Family membership entitles one to full member benefits except the publications. One set of publications will be sent to each household

Students are under 18 years of age or full-time college student (Copy of college ID required).
Seniors are 65 years or older
SABR membership is based on the calendar year.

Will you allow SABR to sell your name to baseball-related companies who rent SABR's mailing list? YES NO
Are you interested in regional meetings? YES NO
Are you willing to research? YES NO

Areas of Interest:
1. Minor Leagues
2. Negro Leagues
3. Baseball Records
4. Biographical Research
5. Statistical Analysis
6. Ballparks
7. Hall of Fame
8. 19th Century
9. Socio-Economic Aspects
10. Bibliography
11. Book Collecting
12. Collegiate Baseball
13. Latin America
14. Umpire/Rules
15. Dead Ball Era
16. Women in Baseball
17. Oral History
18. Baseball Education
19. Scouts
20. Pictorial History
21. Baseball Music and Poetry
Other: _____

Baseball's Greatest Hero

*The President of the United States
in the name of The Congress
takes pleasure in presenting
the Medal of Honor
to John Joseph Pinder, Jr.*

Dick Thompson

The time was shortly after 7 AM. The place was a stretch of seashore on the Normandy coast of France designated Omaha Beach. The date was June 6, 1944. Less than sixty minutes had passed since H-Hour, when the first wave of men from the 16th Infantry Regiment of the 1st Infantry Division, the only first-wave assault unit on D-Day with combat experience, hit the beach.[1] A landing craft containing the 16th's Regimental Headquarters Company was headed for the Easy Red sector of the beach. Among the men in the boat was Technician 5th Grade Joe Pinder.

Pinder had enlisted right after Pearl Harbor. He had seen action in North Africa and Italy and had been awarded the Combat Infantryman Badge on March 24, 1944.[2] Joe Pinder was also a veteran of six minor league baseball seasons. A righthanded pitcher from the Pittsburgh area, he had worked in the Cleveland Indians, New York Yankees, Washington Senators, and Brooklyn Dodgers farm systems. Pinder had notched 17 pitching victories in 1941 but his goal of reaching the major leagues had been put on hold. There was a bigger task at hand.

Omaha Beach was quickly turning into a disaster. Launched from landing barges still out at sea and de-

signed to swim to shore under their own power, all but five of the thirty-two amphibious tanks expected to provide support for infantry in 1st Division areas sank in the heavy surf.[3] Naval fire support had also ceased so as not to hit American troops landing on the beach. Navy gunners waited anxiously for target coordinates to be radioed from their fire-control officers who had gone ashore with the initial infantry wave, but those that did make it to the beach no longer had working radios.[4] Historian Stephen E. Ambrose wrote, "The 16th Regiment first and second waves D-Day was more reminiscent of an infantry charge across no-man's land at the Somme in World War I than a typical World War II action."[5] Cornelius Ryan, author of *The Longest Day*, wrote:

> They came ashore on Omaha Beach, the slogging, unglamorous men that no one envied. No battle ensigns flew for them, no horns or bugles sounded. But they had history on their side. They came from regiments that had bivouacked at places like Valley Forge, Stoney Creek, Antietam, that had fought in the Argonne. They had crossed the beaches of North Africa, Sicily and Salerno. Now they had one more beach to cross. They would call this one "Bloody Omaha."[6]

A German artillery shell exploded just a few feet from Pinder's landing craft, shrapnel punching several large holes in the boat's hull. As the helmsman fought

Dick Thompson *wrote about Wes Ferrell in* The National Pastime *earlier this year. He wishes to thank the following people for their help with this article: LTC Steven Clay and LTC (Ret.) Herbert Payne of the 16th Infantry Regiment Association; Ellen Roberts of the Butler, Pa., Chamber of Commerce and Sarah Zavadsky of the Butler County Historical Society; Andrew Woods of the First Division Museum; and the staff of the Bridgewater, Mass., Public Library. Also the following SABR members: Dick Beverage, Kit Crissey, Alan Denman, Scott Flatow, Jerry Jackson, David Nemec, Ray Nemec, Denis Repp, and Ron Selter.*

to control the craft, it started to fill with water.[7] The ramp dropped to disembark the men, still 100 yards from the beach. They immediately began taking machine gun fire from the enemy gun installations on the cliffs above the shoreline. Confusion reigned as the men broke for the beach. Some were killed outright, others stopped to help the wounded. Much of the vitally important radio equipment remained in the boat as the men scattered in the carnage. In his 1994 article, "D-Day Plus 50 Years," General Gordon R. Sullivan, then Chief of Staff of the United States Army, wrote:

> In a time before transistors and microprocessors, radios capable of reliable shore-to-ship communications bulked out at 86 pounds, roughly the weight, size and shape of a modern window air conditioner. Getting one of these beasts ashore under pleasant conditions would challenge an Olympian. Wrestling a radio through the tortured surf of Omaha Beach bordered on the impossible.[8]

General Sullivan devoted a full page of his story to Pinder.

> Pinder shouldered one of the big radio systems and staggered forward out of the tilted, smashed landing craft. Head bowed, deliberately putting one water-logged leg in front of the other, he pushed through 100 yards of bullet-torn waves. A German bullet clipped him, and he stumbled. But he rose again, a little unsteady, and kept going. He made it to the pile of stones where his soaked partners lay gasping for breath.[9]

Pinder sustained several wounds. Second Lieutenant Leeward Stockwell said, "Almost immediately on hitting the waist-deep water he was hit by shrapnel. He was hit several times and the worst wound was the left side of his face. Holding the flesh with one hand he carried the set to shore."[10]

> That trip alone was beyond the power of most people. But Technician 5th Grade Pinder knew that one radio would not be enough in this firestorm. He turned back, heading into the deadly waters.
>
> Once again, his comrades marveled as he waded out to the half-sunken landing craft to retrieve a backup radio set and some other

items. He managed to get the second load ashore without incident, weaving slowly around rusty obstacles, through geysers and long strings of machine-gun bullets.[11]

Pinder's company commander, Captain Stephen Ralph, said, "He knew the equipment was sorely needed. Three times he made trips into the water and each time drew a deadly hail of fire from the cliffs above. He knew he was critically wounded."[12] Pinder made it back to the landing craft a third time to pick up spare parts and code books.

> As he started back, a German machine gunner found the range. Bracketed by water spouts that showed the path of the bullets, Pinder sped up. But his luck ran out. A burst caught him full on and ripped open his side. He fell, somehow got up, and struggled to the beach, and his radios. His fellow communicators took his burden and turned to help him, but Technician 5th Grade Pinder waved them off. He would be all right. Rather than seek a medic, he looked to his radio sets. Pinder seemed fixated on getting them operational. The radioman was still fiddling with the devices when he passed out from loss of blood. He died later that morning. But his embattled regiment had found its electronic voice.[13]

Early life—John Joseph Pinder, Jr., was born on June 6, 1912, in McKees Rock, Pennsylvania, the oldest of John and Laura Pinder's three children. John Pinder, Sr., worked in the steel mills and the family moved around Pennsylvania, living in McKees Rock 1912-1925, Vanport and Coraopolis until 1929, and Butler from 1929 until the family moved to Burgettstown in 1939. Two other Pinder children, Martha and Harold, were born in 1915 and 1922. Martha died in 1996. Harold, who still lives in Pittsburgh, provided much of the information for this article.

Joe Pinder graduated from Butler High School in 1931. His high school yearbook, *The Senior Magnet*, included a western short story, "On the Road to the Bar X," that Joe wrote. The yearbook referred to Pinder as John and Johnny, but his brother Harold says that everyone called him Joe.

Pinder spent the next several years pitching semi-pro baseball in the greater Pittsburgh area. The Depression was in full swing and minor league jobs, like work in general, were scarce.

Joe's professional debut came late in the 1935 season for his hometown club, the Butler Indians of the Class D Pennsylvania State Association, then the lowest rung of the Cleveland Indians farm chain. Joe was unimpressive in his first game, so nervous that he "couldn't get his fast ball over and his curve swept wide of the plate."[14] Several days later he turned in an excellent mound performance, limiting his opponents to three hits over seven innings. Pinder appeared in eight league games in 1935, turning in a 3-2 won-lost record with 29 walks and 35 strikeouts in 46 innings of work, and Butler reserved his contract for 1936. At least two of Joe's teammates, Mike McCormick and Oscar Grimes, eventually made their way to the major leagues.

Cleveland dropped their sponsorship of the Butler team over the winter and the New York Yankees began what would be a long working relationship with Butler. In 1947, his rookie season in professional ball, Whitey Ford played for the Butler Yankees, then in the Class C Middle Atlantic League.

Joe's time on the Yankees payroll was short. He appeared in only a few games for Butler in 1936 before being released in late May.

Before the release, Butler played exhibition games with the Homestead Grays and the Pittsburgh Crawfords. Pinder drew a start against the Crawfords, whose batting order included Hall of Famers Cool Papa Bell, Judy Johnson, Josh Gibson, and Oscar Charleston. The Crawfords, possibly the greatest Negro League team ever assembled, had little trouble with the Class D club and waltzed their way to an 11-3 win. Pinder gave up just three hits in his three innings but his teammates booted routine plays and he allowed six runs. Joe retired Gibson both times he faced him, once on a fly to center and then on a routine grounder to the shortstop. Bell was 0-for-1 with a walk, Charleston flied out and singled, and Johnson doubled and walked.

Hard luck—Joe played semipro ball for the remainder of 1936 and all of 1937. He tried out with the Washington Senators' Class D Sanford Lookouts in the Florida State League in 1938 and made the team. The Lookouts finished last with a 53-87 record, 34-1/2 games out of first place. Pinder turned in nine wins and 18 losses, completing 16 of his 29 starts. His ERA was 4.04 and his strikeout to walk ratio was dead even, 155 passes and 156 strikeouts in 234 innings pitched. On June 23, 1938, the Sanford *Herald* wrote:

> The hardest luck pitcher in the Florida State League or any other league is none other than Joseph Pinder, youth from Butler, Penn., who has lost 12 games this season and won only two. Pinder has gained a considerable amount of control and has picked up on his pitching in general during the last month or so regardless of the fact he has lost the last 10 games in a row. Each time Pinder walks on the hill his mates make up their minds to win one, and they have come so close that it would be impossible for anything else to happen other than someone dropping dead. Pinder hurled 15 innings against DeLand and lost. Tuesday night he hurled a beautiful game and lost 3 to 2. In Gainesville the other evening he held them scoreless and in the fifth inning had to retire due to a sudden ailment in his right arm. So Pinder is still working hard and one of these days we are going to see him walk off the mound with that victory under his belt.

Pinder's luck, and his pitching, improved dramatically after that point in the season. He tossed one-hitters versus St. Augustine on June 30 and the DeLand Reds on July 29. Wildness continued to be his main problem. He beat DeLand on August 10, 11-1, allowing five hits but passing eleven batters. On July 9, 1938, this article appeared in the Sanford *Herald*:

> One of the most promising rookies on the Lookouts squad this season is John Joseph Pinder, ace right-handed pitcher who nearly entered the hall of fame last week when he hurled a one-hitter against the St. Augustine Saints...
> Pinder was the workhorse of the Lookouts hurling corps earlier in the season, starting games and also doing a bit of relief work. At the present, however, Joe has become a regular starter and gets his four days rest between hurling duties.
> Pinder has a lot of stuff and his curve ball is dreaded by the other clubs in the league. His fast ball comes in very handy after he slips a curve ball by and it hops and travels with more speed than one of an average hurler. The youngster has the stamina and courage to make a big leaguer some day and he takes his work very seriously.

Pinder was retained by Sanford for 1939. Former

American League batting champion Dale Alexander came down from the Chattanooga Lookouts to manage Sanford, and the team responded to his leadership by copping the league pennant with a 98-35 record. The team's strength was its pitching staff which consisted of Sid Hudson (24-4), Cleo Jeter (22-9), J. Harry Dean (21-4), and Pinder (17-7). Hudson won the league's triple crown of pitching, leading in strikeouts (192) and ERA (1.79) as well as wins, and when the season was over the Washington Senators purchased the contracts of both Hudson and Dean. Pinder tossed 211 innings in 35 games. His ERA was 3.94 and he again walked as many batters (115) as he fanned (117). Hudson was Pinder's teammate in 1938 and 1939. He compiled a major league won-lost record of 104-152 over twelve seasons, then became a successful big league pitching coach. Today, at age 85, he resides in Waco, Texas. On Veterans Day, November 11, 2000, Hudson wrote to the author:

In 1938 Joe Pinder and I were room mates in spring training at Sanford, Florida—at the hotel there.

We got to know each other quite well, but, of course, most of our talk was about baseball-trying to learn different pitches from each other.

He was a very nice fellow, and a real gentleman.

We had a four-man starting pitcher staff and he was one of them. We four pitchers won 84 games that year—winning the pennant.

As well as I remember, he had a good curve ball, and change, and an average fast ball. I suppose his only problem was his control, at times.

I certainly feel honored to have been associated with him in baseball.

One other member of the 1939 Sanford club, Hillis Layne, went on to the majors. Layne compiled a minor league batting average of .335 over a career that ran 1938-1958, and he won the 1947 Pacific Coast League batting crown. His major league career consisted of 107 games, all with Washington, in the 1940s. While Hudson knew that Pinder had been killed in the war, Layne didn't. On July 30, 2000, he wrote to the author:

Thanks for your letter as it brings back memories of perhaps my most enjoyable year

in baseball. As one who played Class D-C-B-AA-AAA and the major leagues, the Sanford team of 1939 could hold its own with many of the teams I played with. This club was called the best Class D club that was ever assembled. The club had five pitchers with outstanding ability and all could pitch with any club today. Hudson, Pinder, Jeter, Dean and Al Nixon.

I especially remember Joe Pinder, a stocky built right hander. A real competitor with a live fast ball and good curve. As a teammate of Joe's, I can see why Congress presented him with the Medal of Honor. Aside from being a fine ball player he was a great person and a good friend.

I have wondered what happened to Joe since we played at Sanford and although I am sorry he is gone, it makes me proud of what he did in the service of our great country.

Oddly, Washington had two minor league teams in the Florida State League in 1939, and on July 10, Pinder faced an Orlando Senators lineup that included former University of Michigan football and track star Elmer Gedeon. Gedeon appeared briefly in September that year for Washington and, like Pinder, would be killed in action during the war.[15] Pinder began this third year with Sanford in 1940. The team had changed its name from the Lookouts to the Seminoles, and Alexander, Hudson, and Layne had all moved on. Stan Musial played for Daytona Beach in the Florida State League in 1940. Sanford and Daytona Beach met three times in late April and early May but Pinder and Musial never appeared in the same game. On May 14, 1940, the Sanford *Herald* wrote:

Joe Pinder, for two years one of the mainstays of the Sanford pitching staff, yesterday joined the hurling corps of the Macon Peaches, Manager Whitey Campbell announced as he released the information to the public that he had permitted Joe to leave the Seminole staff to better himself.

Campbell said he was sorry to see Pinder go but that if he had an opportunity to rise, he did not want to see him held back.

Macon was in the Class B South Atlantic League, and Joe's short time there would be his highest level of professional competition. A Brooklyn Dodgers farm team, Macon was managed by former major leaguer Milt Stock. The team's star player was Stock's son-in-law, Eddie Stanky.[16] Pinder won a game and lost a game for Macon. On June 11, 1940, the Fort Pierce *News-Tribune* announced that the Fort Pierce Bombers of the Class D Florida East Coast League had secured Joe from Macon. Fort Pierce finished the season in fifth place and Pinder turned in just 4 wins against 12 losses. His earned run average, a nifty 2.91, was indicative of his luck that year. Joe arrived in Fort Pierce the next January, hoping to get a jump on the 1941 baseball season. On February 2, the *News-Tribune* wrote:

Joe Pinder, the stocky, square-set little Pennsylvanian with the blinding fast ball, is back in town and is ready for the Fort Pierce Bombers 1941 baseball season.

This quiet, amiable and almost shy person, who had some of the toughest luck last season besides a disastrous record of four wins and 12 losses, has spent the fall and winter months in Pennsylvania with his parents where he worked like the dickens and hunted plenty. Joe registered for the selective service while there. Being outdoors most of the time and quite frequently on the pivot end of an axe, Jo-Jo is in tip top condition.

Pinder thinks 1941 will be his greatest year in professional ball and believes Fort Pierce will be high up in the league race. His ambition is to become a major league player and

Joe Pinder in 1939 or 1940.

Sanford Herald

without any flowery ado he will tell you that his whole life is based on reaching the top in pro ball...

A little more about Joe: He hails from Burgettstown, Pa. and went to high school there, later attended Pennsylvania State College for one year. Not much of an athlete during his high school days, he stuck to books and don't think he isn't smart. However, when 18 years of age, he was clocked at 10 seconds for a 100 yard run—which shows his speed on the local diamond last summer was no flash in the pan.

Joe, despite his bad season, was considered one of the most promising moundsmen Fort Pierce had last summer. The 24-year-old hurler will go places this year if the breaks are 50-50.

Shaving a few years off one's age is a time-honored tradition in baseball, and at the time this article was written Pinder was 28 years old, not 24. Another biographical sketch on Pinder that appeared later in the season gave his birth year as 1917.[17]

Pinder won 11 games and lost nine with Fort Pierce in a little more than half a season. At the beginning of July, Joe's contract was optioned to the Greenville Lions of the Alabama State League, another Class D organization. The Greenville manager, former St. Louis Browns pitcher Ernie Wingard, was fired due to the team's horrible 17-47 record, and Herb Thomas, a native Floridian who had played with the Boston Braves and the New York Giants, was brought in as Wingard's replacement. Thomas had managed the Fort Lauderdale team in the Florida East Coast League in 1940 and early 1941 and, being familiar with Pinder's ability, arranged for his transfer.

The Lions went 28-25 after Thomas took over, and Joe's 6-2 record in just over a month with the team played a vital part.

> Joe Pinder has taken part in seven games, winning four and losing one, since he joined the Lions two weeks ago. Had the locals been able to secure him two weeks earlier, the Lions would almost have been assured a place in the play-offs. As it is they are making a strong, though belated, bid for a first division berth—with only three bona fide hurlers on the squad.[18]

Pinder made an "iron man" attempt on August 18 and started both games of a doubleheader. He tossed a shutout in the opener and received a no-decision in the second game. Joe's last professional game came on August 28, 1941.

> Joe Pinder mastered the Tallassee Indians here Thursday night with a 6-hit pitching effort, and his teammates backed him with a 12-hit assault on two visiting hurlers, to tally a 7-1 triumph.
> Except for a much discussed play in the seventh, the little Lion right-hander would probably have scored a shutout.[19]

Joe's final tally in 1941 was 17 wins and 11 losses with a 2.93 earned run average. He struck out 136 batters and walked 125. His contract was still owned by Fort Pierce, but as the team departed for the winter, Joe told the Greenville *Advocate* than he hoped to secure his release and return to Greenville for the 1942 season. He had no way of knowing it at the time, but his professional baseball career was over. His dream of reaching the major leagues would never be realized.

Battlefield—The following information was taken from the history of the 16th Infantry Regiment Association.

> The 16th Infantry's mission was "To assault Omaha Beach and reduce the beach defenses

in its zone of action, and proceed with all possible speed to the D-Day Phase Line, and seize and secure it two hours before dark on D-Day."... The assault began in the early hours of 6 June 1944 as the 16th Infantry Regiment moved toward the shore of Normandy. 600 yards offshore, the LCVP's encountered intense antitank and small arms fire, but continued to move forward without hesitation. As the first elements hit the beaches, it was apparent that many of the enemy's strong points had not been eliminated by the preinvasion bombardment. Those men who lived to get ashore immediately dug holes in the sand, but waves washed them out as fast as they were scooped. To make matters worse, weapons became clogged with sand, and the enemy had reinforced with an added Infantry division, thus almost doubling his firepower. The survivors of the first wave built up a hasty firing line along a low pile of shale. As more men arrived, they found the troops pinned down, congested and trapped... Colonel George Taylor, Regimental Commander, jumped to his feet and said, "The only men who remain on this beach are the dead and those who are about to die! Let's get moving!" The 16th rallied, and soon, by vicious fighting, much of it hand-to-hand, was pushing toward Colleville-Sur-Mer. Early the following day, the 16th Infantry had seized the beach and an initial foothold that made the invasion a success.[20]

While baseball chroniclers may be unaware of the importance of Pinder's actions early on that long-ago June morning, military historians are cognizant of the strategic value of his deeds and sacrifices. The 116th Infantry Regiment, belonging to the 29th Infantry Division but loaned to the 1st Infantry Division for the invasion, landed on the western half of Omaha Beach. Previously untried in combat, the 116th never got a radio working until late in the day and as a result did not receive effective naval fire support. The best the 116th could do at one point was send blinker light signals. The 16th attacked on the eastern half of the beach, and General Sullivan's 1994 historical assessment of the situation credits Joe Pinder as being the reason the 16th was able to sidestep the communications problem that haunted the 116th.

Things turned out differently over in the

Big Red One's 16th Infantry regiment, mainly because of the unflagging willpower of one man—Technician 5th Grade John J. Pinder of Pennsylvania. Pinder and the rest of his communications section carried about half of the regimental headquarters' radio devices in their pitching little landing craft.[21]

Pinder's hometown paper, the Butler *Eagle*, announced his death in July:

Killed in Action.

A former Butler soldier and baseball pitcher, Private First Class J. Joseph Pinder, Jr., of Burgettstown, Pa., has been killed in action in France, it was announced by the War department.

Private Pinder was the son of J. J. Pinder, Sr., and had taken part in three different invasions at the time of his death.

A veteran infantryman, Pinder received his first action in the invasion of North Africa and later took part in the invasion of Italy. When the American army landed on the French coast, Private Pinder was with the first assault waves and June 6 was killed in action.

Well Known Here

Private Pinder was well known in Butler and was a graduate of the Butler Senior high school. He signed with the Yankee team of Butler as a pitcher and later pitched in the Florida State League.

Entering the army on January 27, 1942, he received his basic training at Camp Wheeler, Ga., Fort Benning and Indiantown Gap and then left this country for England. He left England in November of 1942 and had been in action since that time.

Private Pinder leaves his father, J. J. Pinder, Sr., of Burgettstown, Pa., a sister, Martha, of California, and a brother, Lieutenant Harold Pinder, who has been reported missing in action after a bombing mission over Germany in January of 1944.[22]

Harold Pinder was a B-24 pilot stationed in England. He was shot down on a bombing raid enroute to Frankfurt, Germany, on January 29, 1944. He was in a POW camp when he received a letter from his father informing him of Joe's death.

The War Department issued a press release on Janu-

ary 3, 1945, to announce that Pinder had been posthumously awarded the Medal of Honor. *The Sporting News* followed suit in its January 11, 1945, issue:

U.S. Honors Ex-Minor Ace
Posthumously

One of the nation's highest awards, the Medal of Honor, has been awarded posthumously to John J. Pinder, T5/G, of Burgettstown, Pa. former minor league pitcher, before he entered the Army, January 8, 1942.

The 32-year-old infantryman scorned terrible wounds in a race against death to establish vital radio communications on a beachhead in France on D-Day, last June 6, the War Department announced.

Torn by shrapnel and machine gun fire, Pinder lived to see radio parts which he had salvaged from the surf, set up to summon air and sea support.

Pinder's official Medal of Honor citation reads as follows:

For conspicuous gallantry and intrepidity above and beyond the call of duty on 6 June 1944, near Colleville-sur-Mer, France. On D-Day, Technician 5th Grade Pinder landed on the coast 100 yards off shore under devastating enemy machine-gun and artillery fire which caused severe casualties among the boatload. Carrying a vitally important radio, he struggled towards shore in waist-deep water. Only a few yards from his craft he was hit by enemy fire and was gravely wounded. Technician 5th Grade Pinder never stopped. He made shore and delivered the radio. Refusing to take cover afforded, or to accept medical attention for his wounds, Technician 5th Grade Pinder, though terribly weakened by loss of blood and in fierce pain, on 3 occasions went into the fire-swept surf to salvage communication equipment. He recovered many vital parts and equipment, including another workable radio. On the 3rd trip he was again hit, suffering machine-gun bullet wounds in his legs. Still this valiant soldier would not stop for rest or medical attention. Remaining exposed to heavy enemy fire, growing steadily weaker, he aided in establishing the vital radio communication on the beach. While so engaged this dauntless soldier was hit for a third time and killed. The indomitable courage and personal bravery of Technician 5th Grade Pinder was a magnificent inspiration to the men with whom he served.

Joe Pinder was initially laid to rest in Normandy, but his family had his remains returned home in September, 1947. The Pinder family plot is in the Grandview Cemetery in Florence, Pennsylvania. There is a special stone commemorating his Medal of Honor.

Close to sixty years have passed since Joe's death. Time marches on, and, although we shouldn't, we tend to forget the past. Major league stars today make millions of dollars per year, and that seems an eternity away from the bloody reality of our army storming ashore that June morning trying to free an entire continent.

Ralph Houk won three pennants and two world championships as manager of the New York Yankees. He also won a Silver Star for leading a reconnaissance platoon across France. Houk, like all men who had experienced combat firsthand, knew that war contains a lot more horror than it does glory. In his autobiography he wrote:

> Ruined villages, aerial bombardments, strafing, the crackle of snipers' bullets, corpses, the stink of war—that stuff reads well in magazines and books. It happened, it was all there, but not in gaudy words. To the individual soldier nothing mattered except to

take orders, to execute them to the best of his ability—and to survive.[23]

Houk, in answering a letter about Pinder, wrote to the author:

> I did not know or play with Joe Pinder, Jr., but we should not forget what so many people went through in World War Two. I also landed at Omaha Beach a few days after the first wave and it was hard to get through that alive. Baseball should not forget the Joe Pinders of baseball.[24]

Allan "Bud" Selig, the Commissioner of Baseball, wrote:

> He was a very heroic man who represented his country magnificently. He did what so many other baseball players did, at both the major and minor levels, and that is willingly give up their careers to fight for their country. Joe Pinder stands as a great symbol for future generations of baseball players, for his bravery and courage.[25]

Few men find themselves participants in events that determine world history. Fewer still are at the fulcrum of that event's failure or success. Pinder was such a man, an ordinary-Joe selected by fate for an extraordinary role.

So here's to you, Joe Pinder, belated as it may be, a collective tip of our baseball caps, for you will always be baseball's greatest hero.

Notes:

1. Stephen Ambrose, *D-Day. June 6, 1944. The Climactic Battle of World War II*, 1994, p. 346.

2. U.S. War Department press release, January 3, 1945.

3. Cornelius Ryan, *The Longest Day*, 1959, pp. 194-5.

4. Ambrose. p. 346.

5. Ibid, p. 347.

6. Ryan, p. 196.

7. General Gordon R. Sullivan, "D-Day Plus 50 Years," *Army Magazine*, June 1994. p. 26.

8. Ibid.

9. Ibid.

10. U.S. War Department press release, January 3, 1945.

11. Sullivan, p. 26.

12. U.S. War Department press release, January 3, 1945.

13. Sullivan, p. 26.

14. Butler *Eagle*, August 22, 1935.

15. See Joseph D. Tekulsy, "Elmer Gedeon," *The National Pastime*, 1994, p 68-9.

16. *The Sporting News*, September 10, 1942, p 10.

17. Fort Pierce *News-Tribune*, June 22, 1941.

18. Greenville *Advocate*, August 21, 1941.

19. Ibid, September 4, 1941.

20. 16th Infantry Association web site, http://16thinfantry-regiment.org/History/ WWII/wwii.html.

21. Sullivan, p. 26.

22. Butler *Eagle*, July, 1944.

23. Ralph Houk and Charles Dexter, *Ballpayers Are Human, Too* (New York: Putnam's, 1962), p. 37.

24. Letter from Ralph Houk to author., September 2000.

25. Letter from Allan "Bud" Selig to author, September 18, 2000.

Another Perspective on *Fair Ball*

Disputing the Costas analysis

Michael D. McDermott

Say a prayer for baseball's competitive balance. The topic is discussed strictly to be mourned or vilified. Testifying to the Senate Judiciary Committee on November 21, 2000, Commissioner Bud Selig warned, "At the start of spring training, there no longer exists hope and faith for the fans of more than half our thirty clubs."[1] Syndicated columnist George Will writes ominously of how "today's gargantuan revenue disparities produce ludicrous payroll disparities and competitive imbalance."[2]

These people and others point with particular horror to the 1998 season, during which the Yankees piled up 114 regular season victories while the Florida Marlins imploded and lost 108 games. They also are quick to pounce on the 2000 Subway Series as another grim example of the phenomenon. Belief in competitive imbalance has metastasized into baseball's version of political correctness, an unquestioned dogma shared almost universally by baseball people and the sports journalism establishment. Although there are some scattered dissenting voices, such as Joel Sherman of the New York *Post*, they are a distinct and ignored minority.

The most potent restatement of this theme is the recent book by the distinguished sportscaster and SABR member Bob Costas: *Fair Ball: A Fan's Case for Baseball* (released in paperback in April 2001).

I happen to believe that as an interpretation of baseball history, belief in competitive imbalance is utterly wrong-headed. To the extent that it will inform the impending debate surrounding baseball's new Basic Agreement, it could be downright dangerous.

Defining Deviancy Downward—In the 1983 edition of his groundbreaking *Baseball Abstract* books, Bill James wrote a lengthy essay identifying and defending a concept he called the law of competitive balance. More a series of objective observations than a theory, the law of competitive balance asserts that, in sports as well as in life, there is a natural tendency that narrows the gap between the winners and losers and the best and worst. If a hitter's batting average rises from .289 one season to .360 the next, it will likely decline in the third season. If a football running back rushes for 2,000 yards one year, he will likely rush for fewer the next. Historians and political scientists will tell you that now that George W. Bush has been elected president, the Democrats will rebound and gain seats in Congress in 2002. Schoolteachers will tell you that the kid who scores 100 percent on the first quiz of the semester will probably decline on the second quiz, while the kid who scores only 68 percent on the first will probably improve on the second.

Here is the law of competitive balance in James's own words:

"The law of competitive balance ... is a way of making sense of some observable facts. Its essential claim is that there exists in the world a negative momentum

Michael D. McDermott *is a freelance writer in New York.*

far more powerful than positive momentum, which acts constantly to reduce the differences between strong teams and weak teams, teams which are ahead and teams which are behind, or good players or poor players."[3]

We were already several years into the free agent era when James went public with his ideas. He pointed out that the gloom-and-doom scenarios of the rich getting richer and the poor poorer were not bearing fruit. In fact, his research indicated that the precise opposite trend was in motion, pointing out that the standard deviation in victories among major league teams actually declined slowly but steadily between 1978 and 1982.

(I am well aware that Costas lists Bill James in his book's Acknowledgments. If James has recently changed his tune on this issue, he is mistaken and the proof is on these pages. James does have a generous history of supporting people he does not necessarily agree with.)

In statistical parlance, a standard deviation is a "measure of dispersion." It is calculated to assess how close a given set of numbers clusters together. If someone were to tell you that the standard deviation in victories among big-league teams was 14.7 in 1969, that fact, by itself, would probably mean nothing to you. But if you were then told the standard deviation declined to 12.3 in 1970, that would give you an immediate sense of the trajectory all or most of the teams were taking. As standard deviations trend *downward*, that indicates the elements are converging closer to the "mean" or average, narrowing the gap between the best and worst. As standard deviations trend *upward*, that indicates the elements are polarizing, breaking away from the mean, increasing the gap between the best and worst.

Inspired by James's original research and eager to see how well the law of competitive balance has held up in recent years, I devised a study of my own. It is generally agreed that the "modern" era of major league baseball began in 1901. So I calculated standard deviations in regular-season wins at five-year intervals between 1905 and 1990 (except 1945, which was a war year; I used 1946 instead). I also included standard deviations for all six expansion seasons and year-by-year standard deviations between 1995 and 2000. The results are presented in Chart 1.

Despite occasional blips and spikes, there was a steady overall decline in standard deviations throughout the twentieth century. You may notice sharp upsurges in 1961, '62, '77, '93, and '98. These took place for an obvious reason: expansion. Everyone

knows that first-year expansion teams are wretchedly bad. The established teams stomp on them, thereby destabilizing competitive balance, thereby driving up the standard deviation.

Chart 1

Year	Standard Deviation
1905	16.7
1910	15.7
1915	15.0
1920	14.0
1925	11.8
1930	15.0
1935	15.8
1940	13.4
1946	14.8
1950	15.4
1955	13.6
1960	12.4
1961	**15.0**
1962	**15.5**
1965	13.9
1969	**14.7**
1970	12.3
1975	11.4
1977	**14.1**
1980	11.4
1985	12.3
1990	8.9
1993	**11.9**
1995	10.1
1996	9.8
1997	9.5
1998	**13.3**
1999	12.3
2000	9.8

Expansion seasons in bold print.

But the law of competitive balance is a persistent little bug. Chart 1 also shows that expansion's destabilizing impact is always short-lived. By 1965, the standard deviation dropped to 13.9, which was lower than it was in 1950. By 1975, six years after both leagues expanded again, it was down to 11.4, and that despite the resounding success of the Big Red Machine that year. The pattern is remarkably consistent: Every time one of the leagues expands, the standard deviation briefly flares up, then gently glides back down.

Competitive balance has been alive and well and arguably better than ever in recent years. The standard deviation actually plunged to historic lows at points in the previous decade. Moreover, the 13.3 standard deviation of 1998 is not terribly high by historical standards. As the law of competitive balance would have predicted, it dropped to 12.3 in 1999 (the same perch it occupied in 1970 and 1985) and to just 9.8 in 2000. Unless the goal is to cut the standard deviation to zero and have everyone go 81-81, competitive balance has rarely been better than this.

An important subheading of the law of competitive balance is something James called the "70/50 Rule." The first half of the rule asserts that about 70 percent of teams with winning records in a given season will tend to decline in the following season, while about 70 percent of losing teams will tend to improve. Lo and behold, ten of the twelve teams with winning records in 1999 declined in 2000; twelve of the eighteen losing teams improved. Overall, twenty-two of the thirty teams reversed course. That equals 73 percent, which accords beautifully with James's 70 percent figure.

The second half of the 70/50 Rule holds that most of these rises or declines will bring a team 50 percent closer to .500. Applied to the 1998 Yankees, who won 114 games, such a team should drop to 97 or 98 wins (halfway between 114 and 81) the next season; in fact, the '99 Yankees won 98 games. A team winning 98 games will tend to drop to 89 or 90 wins in the follow-up year; the 2000 Yankees won 87 games. The gap between the Yankees and the Florida Marlins in 1998 was a whopping 60 games; in just two years, the law of competitive balance chopped it to eight games.

All well and good, the skeptic may respond, but the damn Yankees still went out and won another World Series, right? Indeed they did. But whereas the '98 and '99 Yankees can be legitimately compared to the great teams in history, the 2000 Yankees bear a suspicious resemblance to teams like the 1985 Royals or the 1987 Twins—champions who were very lucky, not very good. The Yankees would never have made the playoffs at all but for a quirk in the American League alignment, which permitted them to finish first in a mediocre division while the Indians went home for the winter despite winning 90 games. (At only 87-74, the Yankees were one of the worst first-place teams in history. The Mets had only the fourth best record in the National League.)

Take a good close look at the rubber game of the 2000 Division Series. When it boils down to playing one game, bizarre events may transpire. What happened this time was that Terence Long lost Tino Martinez's fly ball in the Oakland twilight, allowing what proved to be the winning runs to score. If Long

makes that catch, either the A's or Mariners advance to the World Series. One botched defensive play in the postseason should not obscure an entire regular season of exceptionally good competitive balance.

Looking back on the early years of free agency, Costas makes an interesting observation that is far more telling than he realizes. As he sees it, the late '70s, '80s and even the early '90s were the halcyon days for competitive balance. "Despite the wailings of Chicken Little types, free agency—at least at first—actually enhanced competitive balance, improved the game, added excitement and life to it."[4]

What a deadly concession that is. The standard deviation declined from 14.1 in 1977 to 11.4 in 1980, whereas it declined from 13.3 in 1998 to 9.8 in 2000. Either *both* eras were characterized by good competitive balance—or neither was.

Anecdotal Evidence—Those who fret over competitive balance make the laughable assumption that large markets are unalloyed sweetness and light. Costas scrupulously details how teams in the largest markets take in more local cable and broadcast revenue, but that only focuses on one side of the ledger. The large market teams may have larger revenue sources, but they also pay higher taxes, incur higher expenses, and cope with a higher cost of doing business. New York is not famous for being a low-cost city. Should not these factors also enter the equation?

There are obvious "quality of life" issues that also hurt the large markets. The lure of less pressure, less scrutiny, and a lower tax bite, if his accountant had a say in the decision, convinced Mark McGwire to stay in St. Louis rather than jump to Anaheim or Los Angeles. Similar considerations led Junior Griffey to thumb his nose at the Mets and Juan Gonzalez to veto a trade to the Yankees. Such are comparative advantages that well-run medium market teams can exploit and have exploited. To some extent, the large market teams *need* that extra revenue. (In fairness to Costas, his proposals would allow the big market teams to continue to take in relatively high local media revenue.)

Another ludicrous assumption enjoying wide currency is the belief that Cleveland, Atlanta, and Baltimore are among the large markets while Minnesota, Miami and Pittsburgh are among the small markets. A look at the most recent US Census data, available in 1997, refutes that view. The population of the "large market" Cleveland metropolitan area is 2.9 million people; the population of the "small market" Minneapolis-St. Paul metropolitan area is 2.8

million people. The population of "large market" Greater Atlanta is 3.6 million; the population of "small market" Greater Miami is 3.5 million. Greater Baltimore has a population of 2.4 million; Greater Pittsburgh's is 2.3 million. To be sure, metro Baltimore could be classified as a true large market if you attach it to the nearby Washington D. C. metro area. Doing so creates the fourth largest metropolitan area in America (7.2 million people). The bad news for believers in large market/small market disparities is that the Orioles have been terrible of late: 2001 was their fourth straight losing season.[5]

We know what the Mets and Yankees have done. In fact, we may never hear the end of it. But what about the teams in the other big markets—Los Angeles, Chicago and Philadelphia? The Dodgers have not won a postseason game since Game 5 of the 1988 World Series. Sharing the second largest market in the country with the Dodgers, the Anaheim Angels have not gone to the playoffs since 1986. The White Sox have not gone to a World Series since Dwight Eisenhower was president and the Cubs have not gone to one since Harry Truman was. Playing in the fifth largest central city and sixth largest metro area in the country, the Phillies have one pennant to show for the last seventeen years.

As a fallback position, Costas and company would stand on more plausible ground if they relinquished this discredited "large market/small market" disparity and focused instead on a "large payroll/small payroll" disparity. Such a disparity is real, but far from reflecting a systemic meltdown of baseball's competitive balance; there is an obvious element of self-selection behind it. In recent years, there have been medium market teams with big payrolls (the Indians, the Diamondbacks) and large market teams with small payrolls (the Phillies, the White Sox).

The ups and downs of the San Diego Padres in the '90s are a compelling illustration of this point. In 1992 the Padres contended for the National League West title until a late-season fade eliminated them. Management embarked on a fire sale the following winter not unlike that of the post-1997 Marlins, dumping salaries and giving away people like Gary Sheffield, Fred McGriff and Tony Fernandez. Predictably, the team crashed, burned and lost 101 games the next year. After that traumatic 1993 season, the Padres had every symptom of a helpless "small market" team that had "no chance" to contend again. Yet the franchise regrouped under smart new ownership, won a division title by 1996, and returned to the World Series by 1998.

In Costas's lurid universe of entrenched competitive imbalance, the revival of the Padres should never have happened—but it did. Yes, the Padres relapsed in 1999—just as championship teams throughout history have returned to earth the year after winning a pennant.

Costas loathes the wild card. His proposal to abolish it and have the second- and third-best division champions in each league face each other in the first round, while giving the best team in each league a bye, has advantages to recommend it. But in his opposition to the wild card, Costas resorts to some misleading arguments. Citing the list of wild card teams between 1995 and 1999, he wonders, "Where, pray tell, are the small- and middle-market teams? ... The evidence is clear: The wild card is a helping hand for the Haves."[6]

That misstates the issue. Aside from the obviously greedy purpose of creating extra rounds of playoffs for extra revenue, another purpose of realignment (in 1969 as well as 1994) was to create more races and therefore more *opportunities* for weaker teams to compete—opportunities, not guarantees. Moreover, in his original article on the law of competitive balance, Bill James presented a chart detailing the percentage of teams finishing within ten games of first place in the first five years of each decade from the early 1900s to the early 1970s. I updated the chart to include the early 1980s (excluding 1981) and the late 1990s; the results are in **Chart 2**.

Chart 2

Years	% of Teams Finishing Within 10 Games of 1st
1900-1904	33%
1910-1914	18%
1920-1924	34%
1930-1934	30%
1940-1944	24%
1950-1954	32%
1960-1964	32%
1970-1974	41%
1980-1984	43%
1995-1999	42%

1900-04 to 1970-74 data is from the *1983 Bill James Baseball Abstract*. Remaining data is the author's.

Chart 2 is powerful confirmation of the point made by Chart 1; the two are mutually reinforcing. The percentage of teams finishing within ten games of first place has hovered in the low forties throughout the divisional era. Including teams finishing within ten games of the wild card, the 1995-99 figure rises to an unprecedented 50 percent: excellent balance.

Yet another gospel in the theology of baseball's endangered competitive balance is the claim that there is vastly superior parity in the NBA. Costas is impressed by the fact that the NBA has some franchises in medium markets that lack baseball teams, and that some of them seem to win on occasion. "[W]hat do these cities have in common: Sacramento, Portland, Indianapolis, and Salt Lake City? Not only do they all have NBA franchises, they all have *contending teams* ... Fans of every NBA team ...have reason to believe they have a chance to win ..."[7]

There is less to that claim than meets the eye. In the '90s (1990-91 to 1999-00) each NBA team played 788 regular season games, or nearly the equivalent of five baseball seasons of 162 games apiece. In that span, the "contending" Sacramento Kings posted a .402 winning percentage, analogous to a baseball team losing about 95 games per year for five years. They did indeed squeak into the NBA playoffs in 1999 and 2000 (as if that were an accomplishment). Is it so "unthinkable" to envision a successful baseball team in Indianapolis or Portland? The Cincinnati Reds—winners of a World Series in 1990, a division title in 1995, and 96 games in 1999—play in a metropolitan area of 1.9 million people, compared to, say, the Indianapolis metro area of 1.5 million, and which is actually *smaller* than that of Portland (2.1 million).[8]

How about the Dallas Mavericks? They went through the '90s without a single winning season— not one. Their aggregate winning percentage was only .303, analogous to a baseball team averaging 110 losses per year for five years. How did that happen, if the NBA's competitive balance is so marvelous? It would be a safe assumption to say the Royals, Brewers, Twins, Pirates and Expos have not scraped that depth in quite a while.

At the other end of the NBA's recent spectrum are the Chicago Bulls—a large market monster if ever there was one. You might remember them; they won six titles in eight years and might well have won eight in a row had Michael Jordan not decided to flail at curveballs for two years. They posted an aggregate .660 winning percentage in the '90s—comparable to a baseball team averaging 106 wins per season for five seasons. By the way, the NBA boomed throughout that period. If there is a greater *perception* or expectation of parity in the NBA, it is nourished by the league's perpetual playoffs, not by a demonstrably superior balance of power on the court.

Costas, Selig, and Will are shocked—*shocked*—by

data showing that only three of 189 postseason baseball games between 1995 and 2000 were won by teams that had payrolls in the bottom half of the league. Okay ... isn't that more or less to be expected? In the NBA, as Peter Vecsey noted in a recent New York *Post* article, the Final Four teams in the 2000 playoffs also just happened to have the top four payrolls in their own league.[9] All that this proves, in either sport, is that good players tend to make more money than bad players.

Modest Proposals—Costas unfolds an entire shopping list of proposals. The fact that the rationale behind them is mistaken or overblown does not necessarily discredit them.

Here are the two highlights: first, minimum team payrolls equal to the per-team average of TV revenue and maximum payrolls no higher than twice that figure. Second, a "superstar salary cap" to limit any single player's salary to one-quarter of the minimum team payroll or one-eighth of the maximum payroll.

Costas is certainly right that imposing a ceiling on payrolls is unacceptable unless it is accompanied by a floor on payrolls as well. Although the proposed limits sound rather tight, I would actually agree with Costas that the general idea is worth exploring, but for a different reason: it would inject accountability into the system. A mismanaged franchise could no longer scapegoat Steinbrenner or Ted Turner for its own ineptitude or sloth.

Meeting a salary floor must be a condition to qualify for revenue sharing. If there is going to be revenue sharing, there have got to be strings attached. Indeed, a case can be made that *unconditional* revenue sharing actually worsens competitive balance by subsidizing failure. Look at the Bengals and Cardinals in the NFL. With characteristic bluntness, Whitey Herzog warns against such NFL-style revenue sharing. "In the NFL, you have owners who are guaranteed huge revenue even if their teams never throw a pass ... The NFL rewards people for being lazy and stupid. So that's out."[10]

We should also beware of any one-size-fits-all proposal. The Tampa Bay Devil Rays, operating in a region with a relatively low cost of living and in a state with no income tax, should not be held to the same financial standard as the Mets or Yankees. A team in New York should be permitted a higher maximum payroll than most others. By the same token, a team in Tampa Bay should be permitted to meet a lower minimum payroll to qualify for revenue sharing. Payroll limits at both ends of the spectrum could be a good thing, but the devil is in the details.

The "superstar salary cap," on the other hand, is, I think, a deplorable idea. Philosophy aside, it seems redundant if you already are imposing a ceiling on payrolls. Even in the absence of such a ceiling, a superstar salary cap does not address the real problem. The most overpaid players are not the A-Rods or Derek Jeters, but the Bobby Bonillas and the David Cones. As we know from the research of Bill James, Pete Palmer and others, a typical athlete's value takes a steep plunge after the age of thirty, and just about all athletes display their rust by thirty-two or thirty-three. The most overcompensated player is one who signs an eternal contract in his late twenties or early thirties. Suddenly he is further into his thirties, falling out of shape, becoming more injury-prone, playing like dog meat, but still drawing the salary of a stud in his twenties.

So rather than seeking an annual salary cap, why not seek what I call a "term cap" on contracts instead? No player between the ages of twenty-eight and thirty-one should be permitted to sign a contract running more than four seasons; no player between thirty-two and thirty-four should be allowed to sign for more than three seasons; no player thirty-five or over should be allowed to sign for more than two seasons. The beauty of a term cap is that it would tie an aging player's salary more closely to what his value is today, not to what it was four years ago. It would also create a glut of aging players on the free agent market, which would exert *downward* pressure on salaries. Economics 101: As the supply of a commodity increases relative to demand, the price tends to drop.

I would actually go one step beyond Costas and propose the utter, total and complete abolition of arbitration. Salary arbitration—salary abomination is a better description—is the most combustible element fueling salary inflation. At least free agency possesses some semblance of the checks and balances of supply and demand; there is nothing self-correcting about arbitration. Costas's proposal to impose a "graduated scale" on arbitration awards just tinkers with a fundamentally flawed process. Dispose of it altogether. In exchange for that, we can implement another one of his proposals. Allow players to become free agents two years earlier. But go one step further: Allow them to become "unrestricted" free agents two years earlier. Recalling Economics 101, it becomes clear that abolishing arbitration and opening the doors to free agency sooner would call the bluff of the Players Association. For the past generation, Marvin

Miller and Donald Fehr have claimed that all they seek for their clients is the same "freedom" that other employees enjoy. Give them some, then see how they like it.

During an appearance on the *Charlie Rose Show* on PBS to promote the hardcover release of *Fair Ball*, Costas remarked that there are more owners than ever in a fighting mood. I believe it. More and more mega-corporations have swallowed sports franchises in recent years. In the real world in the last quarter century, corporate America has waged what author and political pundit Michael Lind has described as a "low-key, bipartisan class war" against the wage-earning middle class in terms of declining union membership, declining fringe benefits and (until very recently) declining wages.[11]

The new breed of corporate owners now brings this confrontational attitude into the sports world. They have little or no institutional memory of the principles that were at stake in the *Flood vs. Kuhn* Supreme Court case in 1971 or in the legal rulings from the mid-1970s that broke down the indentured servitude enshrined in the old Reserve Clause. All they know is that if they can tell the AFL-CIO to go pound sand, then maybe they can tell the same to the Major League Baseball Players Association (which is interesting since the MLBPA is probably the strongest private sector union in America).

The key variable, the X factor, in the upcoming battle over baseball's new Basic Agreement will be the hearts and minds of rank-and-file baseball fans. The fatal flaw in *Fair Ball* is that by recycling and legitimizing the central myth peddled by the owners—that baseball's competitive balance is destroyed and therefore "something" must be "done" about it—Costas misinforms and disorients the public and unwittingly fans the flames of ownership militancy. For all of its sometimes trenchant criticisms of the wild card and of Selig's counterproductive "radical realignment" scheme and of that hideous behind-the-plate advertising blighting stadiums from coast to coast, *Fair Ball* ultimately poses no threat to the corporate lords of baseball. A few of them may also have something more radical and heavy-handed up their sleeves than Costas himself ever contemplated.

For all of Costas's thoughtfulness, integrity, and good intentions, the ironic upshot of *Fair Ball* could be to make another 1994-style train wreck *more* likely, not less, and that cannot be good news for anyone concerned about the state of the game.

Notes:

1. "Selig Tells Senate Panel Money Gap Is Widening," AP report, *Long Island Newsday*, November 22, 2000, p. 89.

2. George Will, "Oh Swell: New York Wins Again," *Newsweek*, October 30. 2000, p. 104.

3. Bill James, *1983 Bill James Baseball Abstract* (New York: Ballantine Books, 1983), p. 12.

4. Bob Costas, *Fair Ball: A Fan's Case for Baseball*, (New York: Bantam Doubleday Dell, 2000), p. 37.

5. www.census.gov.

6. Costas, *Fair Ball*, p. 142.

7. Ibid., p. 53.

8. www.census.gov.

9. Peter Vecsey, "Nets' Search Down to Four," *New York Post*, May 30, 2000, p. 78.

10. Whitey Herzog, *You're Missin' a Great Game* (New York: Berkley Books, 1999), pp. 286-287.

11. Michael Lind, *The Next American Nation: The New Nationalism and the Fourth American Revolution* (New York: Simon and Schuster, 1995), p. 101.

Bonesetter Reese

Youngstown's "baseball doctor"

David W. Anderson

He was neither a physician nor a trainer, but John D. "Bonesetter' Reese was probably the best known treater of injured ballplayers in the first three decades of the twentieth century.

He built a practice in which he saw athletes, entertainers, and statesmen, but also the mill workers of his adopted Youngstown, Ohio. He beat off and eventually surmounted challenges from the medical establishment, and he became a treasured citizen of his hard-working city.

Reese's origins were as humble as they were harsh. Born May 6, 1855, in Rhymney, Wales, he lost his father three months later. When he was eleven, his mother died. Orphaned, Reese went to work in the Welsh iron works. He was taken in by an ironworker named Tom Jones who taught him the trade of bonesetting, a term Welshmen used for the manipulative treatment of muscle and tendon strains, not the setting of breaks. Reese remained under Jones' tutelage until he left for the United States in 1887.

Like many immigrants of the times, Reese was compelled to come to America because there were no jobs in the old country. He sailed steerage class to America without his family, sending for them six months later. When they arrived, Reese left his job as a roller's helper at Jones & Laughlin Steel in Pittsburgh and moved to Youngstown, where he took a job at the Brown-Bonnell Mills. Family history says he successfully treated an injured mill worker for a dislocated shoulder in 1889. From this point on, other workers began coming to Reese for help with their injuries.

Eventually, the call on his skills became so great that he became a fulltime bonesetter in 1894. This called down the wrath of the medical establishment, which charged him with quackery and practicing medicine without a license. To get around this charge, Reese took advantage of the strict language of the state law and began charging patients what they could afford rather than a set fee. His policy, primarily applied to factory workers, was tersely stated: "Pay me when you get it."

Simultaneously, Reese did what he could to satisfy his critics. He even enrolled in medical school at Case University in Cleveland, in 1897. He didn't last long, because he couldn't stand the sight of blood during surgery. His teachers recognized his skill, though, and gave their blessing to his practice of muscle and ligament manipulation, which resembled osteopathy, a medical theory founded in the United States during the late nineteenth century.

Reese's struggle with the medical community ended in 1900. By then he had developed strong ties in the community, had made influential friends, and had made it clear that he refused to treat acute illnesses and was practicing his trade within strict limits. His practice was formally recognized by the State of Ohio, and open opposition by medical authorities ceased.

David W. Anderson is author of More Than Merkle, *a history of the 1908 baseball season, published in 2000 by the University of Nebraska Press. During his research he 'met' Bonesetter Reese and this article is his tribute to him. Mr. Anderson lives in Olathe, Kansas.*

Treating ballplayers—According to David Strickler, Reese's grandson-in-law, who wrote his biography, *Child of Moriah* (Four Corners Press), the first baseball player treated by Reese was Jimmy McAleer, a Youngstown native who was an outfielder for the Cleveland Spiders at the time. McAleer, who later became manager of the St. Louis Browns, spread the word about Reese's talents. In 1903, the Pittsburgh Pirates offered Reese the position of full-time team physician. Reese, preferring to stay at home, refused the offer and continued to treat any ballplayer who came to him for help.

Many did. Strickler's book lists fifty-four players treated by Reese, twenty-eight of whom are in the Baseball Hall of Fame, including Honus Wagner, Cy Young, Ty Cobb, Rogers Hornsby, Eddie Collins, Grover Cleveland Alexander, Walter Johnson and John McGraw. Scores more visited him but weren't listed because Reese never sought publicity and some players did not want anyone knowing they might be hurt. In the mid-twenties, *Sporting Life* paid tribute to Reese's contribution to baseball this way: "[he] has prolonged the active life of countless baseball stars and preserved them for the fans of the country to cheer."

From his experience with players, Reese became an expert in treating sore arms, bad backs, and charley horses. Reese noted that most of his patients were pitchers. "It's not the curve ball pitchers who come the more often…but the boys who try to throw the ball past a batter, the speed ball pitchers…If the soreness is in the elbow it's a speedball pitcher nine times out of ten; if in the shoulder, a curve ball pitcher."

Several players credited Reese with saving their careers, including longtime Cleveland pitcher George Uhle and Pittsburgh and Brooklyn infielder Glenn Wright. While Reese provided cures, the repairs were not painless. Wagner said Reese hurt him, "like the devil, but always does the work." Reese himself liked Wagner and described their first meeting, "because they call me 'bonesetter' he [Wagner] was trembling clear down to his shoes. And the minute I placed my hands on his back he fainted dead away."

The Bonesetter was not always happy with his ballplaying patients. He believed many of them reinjured themselves because they would not follow his directions. Reese disliked sports that put their participants in harm's way. Present-day Youngstown is a gridiron hotbed, but Reese did not share the passion.

He hated football. He treated George Halas only after the future 'Papa Bear' persuaded him his bum knee came from sliding into a base and not from being hammered by a tackler.

Reese's patient list was not confined to athletes. He treated Theodore Roosevelt, presidential candidate and Chief Justice Charles Evans Hughes, and fellow Welshman and former British Prime Minister David Lloyd George. Will Rogers was among his show business clients, along with countless showgirls who needed treatment for strained muscles or twisted ankles. Billy Sunday was also among his patients, both as a player and an evangelist.

Reese died of heart failure in 1931 at the age of seventy-six. His passing was heavily covered by the Youngstown *Vindicator*. His obituary noted that he had always treated patients in order of appearance. The famous had to stand in line like everybody else. Patients paid what they could afford, while the widows and orphans of mill workers were not charged at all.

John D. 'Bonesetter' Reese came to America to seek a better life for himself and his family, a motive the sons and daughters of immigrants understand. He built his life around the opportunity given him in his adopted nation. That simple fact best describes 'Bonesetter' Reese's life and his contribution to his fellow citizens of Youngstown and to our national game.

Bonesetter's All Star Clients Team

Pitchers: Cy Young, Christy Mathewson, Big Ed Walsh, Grover Cleveland Alexander, Addie Joss, Chief Bender and Stanley Coveleski.

Catchers: Gabby Hartnett and Roger Bresnahan.

First basemen: George Sisler and Frank Chance.

Second basemen: Eddie Collins, Rogers Hornsby and Napoleon Lajoie.

Third basemen: Home Run Baker and Jimmy Collins.

Shortstops: Honus Wagner and Donie Bush.

Outfielders: Ty Cobb, Shoeless Joe Jackson, Tris Speaker, Edd Roush and Max Carey.

Manager: John McGraw

El Tiante

Loo-Eee, Loo-Eee

Mark Armour

On June 3, 1971, the Boston Red Sox purchased the contract of Luis Tiant from their minor league affiliate in Louisville. Three years removed from being the best pitcher in the American League, Luis had been released at the end of spring training by the Twins, had spent thirty days with the Richmond Braves, and had been signed by Louisville in mid-May. The Red Sox could always use more pitching, but did they really think this guy was going to help?

Cuba and Mexico—Luis Tiant was born and grew up in Marianao, Cuba, the son and namesake of a legendary pitcher. Luis Tiant Sr. starred in the Cuban Leagues and the Negro Leagues of the United States for twenty years, and was famous for his variety of pitches (including a spitball), his pick-off move, and his exaggerated pirouette motion. As late as 1947, at the age of 41, Luis Sr. put together a 10-0 record for the New York Cubans and pitched in the East-West All-Star Game.

After failing a tryout with the Havana team in the International League, Luis Jr. started his professional career in 1959, at age eighteen, for the Mexico City Tigers. His performance was poor (5-19, 5.92 ERA), but he followed this up with seventeen wins in 1960 and twelve more in 1961, after having been delayed for two months trying to leave his homeland. At the end of the 1961 season, the Cleveland Indians pur-

chased his contract for $35,000.

During these three years playing in Mexico, Luis returned to Havana to play winter ball and be with his family. In August, 1961 he married Maria, a native of Mexico City, and at the close of the season they were planning to return to Luis' home in Marianao. Unfortunately, the Cuban political situation had worsened, and Fidel Castro's government was no longer letting anyone leave. Upon the advice of his father, Luis did not return home. He would not see his parents for fourteen years.

Moving up the ladder—In 1962, living in an English-speaking country for the first time, Luis had a respectable year (7-8, 3.63) for Charleston (West Virginia) in the Class A Eastern League. In 1963, he was probably the best pitcher in the Single A Carolina League, finishing 14-9 for Burlington, North Carolina, including a no-hitter, with a 2.56 ERA, and leading the league in complete games, strikeouts, and shutouts. He was twenty-three years old.

The following winter, he was not on the Indians' 40-man roster and was therefore available in the major league draft. No team risked $12,000 to claim him. The Indians sent him back to Burlington, but on the eve of the 1964 season an injury opened up a spot for him at Triple-A Portland of the Pacific Coast League. He was one step away from the majors.

The Portland Beavers pitching staff included twenty-year-old phenom Sam McDowell, who had spent parts of the last three seasons with the Indians

---

Mark Armour *grew up in Red Sox country, but now does his baseball research and writing in Oregon. His three-year-old daughter, Maya, attended her first minor league game this past summer.*

and was clearly the star of the Portland team. Tiant was not in the rotation.

Luis picked up a relief win on opening day, and another one a week later. His first start was on May 3, his third appearance of the season in the Beavers' fifteenth game. McDowell, meanwhile, started hot and got hotter, pitching a one-hitter and a no-hitter in consecutive starts in early May, before finally being called up on May 30. His Portland record was 8-0, with a 1.18 ERA, and 102 strikeouts in 76 innings. Sam also won eleven games with the Indians in 1964.

Tiant, meanwhile, was quietly building up his own resume. At the time of McDowell's promotion, Luis himself was 7-0 with a 2.25 ERA. After losing, 2-0, on June 5, Tiant won four more games to finish June at 12-1. On July 2, he beat the San Diego Padres, led by his fellow Cuban Tony Perez, 2-1, in a matchup of the best teams in the PCL's Western Division. The next day, Portland GM Dave Steele said, "At first, I wasn't sure that Tiant wasn't just getting the breaks, but that 2-1 win over San Diego convinced me."

Luis was called up to the big club on July 17. His record in Portland was 15-1 (a PCL record .938 winning percentage) with a 2.04 ERA. He had completed thirteen of his fifteen starts.

Tiant joined the Indians in New York on Saturday morning, July 18, and was asked by his manager, Birdie Tebbetts, if he was ready to pitch. When Luis said he was, Tebbetts replied, "Great, you're starting tomorrow against Whitey Ford." Tiant responded with a four-hit shutout, striking out eleven. Continuing his storybook season, he went 10-4 for the Tribe with a 2.83 ERA. His combined line for 1964 was 25-5 with a 2.42 ERA in 264 innings.

The Road to stardom—Tiant spent the next three years as a .500 pitcher (11-11, 12-11, 12-9) for a mediocre team. In 1966, he started the season with three consecutive shutouts, a streak that ended in the first inning in Baltimore when Frank Robinson hit a ball clear out of Memorial Stadium, the only time that was ever done. Luis hit a rough spell in May and June and spent the last half of the season in the bullpen, notching eight saves in thirty relief appearances. Despite only sixteen starts, his five shutouts topped the American League. His ERAs in 1966 and 1967 were a respectable 2.79 and 2.74.

In 1968, Tiant became a star, going 21-9, with a 1.60 ERA. Luis won the ERA title in this "Year of the Pitcher," and led the league with nine shutouts. He pitched his best game on July 3 in Cleveland when he recorded nineteen strikeouts in ten innings against the Twins. In the top of the tenth, the Twins got runners on second and third with no outs. Luis struck out the side. The Indians finally pushed across a run in the bottom of the tenth to give Tiant a 1-0 victory.

The following week, Luis started and lost the All-Star Game, giving the NL an unearned run in the first inning, which turned out to be the only run of the game. After a 3-0 loss to Denny McLain in early September, McLain suggested that "Luis and I would each be fighting for 30 wins if he had our kind of hitting to go with his kind of pitching." Catcher Bill Freehan took it a step further, insisting that Luis would be "going for 40 wins." In the event, McLain finished 31-6 with a 1.96 ERA, and won the Cy Young and MVP Awards unanimously.

After a September game in which Luis left with elbow stiffness, manager Alvin Dark told the press that arm trouble was inevitable with his "extreme motions." Throughout Tiant's tenure in Cleveland, there was grumbling in the media and from management that his trademark exaggerated windup and gyrations were unnecessary. Any time Luis had a sore arm or a stretch of poor pitching, somebody would bring up his delivery—or his weight.

After his great season, Luis was told not to pitch that winter in Venezuela as he usually did. Luis seethed at what he considered disrespectful treatment after his great year. He openly suggested that if he couldn't pitch in South America he would have an off year in 1969.

The Road to oblivion—The Indians finished 1969 with the worst record in the American League and their worst winning percentage in fifty-four years. Luis declined from 21-8 to 9-20, and posted an ERA of 3.71. It wasn't as bad as it sounds—changes to the strike zone and mound sent the league ERA up to 3.61. Nonetheless, Luis was an average American League pitcher, which was quite a step down from 1968. He insisted that it was all due to his not being able to pitch the previous winter.

Tiant's feud with Dark got progressively worse as the losses mounted. Dark talked first through the media—"You can't throw your head up into the air, then look over the scoreboard and then pitch a baseball"—before finally ordering Tiant to curtail the fancy delivery. Tiant stood his ground, and the relationship never recovered.

In December, 1969, Luis was traded to the Twins in a six-player deal that brought Dean Chance and Graig Nettles to the Indians. In 1970, Tiant won his first six decisions for a strong Minnesota team, but left his sixth victory with a sore shoulder that had been bothering him since spring. Luis went to see a specialist who found a crack in a bone in his right shoulder. He prescribed rest.

Luis sat down for ten weeks and returned to lose three of four decisions in the final weeks of the season. He pitched only two-thirds of an inning in the three-game playoff sweep by the Orioles.

By spring training 1971, Luis considered himself fully recovered, but he pulled a muscle in his rib cage, missed two weeks, and was otherwise ineffective in just eight innings. On March 31, he was given his unconditional release. The Twins and their doctors believed that he was finished at age thirty.

The only team willing to give him a job was the Atlanta Braves, who signed him to a thirty-day trial in Richmond. After giving him limited work, the Braves were unwilling to promote him, so he signed with Louisville, the Red Sox Triple-A affiliate in the International League. He pitched well in thirty-one innings—twenty-nine strikeouts and a 2.61 ERA— and was summoned to Boston on June 3.

The Road back—Tiant was not an immediate success in the Hub. In his first appearance on June 11, he gave up five runs in only one inning. Cliff Keane wrote in the Boston *Globe*: "The latest investment by the Red Sox looked about as sound as taking a bagful of money and throwing it off Pier 4 into the Atlantic." Tiant remained in the rotation, but he dropped his first six decisions. After one loss, Keane led his game story with, "Enough is enough." The team was in first place when Luis was recalled, but would be out of the race by the end of July.

Nonetheless, manager Eddie Kasko believed there were signs that Tiant might regain his old form. He shut out the Yankees for seven innings before losing, 2-1, on a two-run home run by Roy White. He threw ten shutout innings, and 154 pitches, in his return to Minnesota, but did not figure in the decision.

Kasko finally took him out of the rotation in early August. He was better out of the bullpen—he finished 1-1 with a 1.80 ERA as a relief pitcher. Nevertheless, after his four-month trial, there was certainly no guarantee of a job next spring. A lot of Sox watchers were surprised he was still on the 40-man roster in the spring.

On March 22, 1972, the Red Sox traded Sparky Lyle to the Yankees for Danny Cater, a trade that many Boston fans still rank among the worst that the Red Sox have ever made. However, it might be worth reconsidering the trade in light of the fact that it

probably saved Luis' spot on the team. Kasko, who never stopped believing in Tiant, remembered his effectiveness in the bullpen in 1971, and wanted him out there. The team believed it had a solid group of starters in Ray Culp, Sonny Siebert, Marty Pattin, and Lew Krausse.

By the end of July, Kasko's faith in Tiant seemed to have been justified. Luis was effective in a variety of roles—the occasional spot start, a ninth-inning save, or a long relief stint. The team started poorly, thanks in part to the ineffectiveness of Siebert and Culp, and remained under .500 for months.

Led by the emergence of rookie pitchers John Curtis and Lynn McGlothen, the Red Sox climbed to within five games of first place at the start of August. They went neck-and-neck with the Tigers, Orioles, and Yankees right through September. The drive for the pennant was led by two players who were hardly considered part of the team's plans at the start of the season: rookie catcher Carlton Fisk and a sensational Luis Tiant.

On August 5, Tiant got a start at Fenway because Siebert wasn't feeling well, and beat the Orioles. A week later, he faced the Birds again in Baltimore and pitched six no-hit innings before settling for a three-hitter. After picking up a save, he started in Comiskey Park on August 19, and had a no-hitter with two outs in the eighth before finishing with a two-hitter. After this game, Kasko announced that Luis was in the rotation to stay.

Over ten starts, beginning with this game in Chicago, Tiant went 9-1 with six shutouts and a 0.96 ERA. All nine victories were complete games. The first four were shutouts, his streak of 40 scoreless innings ending during a four-hit victory over the Yankees at Fenway. After a loss in Yankee Stadium, Luis shut out the Indians back home.

Before the second game of a twi-night doubleheader against the Orioles on September 20, the fans rose to their feet as Luis walked to the bullpen to warm up and gave him such an ovation that his teammates joined in the applause, and several reported that they had goose bumps. The crowd spent most of the evening chanting "Loo-Eee, Loo-Eee, Loo-Eee," a sound that brings a smile to countless middle-aged people in Boston to this day.

When Tiant came up to bat in the bottom of the eighth on his way to yet another shutout, the crowd rose to give him an ovation that continued throughout his at-bat, during the break between innings, and throughout the entire top of the ninth. Larry Claflin, writing in the Boston *Herald* the next morning, compared it to "the last time Joe DiMaggio went to bat in Boston, or Bob Cousy's final game." Carl Yastrzemski, who had had one of baseball's most famous Septembers himself only five years earlier, said "I've never heard anything like that in my life. But I'll tell you one thing: Tiant deserved every bit of it."

After two more clutch victories over the Tigers and Orioles, Tiant lost his final start in Tiger Stadium, 3-1, a game that clinched the pennant for Detroit on the next to the last day of the season. Though he was essentially a relief pitcher for the first four months of the season, Luis finished 15-6 with a 1.91 ERA, good enough for his second ERA title. He was the obvious winner of the Comeback Player of The Year Award. He was thirty-one years old and the most popular player on a team with a suddenly bright future.

Why had Luis struggled for so long and regained it all so quickly? There is no way to be certain, but perhaps after his shoulder injury he just needed some rest. He took only ten weeks off to recover from a broken bone in his shoulder, and he never really stopped pitching after that. When the Red Sox brought him up in 1971, they put him in the rotation and let him throw as many as 154 pitches. Once they sent him to the bullpen he was fine, and by August of 1972, when his brilliant comeback really began, it had been a full year since he had been in the starting rotation.

A Star in Boston—The next four years are the most well known of Tiant's career. He won eighty-one games and became a star on the national stage. He capped his comeback by winning twenty for the second time in 1973, as the Red Sox finished in second place again.

In 1974, Luis won his twentieth on August 23 to give the Red Sox a seemingly safe seven-game lead. The team then went into a horrific batting slump and faded to third, eight games behind the Orioles. Tiant, who had been considered an MVP candidate in August, won only two of his final seven decisions, though he continued to pitch well. In his next four starts after winning his twentieth he lost 3-0, 1-0, and 2-0, then took a no-decision in a game in which he gave up one run in nine innings. He finished 22-13, with a league leading seven shutouts.

Tiant was revered by his teammates in Boston, much as he had been elsewhere. In 1968, Thomas Fitzpatrick wrote an article about Tiant in *Sport* entitled "The Most Popular Indian." When he was released in Minnesota, the Twins long-time publicist called the scene in the locker room , "the most forlorn experience I've ever had in baseball."

The Red Sox had traditionally been a fractured team, but Luis was loved by teammates as different as Bill Lee and Carl Yastrzemski. They loved him because he kept them laughing, largely by making fun of everyone, including himself. He called Yastrzemski "Polacko" and Fisk "Frankenstein," among some of his cleaner sobriquets. A barrel-chested man who looked fatter than he really was, he would emerge from the shower with a cigar in his mouth, look at his naked body in the mirror and declare "good-lookeen sonofabeech" in his exaggerated Spanish accent. After the 1972 season, Red Sox pitcher John Curtis wrote a newspaper story about trying to explain to his wife why he loved Luis Tiant. Dwight Evans later said, "Unless you've played with him, you can't understand what Luis means to a team."

Though 1975 was destined to be a great year for the Red Sox, Luis struggled for most of the summer. As Boston took over the lead for good in late June, Tiant was seen more and more as an aging back-of-the-rotation starter. Luis may have had a reason for his struggles though: his heart and mind were occupied with a long overdue family reunion.

In May 1975, Senator George McGovern made an unofficial visit to Cuba to see Fidel Castro. Although not the principal reason for his trip, he carried with him a letter from Senator Edward Brooke of Massachusetts making a personal plea that Luis's parents be allowed to visit Luis in Boston. The letter suggested that "Luis's career as a major league pitcher is in its latter years" and "he is hopeful that his parents will be able to visit him during this current baseball season." The very next day, Castro approved the request and put the diplomatic wheels in motion for a visit for "as long as they wish." Three and a half months later, there was a tearful reunion at Boston's Logan Airport, with cameramen in full battle array.

On August 26, the Red Sox arranged for Luis's parents to be introduced to the crowd and for Luis Sr. to throw out a ceremonial first pitch. After a prolonged ovation, the sixty-nine-year-old Tiant, standing on the Fenway Park mound adorned in a brown suit and Red Sox cap, went into his full windup and fired a fastball to catcher Tim Blackwell—alas, low and away. Luis Sr., looking annoyed, asked for the ball back. Once more he used his full windup, and delivered a fastball across the heart of the plate. The fans roared as he left the field. His son later commented, "He told me he was ready to go four or five."

Luis Jr. proceeded to get hit hard that night and again five days later, and shut it down for ten days to rest his aching back. Reporters privately lamented that it was a shame that his parents hadn't gotten here a year earlier, when Luis was still good.

On September 11, manager Darrell Johnson decided to give Luis one last chance to get it going, against the Tigers. The Red Sox lead, once as high as 8-1/2 games, was now down to five. If Luis was going to help out, it had to be *right now*. Tiant responded with seven and two-thirds innings of no-hit ball before giving up a run and three hits. When asked about the bloop hit by Aurelio Rodriguez that ruined the no-hitter, Luis Sr. responded, "Don't talk about a lucky hit. The man hit the ball pretty good."

Luis's next start, on September 16, was the biggest game of the year and one of the legendary games in the history of Fenway Park. The hard-charging Orioles, now 4-1/2 games out, were in town, and Jim Palmer would face Luis. Many observers claim that there were well over 40,000 people in the park that night, several thousand over capacity. Tiant pitched his first shutout of the year, a 2-0 five-hitter, and the crowd was chanting for most of the night ("Loo-Eee, Loo-Eee, Loo-Eee"). At the end of the month Tiant pitched another shutout in Cleveland, and the Sox won the pennant by 4-1/2 games.

After these three remarkable performances, Tiant had evolved from an afterthought in the rotation to the obvious choice to start the first game of the playoffs against the three-time defending champs. He three-hit the Athletics to start a Red Sox sweep, and followed with a five-hit shutout in the first game of the World Series against the Reds. In Game 4, in perhaps the quintessential performance of his career, he threw 163 pitches, worked out of jams in nearly every inning, and recorded a complete game 5-4 win. He couldn't hold a 3-0 lead in Game 6, and was finally removed losing 6-3, before Bernie Carbo and Carlton Fisk bailed him out with legendary home runs.

Winding down—Tiant won twenty-one games for a struggling Red Sox team in 1976, and followed that with twelve and thirteen wins the next two years. After the team's stunning collapse late in the 1978 season, the Red Sox found themselves 3-1/2 games behind the Yankees with eight games to go. Before a game in Toronto, Luis said, "If we lose today, it will be over my dead body. They'll have to leave me face down on the mound." He won, of course, and Boston went on to win its last eight games, including two more Tiant wins on three days' rest. On the last day of the season, the Red Sox needed a win and a Yankee loss to force a playoff. Cleveland beat Catfish Hunter while Tiant dazzled the Fenway crowd with a

two-hitter against the Blue Jays. His career record for the Sox in September and October was 31-12. It was his last game in a Red Sox uniform.

In the off-season, the Red Sox management decided to let Tiant and Bill Lee leave, and Tiant signed with the Yankees. Dwight Evans was devastated at what he considered management's ignorance of what Luis meant in the clubhouse. Carl Yastrzemski says he cried when he heard the news: "They tore out our heart and soul."

Luis had one good year with New York, winning thirteen games in 1979, before falling to 8-9 in 1980 and not pitching at all in the playoff loss to the Royals. After the season, the Yankees released him. He signed with the Pirates in 1981, but spent most of the season with his old team in Portland. He excelled again for the Beavers—13-7, 3.82—but struggled with the Pirates and was released at the end of the season. He finished his major league career with six games for the 1982 Angels, winning his final game against the Red Sox on August 17, 1982.

Luis Tiant was one of the most beloved and respected players of his time, and certainly one of the most popular players ever to wear a Red Sox uniform. His career was one of streaks, and his best ones, in the pennant races of 1972, 1975, and 1978 and in the 1975 post-season, came when his team needed him most. Given up for dead in the middle of his career, he came back to greatness that inspired a region and two nations. He is a reasonable candidate for the Hall of Fame, but for those of us fortunate enough to see him close up in the 1970s, his career needs no such confirmation. El Tiante is unforgettable.

Sources:

Claflin, Larry, "He Smokes in Shower, Sizzles on Hill," *The Sporting News*, 174:14, October 14, 1972.

Fitzpatrick, Thomas, "The Most Popular Indian," *Sport*, 46:3, September 1968.

Johnson, Lloyd and Miles Wolff (eds.), *The Encyclopedia of Minor League Baseball, 2nd Edition*, Baseball America, Inc., 1997.

Gammons, Peter, *Beyond The Sixth Game*, Houghton Mifflin, 1985.

Gammons, Peter [Danny Peary, ed.], *Baseball's Finest*, J. G. Press, 1990.

Leggett, William, "Funny Kind of a Race," *Sports Illustrated*, 37:13, September 25, 1972.

Schneider, Russell. "'I'm Skinny, Lucky,' Says Winner Luis," *The Sporting News*, 161:19, May 28, 1966.

Schneider, Russell, "Lucky Luis? Modest Hurler Tiant Thinks So," *The Sporting News*, 166:3, August 3, 1968.

Tiant, Luis and Joe Fitzgerald, *El Tiante*, Doubleday, 1976.

The Oregonian (newspaper), April-July 1964.

The Sporting News Baseball Guides, 1963-1979.

Clark, Dick and Larry Lester (eds.), *The Negro Leagues Book*, SABR, 1994.

International League Total Bases

300 TB an endangered species

David Chrisman

Agood indication of what kind of offensive campaign a batter has had is to tabulate his total bases for the season. In most professional leagues, 300 total bases is excellent work. In the International League, that level was reached 121 times from 1884 through 1999. During that same period, 400 total bases have been reached only five times.

As a club, the mighty Baltimore Orioles had the most 300 total bases achievers—39. The Buffalo Bisons had 28 such seasons, although the Buffalo franchise had a much longer stay in the circuit than did the Baltimore club. The Orioles left the circuit after the 1953 season, when the St. Louis Browns came to town and returned Baltimore to the big leagues. Buffalo played in the circuit through the 1968 campaign and re-joined the league in 1998 after a stay in the now defunct American Association.

The 300 level was reached most often in the 1920s—65 times. In the 1930s, players reached the plateau 41 times. No other decade came close. In the 1940s there were thirteen 300 total-base seasons, and in the 1950s, only nine of them. Since 1960, the International League has seen just seven seasons when any player has totalled 300 bases. Since the 1950s (1960-1999), the circuit has had a player reach the 300 level in total bases only seven times.

The five 400-total-bases achievements in the International League follow a similar pattern (twice in the '20s and three times in the '30s). Prior to 1920, no International League batter was successful in accumulating 300 total bases in one season. Rochester's Wally Pipp in 1914 came the closest with 290 while other impressive marks were achieved by the following: 1898, Toronto's Buck Freeman (284); 1896, Wilkes-Barre's Abel Lezotte (283); 1917, Toronto's Napoleon Lajoie (283); 1893, Buffalo's Jake Drauby (281); and 1900, Worcester's Kitty Bransfield (281).

Let's look at the 300 total-base achievers from 1920 through 1999.

1920 (2)

Jack Bentley, Baltimore	354
Merwyn Jacobson, Baltimore	323

1921 (8)

Jack Bentley, Baltimore	397
Homer Summa, Rochester	335
Fred Thomas, Reading	335
Merwyn Jacobson, Baltimore	317
Fred Merkle, Rochester	313
Bob Fothergill, Rochester	313
Ed Goebel, Reading	303
Jewel Ens, Syracuse	300

1922 (4)

Al Wingo, Toronto	350
Jack Bentley, Baltimore	334
John Jacobs	319
Fred Merkle, Rochester	301

David Chrisman *is a retired English teacher and a freelance writer with an interest in the history of minor league baseball between 1900-1960.*

1923 (6)

Fred Merkle, Rochester	354
Bill Kelly, Buffalo	329
Babe Dye, Buffalo	311
Jim Holt, Jersey City	302
Max Bishop, Baltimore	300
Dick Porter, Baltimore	300

1924 (8)

Bill Kelly, Buffalo	346
Jim Holt, Jersey City	337
Joe Kelly, Toronto	329
John Conlan, Rochester	324
Dick Porter, Baltimore	318
Fred Merkle, Rochester	317
Fred Kane, Newark	311
Tom Connolly, Baltimore	302

1925 (6)

Charlie Gehringer, Toronto	337
Bill Kelly, Buffalo	330
Clayton Sheedy, Baltimore	319
Fritz Maisel, Baltimore	313
Vern Spencer, Buffalo	305
Jimmy Walsh, Buffalo	300

1926 (6)

Bill Kelly, Buffalo	386
Fresco Thompson, Buffalo	350
Clayton Sheedy, Baltimore	339
Dan Clark, Syracuse	334
Lew Fonseca, Newark	332
Jimmy Walsh, Buffalo	304

1927 (5)

Del Bissonette, Buffalo	408
Dick Porter, Baltimore	379
Roy Carlyle, Newark	336
Howie Williamson, Syracuse	315
Harry Layne, Syracuse	312

1928 (5)

Dale Alexander, Toronto	400
Al Moore, Buffalo	340
Charlie Gelbert, Rochester	318
Dick Porter, Baltimore	316
Charles Walsh, Reading	303

1929 (7)

Jim "Rip" Collins, Rochester	352
George Fisher, Buffalo	352
George Quellich, Reading	331
George Loepp, Baltimore	330
Al Moore, Buffalo	323
Joe Rabbitt, Toronto	317
Al Bool, Baltimore	311

1930 (11)

Joe Hauser, Baltimore	443
Jim "Rip" Collins, Rochester	426
Vince Barton, Baltimore	361
Wilbur Davis, Reading	347
Beauty McGowan, Baltimore	344
Herb Thomas, Newark	344
Jim Stroner, Baltimore	324
John Gill, Baltimore	323
Al Moore, Buffalo	322
Pepper Martin, Rochester	304
Harry Layne, Newark	301

1931 (4)

John Gill, Baltimore	340
Ray Pepper, Rochester	340
Jim Poole, Reading	310
Ollie Tucker, Buffalo	306

1932 (7)

Buzz Arlett, Baltimore	378
Beauty McGowan, Baltimore	337
George Puccinelli, Rochester	321
Ollie Carnegie, Buffalo	314
Ivey Shiver, Montreal	312
George Detore, Buffalo	306
Ollie Tucker, Buffalo	304

1933 (2)

Julius Solters, Baltimore	358
Buzz Arlett, Baltimore	345

1934 (3)

Fred Sington, Albany	323
Woody Abernathy, Baltimore	312
Jake Powell, Albany	305

1935 (2)

George Puccinelli, Baltimore	435
Ollie Carnegie, Buffalo	331

1936 (5)

Smead Jolley, Albany	345
Woody Abernathy, Baltimore	327
Beauty McGowan, Buffalo	320
Elburt Fletcher, Buffalo	313
Babe Dahlgren, Syracuse	301

1937 (2)
Ab Wright, Baltimore	334
Joe Gordon, Newark	301

1938 (2)
Ollie Carnegie, Buffalo	358
Charlie Keller, Newark	329

1939 (1)
Murray Howell, Baltimore	302

1940 (2)
Murray Howell, Baltimore	330
Nick Etten, Baltimore	305

1942 (1)
Gene Moore, Montreal	305

1944 (1)
Howie Moss, Baltimore	319

1945 (2)
Roland Gladu, Montreal	313
Sherm Lollar, Baltimore	306

1946 (1)
Eddie Robinson, Baltimore	305

1947 (3)
Hank Sauer, Syracuse	362
Howie Moss, Baltimore	325
Jack Graham, Jersey City	308

1948 (1)
Johnny Groth, Buffalo	358

1949 (2)
Sam Jethroe, Montreal	330
Steve Bilko, Rochester	300

1951 (2)
Archie Wilson, Buffalo	328
Marv Rickert, Baltimore	315

1952 (1)
Frank Carswell, Buffalo	300

1953 (2)
Sandy Amoros, Montreal	321
Rocky Nelson, Montreal	320

1955 (1)
Rocky Nelson, Montreal	335

1957 (1)
Luke Easter, Buffalo	300

1958 (2)
Rocky Nelson, Toronto	340
Luke Easter, Buffalo	301

1959 (1)
Frank Herrera, Buffalo	346

1964 (1)
Mack Jones, Syracuse	336

1982 (1)
Greg Wells, Toledo	306

1996 (1)
Phil Hiatt, Toledo	304

1998 (2)
Brian Daubach, Charlotte	314
Alex Ramirez, Buffalo	301

1999 (2)
Steve Cox, Durham	315
D. T. Cromer, Indianapolis	301

It is obvious that Jack Dunn's Baltimore Orioles of the 1920s were prolific total base achievers, with the great Jack Bentley reaching 300 three times and Dick Porter four. Buffalo's Bill Kelly and Rochester's Fred Merkle were equally adept at amassing total bases.

GM George Weiss's Baltimore Orioles of the early thirties were as prolific at producing total bases accumulations in excess of 300 as any comparable group in league history. The high-flying Orioles of 1930 had five players in excess of 300 total bases. In 1932, the Orioles had three players reach the coveted 300 mark, as did the Buffalo Bisons.

Three Rochester Colt players reached the 300 level in total bases in 1921, and Buffalo's Irish Mafia turned the trick in successive years (1925-26). Nobody can deny the impressive nature of Buffalo's Del Bissonette's offensive display in 1927—his golden season. Not only did he lead the circuit in total bases (408), but he was the league's best in home runs (31), runs batted in (167), doubles (49) and triples (20). His 167 RBI count is the Buffalo club record and the circuit's fourth highest ever.

In 1928, Toronto's Dale Alexander won the triple crown with an impressive .380 average. In addition, Big Moose led the league in home runs (31), runs batted in (144), doubles (49), and total bases (400). It was a campaign to rival Bissonette's 1927 season.

Baltimore's version of Babe Ruth (Jack Bentley) just missed the coveted 400 total bases total in 1921 with 397—the league's sixth-highest accumulation. Another Baltimore slugger, George Puccinelli (in 1935) also won the triple crown. Along the way, the Pooch averaged .359, bashed 53 home runs and drove in 172 runs. He also led the circuit in hits (209), runs scored (135), and doubles (49). His 435 total bases achieved in that year stand as the circuit's second highest mark. His home runs and runs batted in marks are the league's third-highest achievements.

Buffalo's Bill Kelly, in 1926, bashed 44 home runs and drove in 151 runs on his way to a 386 total bases attainment. In that campaign, he was joined on the 300 total bases plateau by teammates Fresco Thompson (340) and Jimmy Walsh (304).

An impressive total bases accumulation can come in many forms. For example, in 1936, Albany's Smead Jolley accumulated 345 total bases, fueled by his hits totals (221) and doubles count (52). However, more often than not, the 300 total bases mark is linked to a high home run total.

Interestingly, from 1920 through 1940, at least one batter accumulated 300 total bases each season—with the high water mark of eleven players in 1930. Nobody got there in either 1941 or 1943. In the '50s, the gaps occurred in 1950, 1954 and 1956. Only Syracuse's Mack Jones (in 1964) reached the 300 level in the '60s, and nary a batter accomplished the feat in the '70s. The '80s had only Toledo's Greg Wells with his 1982 mark of 306.

The circuit made a comeback in the 1990s, when it expanded to include half of the defunct American Association.

Here are the International League records by team:

Baltimore (38)

1. 1930- Joe Hauser	443
2. 1935- George Puccinelli	435
3. 1921- Jack Bentley	397
4. 1927- Dick Porter	379
5. 1932- Buzz Arlett	378
6. 1930- Vince Barton	361
7. 1933- Julius Solters	358
8. 1920- Jack Bentley	354
9. 1933- Buzz Arlett	345
10. 1930- Beauty McGowan	344
11. 1931- John Gill	340
12. 1932- Beauty McGowan	340
13. 1926- Clayton Sheedy	339
14. 1922- Jack Bentley	334
15. 1937- Ab Wright	334
16. 1929- George Loepp	330
17. 1940- Murray Howell	330
18. 1936- Woody Abernathy	327
19. 1947- Howie Moss	325
20. 1930- Jim Stroner	324
21. 1920- Merwyn Jacobson	323
22. 1930- John Gill	323
23. 1925- Clayton Sheedy	319
24. 1944- Howie Moss	319
25. 1924- Dick Porter	318
26. 1921- Merwyn Jacobson	317
27. 1928- Dick Porter	316
28. 1951- Marv Rickert	315
29. 1925- Fritz Maisel	313
30. 1934- Woody Abernathy	312
31. 1929- Al Bool	311
32. 1945- Sherm Lollar	306
33. 1940- Nick Etten	305
34. 1946- Eddie Robinson	305
35. 1924- Tom Connolly	302
36. 1939- Murray Howell	302
37. 1923- Max Bishop	300
38. 1923- Dick Porter	300

Buffalo (28)

1. 1927- Del Bissonette	408
2. 1926- Bill Kelly	386
3. 1938- Ollie Carnegie	358
4. 1948- Johnny Groth	358
5. 1929- George Fisher	352
6. 1926- Fresco Thompson	350
7. 1924- Bill Kelly	346
8. 1959- Frank Herrera	346
9. 1928- Al Moore	340
10. 1935- Ollie Carnegie	331
11. 1925- Bill Kelly	330
12. 1923- Bill Kelly	329
13. 1951- Archie Wilson	328
14. 1929- Al Moore	323
15. 1930- Al Moore	322
16. 1936- Beauty McGowan	320
17. 1932- Ollie Carnegie	314
18. 1936- Elburt Fletcher	313
19. 1923- Babe Dye	311
20. 1932- George Detore	306
21. 1932- Ollie Tucker	304
22. 1925- Vern Spencer	305

23. 1926- Jimmy Walsh	304	
24. 1958- Luke Easter	301	
25. 1998- Alex Ramirez	301	
26. 1925- Jimmy Walsh	300	
27. 1952- Frank Carswell	300	
28. 1957- Luke Easter	300	

Rochester (14)

1. 1930- Jim "Rip" Collins	426
2. 1923- Fred Merkle	354
3. 1929- Jim "Rip" Collins	352
4. 1931- Ray Pepper	340
5. 1921- Homer Summa	335
6. 1924- John Conlan	324
7. 1932- George Puccinelli	321
8. 1928- Charlie Gelbert	318
9. 1924- Fred Merkle	317
10. 1921- Fred Merkle	313
11. 1921- Bob Fothergill	313
12. 1930- Pepper Martin	304
13. 1922- Fred Merkle	301
14. 1949- Steve Bilko	300

Newark (7)

1. 1930- Herb Thomas	344
2. 1927- Roy Carlyle	336
3. 1926- Lew Fonseca	332
4. 1938- Charlie Keller	329
5. 1924- Fred Kane	311
6. 1930- Harry Layne	301
7. 1937- Joe Gordon	301

Syracuse (7)

1. 1947- Hank Sauer	362
2. 1926- Dan Clark	334
3. 1964- Mack Jones	336
4. 1927- Howie Williamson	315
5. 1927- Harry Layne	312
6. 1936- Babe Dahlgren	301
7. 1921- Jewel Ens	300

Montreal (7)

1. 1955- Rocky Nelson	335
2. 1949- Sam Jethroe	330
3. 1953- Sandy Amoros	321
4. 1953- Rocky Nelson	320
5. 1945- Roland Gladu	313
6. 1932- Ivey Shiver	312
7. 1942- Gene Moore	305

Reading (6)

1. 1930- Wilbur Davis	347

2. 1921- Fred Thomas	335
3. 1929- George Quellich	331
4. 1931- Jim Poole	310
5. 1921- Ed Goebel	303
6. 1928- Charles Walsh	303

Toronto (6)

1. 1928- Dale Alexander	400
2. 1922- Al Wingo	350
3. 1958- Rocky Nelson	340
4. 1925- Charlie Gehringer	337
5. 1924- Joe Kelly	329
6. 1929- Joe Rabbitt	317

Jersey City (3)

1. 1924- Jim Holt	337
2. 1947- Jack Graham	308
3. 1923- Jim Holt	302

Albany (3)

1. 1936- Smead Jolley	345
2. 1934- Fred Sington	323
3. 1934- Jake Powell	305

Toledo (2)

1. 1982- Greg Wells	306
2. 1996- Phil Hiatt	304

Charlotte (1)

1. 1998- Brian Daubach	314

Durham (1)

1. 1999- Steve Cox	315

Indianapolis (1)

1. 1999- D. T. Cromer	301

Rochester had all of its 300 total bases accumulations prior to 1950. Eight players associated with the New York Giants attained the mark. Seven Cardinal farmhands achieved the coveted 300 total bases attainment (between 1927 and 1960). No Baltimore Oriole farmhand in Rochester has attained the coveted 300 total base attainment. Bobby Grich, with 299 in 1971, came the closest.

As successful as Columbus has been from 1954 to the present, no Clipper or Jet player has yet achieved 300 total bases in one season.

Through 1927, Syracuse was the principal Cardinal farm in the International League and its last season with that affiliation was a great one. Harry Layne achieved 322 total bases and Howie Williamson added 308. Dan Clark had a big year in 1926 (337 total bases). In the '30s and '40s, Syracuse had a Cincinnati Red working agreement. In 1936, Babe Dahlgren had 301 total bases. Hank Sauer's monster year in 1947 set the Salt City's all-time record at 362.

The independent Buffalo Bisons of the 1920s were a murderous hitting team. Bill Kelly accumulated 300 total bases on four separate occasions and Jimmy Walsh turned the trick twice.

In the 1930s, both Al Moore and Ollie Carnegie reached the coveted 300 total on three occasions. In the 1950s, Luke Easter had two 300 total base campaigns. Rochester's Fred Merkle also reached the 300 mark four times, as did Baltimore's Dick Porter.

In 1930, the league saw Baltimore's Joe Hauser set all-time marks in home runs (63) and total bases (443). Who knows the heights that Hauser might have climbed in 1931 if he hadn't been injured. "Unser Choe" started out on a pace to eclipse his 1930 attainments. Still, his home run total (31) was good enough to lead the circuit.

Rochester's precocious Ripper, Jim Collins, had impressive back-to-back campaigns in 1929-1930. In 1929, Collins tied Buffalo's George Fisher in total bases (352) while leading the circuit in home runs (38) and runs batted in (134). One year later, Collins won the batting title with a high water mark of .376. In addition, he set the league's all-time runs batted in mark (180)—five more than Hauser. Collins trailed Hauser in home runs with 40 and total bases (426). This was one of two times in the history of the circuit that two men finished with 40 or more home runs in one season. It was the only time that two men accumulated 400 or more total bases in a single campaign.

Montreal rose to total base prominence in the 1940s and 1950s—mainly on the broad shoulders of Rocky Nelson. In addition, Nelson in 1958 became the first Toronto Maple Leaf since 1929 to reach the 300 level in total bases. Let's look at the stars who had multiple 300 total base seasons in the International League:

Bill Kelly (4)

1926- Buffalo	386
1924- Buffalo	346
1925- Buffalo	330
1923- Buffalo	329

Dick Porter (4)

1927- Baltimore	379
1924- Baltimore	318
1928- Baltimore	316
1923- Baltimore	300

Fred Merkle (4)

1923- Rochester	354
1924- Rochester	317
1921- Rochester	313
1922- Rochester	301

Jack Bentley (3)

1921- Baltimore	397
1920- Baltimore	354
1922- Baltimore	334

Al Moore (3)

1928- Buffalo	340
1929- Buffalo	323
1930- Buffalo	322

Ollie Carnegie (3)

1938- Buffalo	358
1935- Buffalo	331
1932- Buffalo	314

Beauty McGowan (3)

1930- Baltimore	344
1932- Baltimore	337
1936- Buffalo	320

Rocky Nelson (3)

1958- Toronto	340
1955- Montreal	335
1953- Montreal	320

Merwyn Jacobson (2)

1920- Baltimore	323
1921- Baltimore	317

Clayton Sheedy (2)

1926- Baltimore	339
1925- Baltimore	319

Jimmy Walsh (2)

1926- Buffalo	304
1925- Buffalo	300

Harry Layne (2)

1927- Syracuse	312
1930- Newark	301

George Quellich (2)

1929- Reading	331
1931- Newark	310

Murray Howell (2)

1940- Baltimore	330
1939- Baltimore	302

Luke Easter (2)

1958- Buffalo	301
1957- Buffalo	300

Jim Holt (2)

1924- Jersey City	337
1923- Jersey City	302

John Gill (2)

1931- Baltimore	340
1930- Baltimore	323

Jim "Rip" Collins (2)

1930- Rochester	426
1929- Rochester	352

Buzz Arlett (2)

1932- Baltimore	378
1933- Baltimore	345

George Puccinelli (2)

1935- Baltimore	435
1932- Rochester	321

Woody Abernathy (2)

1936- Baltimore	327
1934- Baltimore	312

Howie Moss (2)

1947- Baltimore	325
1944- Baltimore	319

Why have the 300 total bases accumulations begun to dry up in recent campaigns? Perhaps it is the changing nature of the game. These days an impressive farmhand seldom stays all season at the Triple A level. In an earlier era, minor league teams were more independent and often played much longer schedules than they do today. Whatever the reasons, the 300 total bases achievement has become an endangered species at the Triple A minor league level.

Aspects of Nemesis

A look at the phenomenon of "killer" pitchers

Zita Carno

You know the names: Mathewson, Johnson, Alexander, Grove, Hubbell, Ruffing, Gomez, Newhouser, Feller, Chandler, Brecheen, Trucks, Raschi, Lopat, Spahn, Maglie, Maddux, Marichal, Glavine, Martinez, Clemens, Wells…

They and many others throughout the history of the game were, and are, also known by other names: killers, jinxes, hexes, hoodoos, voodoos, and the entire gamut of unprintable epithets. They were, and are, accused of black magic, sorcery, witchcraft, alliance with the devil, and conspiracy with Macbeth's three witches. They were, and are, aspects of Nemesis.

In the ancient Greek mythology, Nemesis was the goddess of retributive justice. In time her name became synonymous with one who destroys inevitably and relentlessly, and from there it was only a short step to the meaning of the term in modern baseball: a pitcher who repeatedly, consistently and with almost monotonous regularity defeats certain teams as if he owns them. A killer.

To list every pitcher who has ever functioned thus would require volumes, so let's go with some representative examples. But first, let's consider what makes a pitcher a killer.

Simply put, such a pitcher is extraordinarily effective against a certain team—or, in some cases, more than one team—over a period of time, usually with a

percentage of .600 or better. There have been instances of pitchers who did this for a year or two and then stopped, either because they were traded out of the league or because their patsies caught on to them. Walter "Monk" Dubiel, for example, who pitched for the New York Yankees in 1945 and 1946, racked up an 8-2 record against the Boston Red Sox before disappearing into the minor leagues. Also with the Yankees was Ernie Bonham, who over a period of seven years went 15-6 against the Cleveland Indians before being traded to the Pittsburgh Pirates at the end of the 1946 season. Detroit Tigers hurler Hal Newhouser, who beat the Yankees six times in 1943 without a defeat, never again exhibited quite that level of mastery, even though he gave them a lot of trouble in subsequent years.

For the most part, however, such pitchers continue to build up winning records against particular opponents over long periods of time, sometimes with devastating psychological results. Let's consider a few of them.

In the beginning—The first recorded instances of pitchers being labeled "killers" occurred in 1908, both in the National League. In July and August of that year the Chicago Cubs' Jack Pfiester won crucial games against the New York Giants, leading sportswriters to call him—what else?—"Jack the Giant Killer." Then, during the final week of the season, the Philadelphia Phillies' Harry Coveleski defeated the Giants three times, thus also earning the nickname,

Zita Carno *is a retired musician and a baseball enthusiast from childhood, particularly the Yankees. She is an especially keen student of pitching in all its ramifications.*

"Giant Killer." (This feat was virtually duplicated in the 1957 World Series by Lew Burdette who defeated the Yankees three times, two of them shutouts.)

In the early days of the game pitchers worked every two or three days, even working both ends of double-headers, and the best of them compiled good records against all comers. Even then there would be one team, maybe two, these aces would beat more regularly than the rest. Look at Babe Ruth—he went 17-5 against the Yankees before they got him. And Walter Johnson, who beat everybody, was most effective against the White Sox, the Tigers, and the Highlanders/Yankees. His 66-42 record against Detroit still stands as the most lifetime victories by an American League pitcher against one club.

In the National League, the record-holder in this department is Grover Cleveland Alexander, with a 70-24 lifetime record against the Cincinnati Reds. Christy Mathewson is not far behind, at 52-24 versus the St. Louis Cardinals and 64-18 against Cincinnati. The most startling record of the era, in either league, belongs to Carl Mays, who during his career with first the Red Sox and then the Yankees racked up a 35-3 (.921) record against the Philadelphia Athletics. (See Kenneth D. Richard's article on page 122.)

The winds of change—In the 1920s, the ball was livelier, home runs were more common, the spitball and other such pitches were outlawed, and hurlers were forced to find other ammunition. George Blaeholder and George Uhle both came up with the slider, and Red Ruffing refined the pitch and made it a staple in the repertoire of almost every hurler. There still were some pitchers who beat everybody, but more who displayed a wider range of "killer" records and percentages. Take the case of Lefty Grove, who was a Red Sox killer from 1925 through 1933 with a 35-8 record against Boston. He didn't do too badly against the Tigers, either, compiling a lifetime record of 39-19. But at the other end of the spectrum we see 31-25 against the Senators and 34-27 versus the Yankees.

Pitchers began to take more time between starts. The era of the relief ace was just around the corner. It took a pitcher longer to build up the kind of record against a team that would earn him the title of Nemesis. And there were trades: on occasion a pitcher who had been beating a certain team to a pulp would end up being traded to his patsy. Grove, who stifled the Red Sox for nine years with Philadelphia, was traded to the Sox and could manage only a 13-5 record against his old team, although he continued to defeat the Detroit Tigers.

The Age of Nemesis—From the 1930s through the 1960s, there were many Nemeses in both leagues. As usual, the great power pitchers were highly successful, but during these years, many finesse hurlers relied on good stuff, accurate control, and brains to enjoy equal success against their chosen victims. In fact, they may have been the deadliest of the lot. I will discuss one in particular later on, because the devastating effect he had on his favorite patsies constituted an extreme case.

Several teams were especially beloved of these "killer" pitchers. In the American League the teams they loved to beat were the Philadelphia Athletics, the St. Louis Browns and the Washington Senators, while in the National League the overwhelming favorites were the Chicago Cubs, followed by the Pittsburgh Pirates and the Cincinnati Reds. Let's look at a few examples.

American League

Pitcher	Opponent	Lifetime Record
Bob Feller	Philadelphia Athletics	40-13, .755
	Washington Senators	30-11, .732
	St. Louis Browns	33-14, .702
	Chicago White Sox	40-20, .667
Lefty Gomez	Philadelphia Athletics	34-11, .755
	Boston Red Sox	23-9, .719
	St. Louis Browns	24-11, .702
	Cleveland Indians	38-20, .655
Frank Lary	New York Yankees	28-13, .683
(Note: Lary's percentage against the rest of the league was .493.)		
Hal Newhouser	Philadelphia Athletics	24-9, .727
Vic Raschi	Philadelphia Athletics	26-6, .813
	Cleveland Indians	22-8, .733
	Chicago White Sox	19-7, .731
Allie Reynolds	Boston Red Sox	25-11, .694
Dizzy Trout	Chicago White Sox	33-16, .673

There were, of course, many others. There was also at least one study in frustration: Mel Harder, the great Cleveland Indians pitcher, defeated the Yankees 25 times—and was beaten by them 25 times, for a grand total of .500. The same thing happened to Bob Feller.

Now to the National League.

National League

Pitcher	Opponent	Lifetime Record
Harry Brecheen	Chicago Cubs	31-12, .721
Lew Burdette	Pittsburgh Pirates	25-9, .735
	NY/SF Giants	32-15, .681
Dizzy Dean	Cincinnati Reds	27-4, .871
Carl Hubbell	Philadelphia Phillies	44-14, .759

	Boston Braves	34-13, .723
	Pittsburgh Pirates	44-14, .700
Sal Maglie	Pittsburgh Pirates	25-6, .806
	Philadelphia Phillies	17-9, .653
	Bklyn./LA Dodgers	22-13, .629
Don Newcombe	Chicago Cubs	21-7, .750
	Cincinnati Reds	21-8, .724
	Pittsburgh Pirates	22-10, .688
	St. Louis Cardinals	23-11, .676
Warren Spahn	Chicago Cubs	47-19, .712
	Cincinnati Reds	62-29, .681
	Philadelphia Phillies	47-28, .627

Later on, Juan Marichal of the San Francisco Giants became a great Dodger killer: 37-18, .673.

Question: Is there any particular kind of pitcher who is more likely to be a killer?

The answer is no. In this sampling of aspects of Nemesis, we find a nice variety. There are the power pitchers, such as Feller, Newcombe, and Raschi. There are the finesse pitchers such as Brecheen. And then we have the "everything bagel" pitchers like Gomez, Reynolds, and Spahn. We have pitchers who zero in on the contenders, pitchers who pick on the lesser lights of the league, and the pitchers who don't discriminate—they get on everybody and beat them to a pulp.

Killer Psychology—There's an old saw in baseball that states unequivocally that all it takes to beat a certain team is for a certain pitcher to throw his glove onto the field.

The morning of a crucial doubleheader finds the Cleveland Indians perusing the paper to see who their mound opponents will be, and what do they find? The starters for the other team are two pitchers who have been waxing them all season. Or just before a night game the Houston Astros learn that Tom Glavine has been scratched because of the flu, and who will take the mound instead? Greg Maddux, who has a 24-9 record against them. Either way, the result is the same: "Oh, no, not again!" or "We've had it!" or—most likely—a string of undeleted expletives, imprecations, invectives, or just plain cusswords.

Why is this? Why does the mere mention of a certain pitcher throw such apprehension into the hearts of a particular team that they are thoroughly convinced the game is over before it has even started and they might as well take their equipment and go home? We may never have the complete and final answer to that question—even the pitchers themselves are at a loss for words—but it may help to look at some psychological angles. Specifically, let's examine three.

The first is known simply as the law of reversed effect, which states that the harder you try to do something the harder it gets. Case in point: the hitter in a slump. No matter what he does, he just can't buy a base hit. He goes 0-for-15, then 0-for-25, then 0-for-30. He's tried everything from a change of stance to a lighter (or heavier) bat to sticking pins in a voodoo doll—nothing seems to help. When does the slump end? Usually when the batter stops struggling and just tries to lay the bat on the ball. Athletes function best when they just do what they do.

Next is the concept of the self-fulfilling prophecy, essentially a matter of supreme confidence, or the lack of it. On the positive side, a pitcher decides he can and will beat a particular team silly. He convinces himself he's going to do it. And he goes out and does it. The Brooklyn Dodgers had been eating lefthanders for breakfast, lunch and dinner, and the Boston Braves had not even sent Warren Spahn out to face them. It was assumed that the situation would stay the same in the 1953 World Series. But Ed Lopat had other plans. He decided he was going to beat the Dodgers in the Series, and what was more, he was going to go nine innings to do it. And in the second game he did exactly that, 4-2.

The third psychological factor is known as learned helplessness, at once a separate and distinct entity and one that incorporates elements of the other two. Earlier in the twentieth century, a group of psychologists ran a series of experiments on laboratory rats in which they first subjected them to a series of shocks and other unpleasantnesses, then taught them how to escape them. Then they repeatedly thwarted, stymied, blocked the rats' efforts to escape. After a while the rats simply gave up. The psychologists then reasoned that the same could be applied to humans.

And so we come to the situation regarding certain teams and their inability to beat certain pitchers.

Jim Brosnan, in his book *Pennant Race*, describes the Reds' effort to battle a losing streak: "The momentum of losing a series of games creates a mental force against which a superhuman effort seems called for." But he fails to mention what happens when the superhuman effort is constantly stymied. For this we need to ask the pitchers involved how they do it, how they beat these teams so consistently—and we get as many answers as there are pitchers. Some don't know. Others say simply that they feel they have to do their best against certain teams, such as Frank Lary who racked up a 28-13 lifetime record against the Yankees. Still others take a scientific approach.

One of the last-named is the special case I mentioned earlier. All three elements combined in his success against one particular team.

An extreme case—On September 23, 1949, the Cleveland Indians held a bizarre ceremony at Municipal Stadium prior to their game against Detroit. It was a funeral rite in which they took down their 1948 American League and World Series flags and the crown that had rested atop the image of Chief Wahoo, proceeded to deep center field, and buried these items along with their pennant hopes. Just three days earlier they had been eliminated from the race. Then they went out and lost the game, 5-0.

Perhaps the most puzzled spectator at this eerie event was Cleveland *News* sports columnist Ed McAuley. He expressed this bewilderment in a long article which appeared in *The Sporting News* on October 5, coincidentally the opening day of the World Series. He called it a post-mortem, an attempt to determine just why the team, only one year after their glorious Series triumph, had finished an ignominious third.

What *had happened* to them?

McAuley began with this inescapable conclusion: the Indians had given up.

They had, he said, lost the will and the desire to win. He then explored some possible reasons for this. He cited such factors as the season-long plague of injuries which had decimated the pitching staff and much of the team, reports of dissension within the team, frequent and vehement clashes between shortstop-manager Lou Boudreau and owner Bill Veeck, rumors that some of the players had taken to excessive drinking, and a number of other possibilities. But McAuley omitted one major element, perhaps because it had never occurred to him.

Nemesis.

Ed Lopat was a heavy-set strawberry-blond lefthander who came up to the Chicago White Sox in 1944 and immediately zeroed in on the Indians, beating them, 2-1, in his first start against them. He continued to beat them with such consistency and such monotonous regularity that within a short time he became the one pitcher they feared more than any other in the league. In 1948, just before the start of spring training, he was traded to the New York Yankees, and by the end of the 1949 season he held a 22-6 record against the Indians and was well into a winning streak—his second—that would not be stopped until the middle of the 1951 season.

The situation had gone far beyond throwing the glove onto the field. All that was needed was for the Indians to know that they would be facing him; the only times they escaped were when his turn did not come up in the rotation. They had become thoroughly convinced that they could not beat him for sour apples, and most of the time they could not, as his eventual 40-13 lifetime record against them clearly demonstrates. They had indeed given up.

Stories and rumors about him

Eddie Lopat

were making the rounds: Ed Lopat practiced sorcery and witchcraft; he dabbled in black magic; he consorted with Macbeth's three witches; he supped with the devil. The word was that he held some arcane, irresistible power over the team. And it wasn't only the team that was affected; the fans, the sportswriters and ultimately the entire city were caught in the trap from which the only escape would come when he retired after the 1955 season.

In fact, Lopat's irresistible power over the Tribe had nothing to do with black magic or witchcraft; they were especially vulnerable to his kind of pitching. He was one of the greatest strategic pitchers in the history of the game—a finesse pitcher of the highest order who knew how to compensate for lack of speed with a bewildering assortment of breaking stuff, an even more bewildering assortment of ways and speeds with which to throw all those breaking pitches, and accurate, pinpoint control that led observers to state that he was wild if he walked more than two in a game. He was particularly adept at keeping batters off balance, disorienting them, messing up their timing and their thinking, and getting them to go after the pitches he wanted them to hit; they would complain repeatedly that after facing him in a game they couldn't get their timing back for a week.

Lopat had an easy, deceptive, almost hypnotic motion which made matters even worse for opposing hitters who found themselves watching and going after it instead of the ball, and there was about him an almost preternatural calmness. Nothing fazed him, not even the events of the June 4, 1951, "Night of the Rabbit's Foot" when his eleven-game winning streak ended before a crowd of rabbit-foot toting Cleveland fans after one Indian rooter had tossed a kitten at him during his warmups. (See "The Night the Indians Rabbit-punched the Yankees," Lenore Stoaks, TNP 94: 45-46.)

Two examples of Lopat's consistency in beating the Indians come to mind here. In June, 1950, on a hot day in Cleveland, he left the hotel for some air and something told him to get down to the ballpark because the Indians might be up to something. He sneaked into the stadium and watched as Sam Zoldak pitched a special batting practice to the Indians in which they practiced hitting slow breaking stuff. That night before the game Lopat took Casey Stengel and Yogi Berra aside, told them what he'd seen, and said "I think we'll have some fun tonight." The game began, and for the first three innings all the Indians saw from him were fast balls and hard sliders, during which they broke several bats. When they switched

back to their free-swinging ways, he went back to control-pitching, and only two runners made it to second. He shut them out, 7-0, on six hits.

A little over a year later he outpitched Bob Lemon, 2-1, the Yankees' winning run scoring on a suicide-squeeze play by Phil Rizzuto that scored Joe DiMaggio from third and caused Lemon to grab both his glove and the ball and hurl them full force into the backstop screen, as well as netting Lopat his 20th win of the season.

The irony of it all was that the Indians could have had him. They could have purchased his contract from Little Rock at the end of the 1943 season; instead, they chose to believe their scouts who said he'd never make it in the majors because he did not have a fastball. That decision came back to haunt them for twelve years.

What next?—Ed Lopat was not the only Nemesis who made life miserable for the Cleveland Indians. In 1947 he was joined by Vic Raschi, who would become his teammate the following year and who ended up with a 22-8 lifetime record against Cleveland. Raschi did not stop there; he was 26-6 against the Philadelphia Athletics and also racked up a 19-7 record against the Chicago White Sox.

Since 1970 or so we've entered a new era of aspects of Nemesis. We simply don't see much of this any more. There have been a number of changes in the game: expansion; the business of pitch counts; and the use of specialist relievers. There aren't as many twenty-game winners as there used to be, let alone true killers. But there are some pitchers who have compiled records sufficient before the 2001 season to earn them the title of Nemesis—or Nemesis-in-the-making.

Jim Palmer: over a period of nineteen years, 30-15, .667 vs. New York. Chuck Finley: known as the Yankee-killer, 16-9, .640, but with an even better record against the Seattle Mariners, 19-7, .731. Roger Clemens: 26-8, .765 against the Angels. Terry Mulholland: with Phillies and then Braves, 17-5, .773 vs. Expos. Ramiro Mendoza: 6-0, 1.000 vs. Indians.

David Cone: 18-7, .720 against the Kansas City Royals. David Wells: 14-8, .636 vs. the Yankees; 13-3, .812 vs. the Indians. Tom Glavine: 19-8, .704 against the Phillies; 14-5, .737 vs. the Mets. Greg Maddux: 24-9, .727 vs. the Astros. Pedro Martinez: 9-1, .900 against Indians.

There will be more to come. Let's await developments.

Tracking Trends

A little historical perspective, please.

David Q. Voigt

To the serious historian, tracking trends is the passion that spurs his working life. Successful trend-tracking is the skill that sets the trained historian apart from analysts, antiquarians, reporters, and other commentators on the human past. It is the logical outcome of research.

A baseball historian's daily routine might find him gathering facts, filing them into categories, and analyzing each category with an eye for trends, counter-trends, combinations of trends, and consequences of trends. It can be a grind, but trend-tracking can be great fun when it lets us correct some addlepated know-it-all.

Of pundits pushing pretentious trends—Mischievous delights aside, baseball historians regularly shoulder the burden of enlightening the clueless and undoing the damage wrought by shallow research probings. Some commentators bedevil readers by touting trends with shaky roots. Sometimes their findings take the form of short term predictions that fall flat; at other times they deal in historical falsities. What's more, purveyors of such errors are notorious for not admitting that they were wrong.

Baseball historians are most likely to be plagued by soothsaying sportswriters spinning phony predictions. Examples crop up almost daily in baseball accounts. Thus, early in the 2000 season a New York scribe projected early winning streaks by the Yankees and Braves into a near-record total of 115 victories for each. Later on, a Gotham tout took note of current Yankee fielding lapses to forecast a record error total for the season. And early in May another seer airily awarded the AL wild card to the Red Sox.

Such baseless predictions are quickly debunked by historians. There's a greater threat from scribes who try to explain a present happening as the outcome of a misinterpreted trend. An example of this blunder was a *Sports Illustrated* writer's assertion that "Scientific evidence irrefutably dates the Big Bang to the 1997 expansion." (SI, July 17, 2000.) Did he ever hear tell of the homer explosion (the original Big Bang) of the 1920s?

An even more wrong-headed example cropped up in *Time* magazine of April 30, 2000. Penned by Charles Krauthammer and entitled "Requiem for the Summer Game," it asserted that "new" trends of the past twenty years were causing the "imminent death" of major league baseball. The "new" problems included carpetbagging star players and the "emergent" caste system dividing the teams; together these trends supposedly just opened a yawning divide between "have" and "have not" clubs.

Had the author gone beyond such shallow research, he would have learned that his putative new trends were actually quite old. After all, carpetbagging stars had plagued professional baseball ever since 1871; moreover, owners abetted such carpetbaggery by trading, buying, and selling star players.

A veteran baseball historian, **David Q. Voigt** *is currently working on Volume IV of his* American Baseball *series.*

As for the author's other "new" problem of the haves and have-nots, that trend may well be the oldest tradition in the game's history. Without breaking a sweat a historian can trace this phenomenon back to the 1860s; thereafter, each passing decade demonstrates that a few teams always have captured an inordinate share of glory. More ironic, in erroneously pinpointing the 1980s as the beginning of major league baseball's competitive imbalance, Krauthammer picked the one decade in history when teams came closest to achieving the dream of balance!

Some sportswriters, of course, are able trend-spotters. Indeed, Buster Olney's article, "Hitters vs. Pitchers" (*New York Times Magazine*, July 9, 2000) is a sparkling elucidation of the ongoing and deep-rooted "cultural war" between these antagonists.

Some Trends to Ponder—For their part, baseball historians should beware of sanctimonious finger pointing. For an antidote to any smugness toward other trend purveyors, we would do well to remember Montaigne's adage that one should never sit so high upon his stool lest he forget that he sitteth upon his own ass!

As a chastened sitter, I am listing a few long term trends with deep roots in major league baseball history. To seasoned historians these might be all too familiar, but they might be interesting to fans and players who want a better appreciation of how some of the game's pressing problems of today came to pass.

#1. The Pitching-Batting Disequilibrium—In the wake of the recent record homer barrages pundits have been urging baseball officials to take action to correct this "new problem." However, the historical record shows that imbalance has been a major problem for baseball at least since the 1870s. Over the decades since then, rules makers have labored to cope, tinkering with such things as pitching distances, ball-strike counts, equipment changes, pitching boxes, pitching mounds, and replacing pitchers as batters, to name only a few. Despite such efforts, imbalance continues. Maybe it is time to accept disequilibrium as the norm and to regard any longterm equilibrium between pitching and batting as a pipe dream.

#2. Players vs. Owners—Like the first trend, this one harks back to the early days of major league baseball. A likely point of origin was the 1876 coup in which club owners overthrew the player controlled National Association and imposed their newly created National League. Ever since, tensions between owners and players have smoldered—and sometimes erupted into fierce struggles like the Brotherhood War of 1890 and the strikes of 1981 and 1994-1995.

#3. Player Militance—If any readers think that the first united action by players against owners came after the players hired Marvin Miller to head the Major League Players Association in 1966, they would be surprised to learn that the player union trend dates back to 1885, when players united against, among other things, the owners' threat to impose salary caps. When the owners rebuffed the demands of the Brotherhood of Professional Base Ball Players, the players formed the Players' League, which came within a hair's breadth of reshaping baseball's structure in 1890.

In 1892 the victorious owners began imposing their salary cap policy on all players of the monopoly National League. In 1900, the Players Protective Association indirectly helped to end both the monopoly League and the salary cap policy by allowing members to join teams of the new American League.

The Baseball Players Fraternity of 1912-1917 died trying to win rights for minor league players, and the American Baseball Guild of 1946 lost its bid to rally players behind a pension rights plan. But the pension issue encouraged major league players to join the Major League Baseball Players Association in 1953. Approved by the owners as a "company union," the MLPA gained limited benefits, but after 1966, under the leadership of Miller, the MLPA became the great countervailing force against the owners.

#4. The Dual Major League Trend—Baseball's grand design of two rival major leagues, each with its own leaders and administrative staffs, united under a National Agreement headed by a Commissioner system, was a sports standard of the twentieth century.

Yet it is rooted in the game's nineteenth century past. Like the version that arose out of interleague war in 1903, the first dual major league agreement settled an interleague war between the National League and the interloping American Association. This shaky union began in 1883 to curb the expenses of interleague war, but ended in 1892 when the NL monopolized the major league game until 1901, when the interloping American League asserted major league status. By 1903, what came to be called the Senior and Junior circuits established the detente that allowed them both to prosper while retaining their rivalry.

As the twenty-first century unfolds, the dual major league trend is giving way to a greater unity. The resulting blurring of the identities of the two leagues, like interleague play, a single umpire staff, and the realignment of teams, is bewildering to older fans. But the seeming loss of identities is counterbalanced by prospects of profitable efficiencies.

#5. The Weak Central Government Trend— Whether dominated by single or dual leagues, major league baseball's 130-year history shows a general trend of weak incumbents in leadership positions. Indeed, we can count only two strong presidents of major leagues, William Hulbert of the National and Byron "Ban" Johnson of the American. The true founder of the National League, Hulbert wielded dictatorial power, even ousting Philadelphia and New York clubs in 1877. But when he died in 1882, owners ousted his forceful successor after two years and named compliant presidents ever after. Likewise in the American League, Johnson was a forceful leader in the struggle for his league's recognition, then became the most influential member of the National Commission that presided over major league baseball. No successor has matched his influence.

And so it was with the High Commissioners. Elected to preside over baseball in 1920, Judge K. M. Landis pontificated much, but by the end of his first seven-year term the owners reasserted their power. And despite a few stirrings by the likes of Commissioners Chandler and Vincent, all succeeding Commissioners were beholden to their owner employers.

Baseball's decision-making power has always resided with owners acting individually or through cabals. The "iron law of oligarchy" applies to baseball as to other organizations.

These few trends are among many to be found and tracked in MLB history. Any student of baseball history can research trends and adduce one's own considered interpretations. Such is the promise of the baseball history enterprise. And the only caution to be heeded is that one remembers Montaigne's advice to high-stool sitters!

The Players' Fraternity

They fought the good fight

Scott Longert

The creation of the National League of Professional Base Ball Clubs in February, 1876, brought stability and strong leadership to organized baseball. The eight-team National League promised a respectable game for its patrons, with no play on Sundays, no liquor sales on the grounds, and no gambling.[1] To insure roster stability and salary control, the owners, over the next few years, instituted the reserve clause, which in essence gave clubs ownership of players.

Ballplayers, at first honored to be important enough to be reserved, soon understood their loss of freedom and its economic ramifications. By 1885 dissatisfaction surfaced in the form of the Brotherhood of Professional Base Ball Players. Led by John Montgomery Ward, a ballplayer with a law degree, the Brotherhood sought to organize its members and have a voice in the governing process of the major league.[2] Finally, locating backers who were willing to finance the operation, Ward and his followers bolted from the National League and began play as the Players' League in 1890.[3] When the Brotherhood was shattered with the folding of the PL after that season, owners solidified their control over the players.[4]

The story of the Brotherhood and the Players' League is reasonably well known to baseball fans interested in the history of the game.

It is less well known that ten years later the players again attempted to organize themselves against the owners. Calling their new alliance the Players Protective Association, they took a more conservative path than the defunct Brotherhood. Players were careful to avoid appointing any officers who had participated in the Players' League.[5] They did, however, attract attention by inviting Dan Harris, a representative of the American Federation of Labor, to speak at their inaugural meeting. Harris brought the greetings of the famed labor leader Samuel Gompers, assuring the players of his moral support.[6] The Association put forward a platform that called for players to receive half the sale price whenever they were sold to another team.

Despite AFL support, the Players Protective Association crumbled when the American League was formed. With the opportunity to jump to the new league for bigger contracts, players quickly lost interest in the Association. By 1903, when the war between the two major leagues ended and the reserve clause began to be strictly enforced again, the Players Association had disappeared.

Renewed interest—Players again began brooding about the lack of a pension fund and the clubs' practice of suspending injured players without pay. By 1908, several ballplayers began to seek out attorney Dave Fultz for advice concerning their individual contracts.[7] Like Ward before him, Fultz was respected because he had been a big league ballplayer.

Scott Longert *has an M.A. in American History from Cleveland State. He is the author of* Addie Joss: King of the Pitchers.

A 1911 event demonstrated the players' renewed willingness to act together in opposition to the owners. When Cleveland's great pitcher, Addie Joss, suddenly died in 1911, his teammates asked the American League to postpone a scheduled game with Detroit so they could attend the funeral in Toledo. American League president Ban Johnson refused, and the players called a one-day strike.[8] Faced with strong player solidarity, Johnson reversed his position.

The next year, Ty Cobb raced into the stands, attacking a fan who had been heckling him. Johnson suspended the American League's best player for ten days without pay. Cobb's teammates met and agreed to go out on strike until their unpopular teammate's suspension was rescinded.[9] Johnson reacted with fines of $100 for each player. After boycotting one game, which the Tigers played with a pickup team, the players returned at Cobb's urging. Their fines were reduced to $50. Once again, though, players had stood together for a principle.

Throughout the summer of 1912, small groups of players began to meet secretly with Fultz to discuss a union. Players believed to be involve in the planning stages were Brooklyn's Jake Daubert, Detroit's Sam Crawford, and Chicago Cubs pitcher Ed Reulbach.[10] Reulbach told F. C. Lane of *Baseball Magazine* that the idea for a union of ballplayers was first described to him by Addie Joss in 1907,[11] the year Joss held out to fight a cut in pay. Reulbach took the conversation to heart, and with several others met with Dave Fultz before the 1912 Cobb strike. Final preparations were made in the Detroit rooms of Tiger players Davey Jones and Sam Crawford. Until the players could meet and hold formal elections, Fultz temporarily named himself president with Crawford and Jones as vice-presidents.[12]

Fraternity—The Base Ball Players' Fraternity was officially incorporated in the state of New York on September 6, 1912. The charter read in part, "To have every reasonable obligation of the players contracts lived up to by both contracting parties…To advise the player concerning any real or fancied grievance, and, in the event the former exists, to prepare his case for him."[13] The charter further stressed the need for adequate protection from rowdy fans and for the players to give owners the best service possible. Fultz made certain the charter conveyed a sense of cooperation to demonstrate the aims of the Fraternity were reasonable.

Provided a monthly forum by *Baseball Magazine*, Fultz, an 1895 graduate of Brown University, wrote eloquently of the rationale behind the formation of his new organization. He responded to assertions that player grievances could be arbitrated by baseball's ruling body, the National Commission. "The National Commission is composed of three members: the presidents of the two major leagues and a third person selected by them; this person at present time is a club owner…The player who has a grievance goes before a body composed of men paid and chosen from the very faction with which he has his controversy. This is contrary to the basic principles of equity."[14]

In addition, Fultz addressed the issue of players being fairly compensated for their efforts. He wrote, "It is argued the player is well paid. That he is well paid is no reason he should not organize. The star is well paid, the average player not so well, and some players very poorly."[15]

Initial reaction to the Players' Fraternity was mixed. Ban Johnson took a wait-and-see approach, declaring that players had a right to organize. Newspapers were divided on the issue. Some, including *Baseball Magazine* and *Sporting Life* were supportive. Others chastised the players. The Philadelphia *North American* sarcastically listed a number of player "grievances," such as having to leave their homes and travel south during the winter while working a total of twenty weeks a year. The writer facetiously protested the fact that the players got free medical care during the season and were forced to travel around the country by rail at the owners' expense.[16]

Star power—To be successful, the Players' Fraternity needed the support of the game's great stars. One by one they came into the fold. Pitching great Ed Walsh of the Chicago White Sox told *Baseball Magazine*, "I consider the fraternity has great work to do and I shall only be too glad to give it my full share of support."[17] Jake Daubert commented, "I know there are many players who are not getting along well, and it is for their interests we have organized."[18] Christy Mathewson, who had attended Bucknell University, and Ty Cobb, already a successful businessman, let it be known they were firmly in support of the Players' Fraternity. With this solid backing, Fultz called for the organizational meeting to elect officers and prepare a formal platform of issues.

The players met in New York on October 20, 1912, to prepare an agenda for the upcoming season. The players officially elected Fultz president. Cobb and Mathewson were elected vice-presidents. The selection of the two stars proved to the public that the Fraternity was a serious effort. Joining Fultz, Cobb, and Mathewson were directors Sam Crawford, Johnny Evers, Miller Huggins, and Washington catcher John Henry. Henry would become one of the most steadfast supporters of the Fraternity, resulting in Ban Johnson's eventual threat to have him barred from organized baseball for his union activities.[19]

Equity and discipline—The first case examined by the Fraternity was that of Boston pitcher Kurt Hageman. Early in the 1912 season, Hageman was optioned to Jersey City. After several weeks the minor league club decided it did not need the pitcher, returning him to Boston. The club then advised Hageman he was being optioned to Denver and would have to negotiate a new contract with that club's owners.[20] The pitcher reacted with anger when Denver offered him $1,500, $900 less than his contract with Boston called for. Hageman demanded his outright release from Boston, citing several offers he'd had from minor league clubs willing to pay him his original salary of $2,400. The Red Sox refused to release him or sell him to another club. Hageman refused to report to Denver, and sat out the remainder of the season. Once the Players' Fraternity opened its doors, he appealed for help.

Fultz sued the Red Sox on Hageman's behalf, citing the Rules and Regulations of the National Commission which read, "A player recalled under an optional agreement or who has been in the service of a Major League Club for a season, shall not be subject to release again under an optional agreement."[21] Fultz correctly stated that Boston's actions were in clear violation of the rules of baseball, and that the club had denied Hageman his right to earn his livelihood.

Fultz's office was on Wall Street, and the case went before the New York State Supreme court. The Red Sox won. Fultz appealed the ruling, watching the case drag through the judicial system for five years. In 1919 the courts ruled in favor of Hageman, awarding him $2,300 in back pay plus interest and court costs.[22]

Though victory in the Hageman case came after the demise of the Fraternity, at the time it was filed the suit demonstrated to major league owners that the players were serious about fighting for their rights in an organized way.

In April, 1913, Fultz wrote to Johnson about the procedure followed when a player was ejected from a game. It had long been the policy of the National Commission to suspend and fine ejected players without a hearing. In a carefully worded text, Fultz wrote, "We...request that when a prima facie case has been made out against a player, that he be accorded the privilege of replying to the charges."[24]

Fultz received a terse reply denying his request. Writing from his office in Chicago, Johnson stated that ninety percent of the ballplayers suspended were dealt with for using vicious and profane language. He explained it had taken years to minimize this evil and that his league would do nothing to alter its policy.[25] Johnson wrote firmly, "Your suggestion , if adopted, would be too obstructive to good discipline, and cannot have our serious consideration."[26]

Fultz printed the letter in *Baseball Magazine* to demonstrate to readers the highhandedness of the National Commission. Johnson claimed that the umpires simply conveyed the facts, and he would not acknowledge the possibility of an error by any of his umpires. Fultz explained the Fraternity's position that the ballplayers merely wanted a chance to respond to the charges against them before a final decision was reached. Although the National Commission did not issue any further statements, within a few years players gained the right to a hearing.

A victory—In January of each year, the National Commission met to discuss business for the upcoming season. The Players' Fraternity assembled in the fall of 1913, developing a list of seventeen suggestions for the Commission to review. In the context of a threatened third major league to begin play in 1914, the National Commission invited a Fraternity delegation to meet and discuss the proposals, although at first it refused to allow Fultz to attend. Cooler heads prevailed, and owner Garry Herrmann announced that Fultz could attend if he did not demand an individual audience.[27]

The most important of the Fraternity's proposals suggested that a player be free to negotiate with any team for his services when he had received ten days' notice of unconditional release by his current club. The existing rule allowed a player to negotiate only with a team in the same league.

Other requests presented were that all teams must furnish two uniforms to each player at no charge; that traveling expenses to spring training must be the responsibility of the owners; and that players must be provided with a copy of their contracts.

The Fraternity asked that any major league player with ten years service be given his unconditional release if his club did not exercise its option on him. It asked the same for minor league players with twelve years of service.[28]

Many of the seventeen requests were granted—a huge victory for the Players' Fraternity. The result, known as "The Cincinnati Agreement," was clearly an effort by the National Commission to appease the players in the face of the coming competition from the Federal League, but no movement would have been likely without the Fraternity. The organization had played its cards skillfully, drawing praise from fans and sportswriters alike.

"A menace to the game"—Fultz still had a difficult task ahead of him. The victory had left owners and league officials full of indignation at Fultz's influence over the players. Cries of "agitator" and "outlaw baseball anarchist" found their way into The Sporting News and other publications. Fultz found himself in a similar position to other labor organizers who had clashed with management. He became the target of the owners, who sought to remove him from the game of baseball.

The threat of the Federal League kept the Fraternity's president temporarily out of harm's way. Fultz skillfully took no official position on the "Outlaw League." He conducted business as usual, while the owners fretted about possible defections to the Federals. For a short time, the Fraternity enjoyed a cease-fire.

In July, 1914, Clarence Kraft sought the protection of the Fraternity after he received notification of his demotion from Brookly, to Nashville of the Class A Southern Association. Kraft had read the Cincinnati Agreement, which stated in Section 18 that, "before a major league player shall be released outright or under an optional agreement to Class A or a lower classification, his services shall first be tendered to all Class AA clubs."[29] Newark, a Class AA club, claimed Kraft, but Ban Johnson, acting for the National Commission, ruled that Nashville had put in a claim first and as such were entitled to his services.

Fultz protested this action, citing a clear violation of the Cincinnati Agreement. He sent a letter to Johnson, informing him that the Fraternity Board of Directors and all members would cease to honor their contracts after July 22 if Kraft was not authorized to report to Newark.[30] Johnson accused Fultz of being a "menace to the game," but he also, according the The Sporting News, advised Brooklyn owner Charles Ebbets to take whatever steps were necessary to reacquire Kraft and return him to Newark. While both sides postured, Ebbets quietly sent $2,500 to Nashville in return for their withdrawal of the claim on Kraft. After a month on the sidelines, Kraft appeared in the Newark lineup on July 22, and celebrated his return to the game with a home run against Provi-

dence. Ebbets' willingness to pay off the Nashville club suggests that the owners took the players' new strength seriously.

In the next year, the Fraternity did not bring any significant actions against major league baseball. However, the organization was busy answering inquiries from members and publishing no fewer than thirty-two articles. In his President's Report of October 1915, Fultz reported a membership of slightly over 1,000 major and minor league players.[31] Income from membership dues of $18 per player totaled $10,316.04, which was earning between three and four percent yearly. Fultz reported thirty-two meetings held with various clubs over the course of the year in which attendance reached ninety per cent.[32] A total of 410 players applied to the Fraternity for advice on contract matters. The President's Report proudly noted that $3,184.35 had been recovered from the owners on behalf of its members. Appeals to the National Commission were being accepted at a higher rate than ever before.

The Fraternity never addressed the question of establishing a pension fund for retired ballplayers, but did on several occasions send money to old players who needed help. For example, Cal McVey, one of the members of the 1869 Cincinnati Red Stockings, had fallen ill and had little savings to pay for medical care. The Fraternity sent him a check for $160. The Players' Fraternity was, in fact, at the peak of its effectiveness.

Baseball's ownership and management had begun an attempt to undermine the ballplayers' solidarity by borrowing the techniques of espionage and blacklisting used by their counterparts in the steel and textile industries.

In the fall of 1914, Fultz revealed that Fraternity member Ira Thomas of the Philadelphia Athletics had attempted to organize a separate union for American League players only. Thomas told American League players that they had fewer grievances than the National's and therefore stood a better chance of gaining ground if they split from the Fraternity. He assured the players that Johnson would recognize the new organization and meet regularly with a players' committee.[33] Fultz immediately expelled Thomas, castigating Philadelphia owner Connie Mack for masterminding the plot. Fultz stated, "We don't for a moment think that every one who opposes us is a crook and a blackleg. But Mr. Mack is against us and will beat us if he can. He wasn't called 'Connie' for nothing."[34]

Two months later Fultz filed a $50,000 libel suit

against *Sporting Life*. The magazine, along with the *Sporting News*, had been stepping up attacks on Fultz and the Fraternity. On this occasion, *Sporting Life* insinuated that Fultz was secretly negotiating with the rival Federal League to become its president. The article further accused Fultz of misappropriating Fraternity funds and claimed that he would shortly lose his job.

Fultz was not the only Fraternity official to feel the anger of the baseball establishment. Ed Reulbach, executive secretary of the organization, came under fire for his activities. The Brooklyn pitcher had been to college and taken an active role since the Fraternity's beginnings. A ten-year veteran, Reulbach gave contract advice to many of the younger players, which drew the ire of Brooklyn owner Charles Ebbets.[35] While players debated jumping to the newly established Federal League, Ebbets approached Reulbach, asking him to help sign players for the next season. Ebbets told Reulbach he would delete the ten-day clause in the contracts, thus rendering them guaranteed. At this time the Players Fraternity took no official stance on the Federal League, leaving it up to the unsigned players to determine their course of action. Ebbets felt he could use Reulbach's influence to keep his team intact.

Reulbach declined to help. Ebbets offered him a two-year contract at a substantial raise.[36] Reulbach asked Ebbets to offer raises to the other players for not jumping to the Federal League but the owner refused. Reulbach declined the offer again, citing unfairness to the other ballplayers. Angered by Reulbach's stance, Ebbets at season's end asked for waivers on the pitcher, but did not inform him until January 27. Strangely, no AL or NL club put in a claim for Reulbach's services. Reulbach signed with a Federal League team. *Baseball Magazine* asserted that Reulbach had been blacklisted for his active role in the Fraternity.

In March, 1916, the Players Fraternity moved back into the courtroom, filing a lawsuit on behalf of William Cristall, manager of the Hamilton club of the Canadian League. Cristall received notice from the National Board, the governing body of the minor leagues, that he was being fined and suspended for unspecified reasons. Fultz discovered that manager Cristall had negotiated with a prospective player, but ultimately decided not to offer him a contract.[37] The player believed he had a verbal agreement, and filed a complaint with the National Board. Without contacting Cristall, the Board ruled on behalf of the player, fining and suspending Cristall for his actions.

Fultz had received copies of the letters sent by Cristall, however, and in no instance did they indicate any agreement between the two parties. Before the suit could be brought forward, the National Board rescinded the fine and suspension, claiming a telegram had been sent to Cristall but was returned due to a incorrect address. In its editorial section, *Sporting Life* found the actions of the Board puzzling. The editorial stated, "He (Cristall) was tried and convicted without the slightest notice to him or anyone representing him."[38] Fultz withdrew the suit, suggesting that the National Board should review its procedures before sanctioning players and managers.

Hard line—The National Commission and National Board convened on December 14, 1916 to discuss business for the new season. The Players' Fraternity submitted a list of four recommendations for review. The first dealt with a clause in the players' contracts that allowed owners to suspend injured players without pay after a certain time period. The other three requests centered on minor league issues, including reimbursement for travel expenses to spring training, and copies of all defenses of player claims submitted to the National Board.[39]

In his annual letter to the Fraternity members, Fultz had included a pledge card which requested the members to delay signing their contracts until the four demands had been approved. Fultz received signed pledges from six or seven hundred major and minor league players.[40] Convinced of the Fraternity's solidarity, Fultz announced the players were prepared to strike if the four demands were not approved.

This was a time when labor throughout the United States was working hard to organize. Large World War I orders from overseas and some support from the Wilson administration had revitalized labor efforts. The climate was such that the Fraternity believed the time had come for collective action.

Ban Johnson vowed to lock the players out if they did not sign. He called Fultz a "half-baked New York attorney."[41] The owners were determined to crush the Fraternity once and for all, and went on the offensive. Ban Johnson falsely announced there had never been an instance where a player was not paid while injured. He further demanded to see a copy of a contract in which a clause existed that would deny payment to an injured player. He threatened to publicly declare Fultz a liar and a falsifier if he could not produce a sample contract.[42]

Fultz retorted that, "[Johnson] may smash the Fraternity, but we would advise him to go slow as it is a bigger job than he anticipates."[43] Then he forwarded a copy of Fraternity vice-president John Henry's contract to Johnson. The contract contained the clause which the National Commission claimed did not exist.

Many fans and sportswriters were confused why major league players would strike for minor league demands. Fultz explained to Fred Lieb of *Sporting Life* that sooner or later most players wound up their careers in the minors, and that they want conditions in the minors brought up to standard.[44]

In January, 1917, the National Commission announced its rejection of the Fraternity's three minor league demands. It stated that it was the jurisdiction of the minor league's ruling board to review the demands and that the Commission could only rule in the event of an appeal.[45] Garry Herrmann stated that he expected the Fraternity to file an appeal and would address the issue at that time. He further added that the demand concerning the injury clause had been addressed in December, when the National Commission had adopted a new clause in the players' contract providing for the full payment of salary for injured players, thus negating any need to issue a ruling.[46]

Several days later, National League President John Tener announced that the National Commission would not hear any appeals from the Players Fraternity. Instead, the Commission advised appeals would have to come from individual players.[47] Fultz replied the players were ready to go to the limit in their fight. To demonstrate their solidarity, Fultz announced the expulsion of Slim Sallee of the New York Giants for signing his contract. Fultz said, "We expect some desertions, but let no one think because a few traitors quit, the Fraternity is crumbling."[48]

Fatal misstep—Several days later the New York *Times* announced the Fraternity had taken action to file for membership in the American Federation of Labor. Samuel Gompers welcomed the ballplayers, stating he heartily approved of the threatened strike.[49] The *Times* revealed that Gompers and Fultz had met numerous times concerning the Fraternity's wish to join the AFL. According to the report, Gompers' full support would strengthen the players' position.

In response to the Fraternity's pending AFL affiliation, the National Commission announced it would no longer deal with the Players Fraternity as an organization, only with players as individuals.[50] The commission also announced it would not accept or respond to any communication from Fultz. This action came as no surprise to Fultz. With the Fraternity's af-filiation with the AFL seemingly imminent, he defied baseball to fight it out with organized labor. He questioned how strikebreakers would fare in opposition to a strong union.[51]

Near the end of the month, Fultz held a meeting of the Fraternity in New York. Twenty-five members attended to reaffirm their support. Tris Speaker sent a wire pledging his support and his regret for not being able to attend.[52] Paul Turner, the attorney for the Actors Equity Association, spoke to the members on the advantages of being affiliated with the AF L[53] A decision on the Fraternity's application was expected in a few days.

Encouraged by the meeting, Fultz announced plans to rent a New York theater and invite fans to hear the players' version of the dispute. He had set a February 20 deadline for the strike, wanting to drum up as much support as possible. He waited anxiously for word from the AFL, which had delayed issuing a ruling. Speculation now existed that the owners had secretly conferred with Samuel Gompers and had persuaded him to moderate his stance on the Fraternity.[54]

Gompers' sudden waffling has never been fully explained. He did issue a statement to the New York *Times* claiming that the AFL was still in sympathy with the ballplayers. However, there is a big difference between being sympathetic and taking direct action. The AFL was, by the lights of the labor movement, a conservative organization, one that concentrated its membership on the skilled workers in the steel industry. It represented no more than ten percent of all workers. Perhaps after some reflection, Gompers concluded that an alliance with the Players' Fraternity was too radical a move for his unadventurous union to take. Whether it was for this reason or that baseball owners were leaning hard on him, Gompers clearly decided to limit his support for ballplayers to cheering from the grandstand.

With the prospects of an AFL affiliation fading, Fultz canceled plans to take the Fraternity's case to the public. Newspapers reported daily on players giving up the fight and signing their contracts. On February 13, 1917, the National Commission passed a resolution revoking the Cincinnati agreement of 1914. According to the owners, the pact made with the Fraternity was void.[55] Fultz issued a statement releasing the players from their strike pledge.[56]

The capitulation by the Players Fraternity effectively crippled the five-year union. It had lost its most important fight, and with it the public support it had gained through *Baseball Magazine* and various other publications. The threatened strike had turned baseball fans against the players, while inadvertently strengthening the owners' position. The promised support of the AFL never materialized, leaving the Fraternity with few allies. Players drifted away from the Fraternity, causing it to cease doing business within months. Dave Fultz left for Europe to become an aviator for the United States Army. Ironically, when Fultz returned home in 1919, he was offered the Presidency of the International League.[57] He served in that office for two years, staying long enough to witness the demise of the National Commission and the dramatic fall of Ban Johnson to mere figurehead under new Commissioner Judge Landis.

Disappointment—Before departing for Europe, Fultz consented to one final interview with *Baseball Magazine* editor F. C. Lane. He elaborated on his reasoning for calling the strike, stating that he wished to unite the members of the Fraternity in a closer bond of union. He believed the time had come to impress organized baseball with the union's strength.[58] Fultz commented on the results, saying, "It has been the biggest disappointment of my life. I staked everything on this one cast and lost."[59] He firmly believed he had the power to force the National Commission to intercede with the National Board, thus compelling the minor leagues to accede to his demands. The magazine noted that at the very end there were still 200-250 ballplayers committed to sitting out.

Before the strike ended, *Baseball Magazine* published an anonymous letter from a prominent member of the Fraternity. The player unknowingly predicted the outcome of the conflict. He wrote, "They don't like Fultz because he interferes with the baseball machinery and brings to light and publicity some of their deals…Suppose the Fraternity was out of the way—it doesn't take much intelligence to see that the players would have a fine chance of dealing with the magnates direct."[60] Unfortunately for the Players' Fraternity, truer words were never spoken.

Legacy—In its five years of existence, the Fraternity won some significant victories over the owners in their struggle for an equal voice in major league affairs on and off the field. The Cincinnati Agreement represented a landmark pact in favor of the ballplayers, something without precedent in baseball's early days. The court battles orchestrated by Fultz gave the Fraternity credibility, and the number of players who regularly paid their membership dues demonstrated a solidarity that truly unnerved the owners.

The collapse of the Federal League took away a large piece of the Fraternity's bargaining power. Fighting a battle with the Federals kept the baseball hierarchy distracted. Without a third league to deal with, the owners could focus all their efforts on the players. It was a time for Dave Fultz to recognize that the Federal League no longer shielded him.

In the end, the owners remained triumphant. It is easy to see in retrospect that the call for a strike was a disaster that lost the Fraternity support from fans, the press, and some of its own members. The Fraternity was crushed. The best that can be said for it is that is that it laid down a gauntlet that would be successfully picked up many years later.

1. Robert Burk, *Never Just a Game* (Chapel Hill, 1994), pp.54-55.

2. Ibid., pp. 95-97.

3. Ibid., pp. 105-106

4. Ibid., pp. 112-114.

5. Lee Lowenfish, *The Imperfect Diamond* (New York, 1980), pp. 61-62.

6. Ibid., p. 61.

7. Harold Seymour, *Baseball: The Golden Age* (New York, 1971), pp. 194-195.

8. Cleveland *Plain Dealer*, April 15, 1911.

9. Burk, *Never Just a Game*, pp. 185-186.

10. *Baseball Magazine*, April, 1917.

11. Ibid.

12. *Sporting News*, March 1969. (Dave Fultz file, National Baseball Library.)

13. *Baseball Magazine*, November, 1912.

14. Ibid.

15. Ibid.

16. Philadelphia *North American*, August 31, 1912 (Dave Fultz file) NBL.

17. *Baseball Magazine*, February, 1913, p. 17.

18. Ibid., p.17.

19. New York *Times*, February 10, 1917.

20. *Baseball Magazine*, December, 1912, pp. 109-110.

21. Ibid., pp. 109-110.

22. Seymour, *Baseball: The Golden Age*, pp. 223-224.

23. *Baseball Magazine* May, 1913, pp. 70-71.

24. Ibid., pp. 70-71.

25. Ibid., pp. 70-71.

26. Ibid., pp. 70-71.

27. Burk, *Never Just a Game*, pp. 197-199.

28. *Baseball Magazine*, January, 1914, pp. 81-84.

29. *Baseball Magazine*, September, 1914, pp. 82.

30. Seymour, *Baseball: The Golden Age*, pp. 228-229

31. *President's Report*, (Dave Fultz file, NBL.)

32. Ibid.

33. *Baseball Magazine*, November, 1914, pp. 88-89.

34. Ibid., pp. 88-89.

35. *Baseball Magazine*, May, 1914.

36. Ibid.

37. *Sporting Life*, March 18, 1916, p. 6.

38. Ibid., March 25, 1916.

39. *Baseball Magazine*, December, 1916, pp. 85-87.

40. Burk, *Never Just a Game*, p. 213.

41. Eugene Murdock, *Ban Johnson, Czar of Baseball* (Westport, 1982), p. 71.

42. *Baseball Magazine*, January 1917.

43. Ibid.

44. *Sporting Life*, December 23, 1916.

45. *Sporting News*, January 1917.

46. Ibid.

47. *Sporting Life*, January 20, 1917.

48. Ibid.

49. New York *Times*, January 16, 1917.

50. *Sporting News*, January 27, 1917., p. 4.

51. Ibid., p. 4.

52. New York *Times*, January 27, 1917.

53. Ibid.

54. New York *Times*, January, 29, 1917.

55. New York *Times*, February, 14, 1917.

56. New York *Times*, February, 15, 1917.

57. Dave Fultz file, NBL.

58. *Baseball Magazine*, April 1917 p. 92.

59. Ibid., p. 92.

60. *Baseball Magazine*, April 1917.

Zeke Bonura

It does not seem possible that 60 years have passed since over 51,000 fans paid their way into New York's Polo Grounds for what proved to be an eventful day as baseball's greatest rivals, the Giants and Dodgers, played a doubleheader. As usual, half the crowd came over from Brooklyn. The date was July 2, 1939. The New York World's Fair, "The World of Tomorrow," was in full swing in Flushing and, along with the Yankees, both teams wore the Fair emblem, the trylon and the perisphere, on their uniform sleeves.

The Dodgers won the first game, 3-2, beating Brooklyn-born Bill Lohrman. The Giant runs came in the eighth, when Mel Ott homered off winning pitcher Luke Hamlin.

It was during the second game that the fireworks started—two days before the Fourth! Giant pitcher Hal Schumacher hooked up in a duel of righthanders with Brooklyn's Whitlow Wyatt. In the fourth inning Brooklyn, trailing 4-0, scored three runs, knocking Schumacher out of the box. As rookie manager Leo Durocher, playing shortstop, hit into an inning ending double play, he deliberately spiked first baseman Zeke Bonura, who had hit a home run on opening day at Ebbets Field, ruining Durocher's managerial debut.

Enraged, big Zeke threw the ball at Leo. As the ball whistled past Durocher's ear, Bonura chased the manager into right field, caught him, and pounded him while holding him in a head lock. The mismatch was quickly broken up as the umpires restored order. Both Leo and Zeke were ejected from the game. Durocher later contended that he spiked Zeke in retaliation because Schumacher was throwing at Dodger hitters. The game was tied until the eighth inning when Giant catcher Harry Danning hit a two-run home run to give the New Yorkers a 6-4 victory and a split for the day.

Before coming to the Giants, Bonura had been one of the American League's outstanding hitters. When Zeke hit .345 in 1937, the righthanded slugger was outhit by only three men—Charlie Gehringer (.371), Lou Gehrig (.351), and Joe DiMaggio (.346). In five seasons with the White Sox and Senators, Zeke drove in 554 runs. A lifetime .307 hitter, he hit .321 for the Giants in 1939 as the team finished fifth.

Zeke's career was cut short by World War II. He was among the first group of ballplayers called before December 7, and served more than five years in the Army. Assigned to Special Services, he set up leagues, laid out baseball diamonds and had 44 service teams playing in North Africa, culminating in the African World Series. Zeke also organized baseball teams for Italian kids in Italy and French kids in France. But he did more than that.

"We were in France," he said, "and they asked me to go back to Italy and round up a band of Italian musicians to play for our group back of the lines, because we had no bands of our own around there and they figured a little music would do our guys some good. So I went back and came up with some band leaders and they got the men for me. I rounded them up and put them on a ship and took them to France.

"Well, they were swell but all they knew were Italian pieces and the officers said to me, 'Those soldiers want some songs from back home. What can you do about it?' One day, without a pass or anything, I sneaked off and got in a jeep and drove into Paris. I went to the Special Services headquarters there and grabbed an armful of sheet music that had just come over from the U.S. and hustled back with it and then we had some real hot stuff, right up to date." That was typical of my good friend, fun-loving Sgt. Zeke Bonura.

For his great job, General Dwight D. Eisenhower conferred the Legion of Merit upon Zeke. "It was on Goat Hill," Zeke said. "They had the troops drawn up and I was called out and General King pinned the medal on me. I was so proud—so proud I can't tell you how much. But I could have cried. I hadn't fired a shot in the war and here I was, getting a medal on Goat Hill—and a lot of our guys had died taking that hill."

Zeke was 78 years old when he died in his beloved New Orleans on March 9, 1987.

—Tom Knight

Don Minnick's Career Year

20-4 for Reading in 1955

Dennis G. Dillon

This story is about the only 20-game winner in the history of the Reading, Pennsylvania, entry in the Eastern League. In 1955, Don Minnick was one of Reading's *fifteen* starters. Minnick and Don Nance started the most games (26), and Minnick also relieved in four. Besides Minnick, three of the other pitchers made it to the majors: Bobby Locke, Dan Osinski, and Jake Striker.

Before playing at Reading, Don lead his Trenton, New Jersey, American Legion Junior team to the 1948 national title. In 1949, his first year in pro ball, he pitched at Pittsfield. In 1951 his record at Wichita was 14-11 with an ERA of 3.12. After two years in the military, he was 7-9 with an ERA of 2.88 with Reading, pitching mostly in relief.

Other future major leaguers who played in Reading that year are perhaps better known: Roger Maris, of course, broke Babe Ruth's home run record. Carroll Hardy was the only man ever to pinch hit for Ted Williams. Larry Raines may be the only player to play in the Negro Leagues, the Japanese Leagues, the minors, and the majors. Dick Brown caught Herb Score in high school. Other teammates included Clell Hobson, Clell "Butch" Hobson's father; Gene Lary, brother of the Tigers' Yankee killer Frank Lary; and Frank Tanana, father of another major league son.

Don was the number three starter. He started his first game April 23 against Elmira, going eight innings for the 7-5 win. He next blanked Williamsport, 9-0,

on the road April 29, for a 2-0 record for April.

On May 4, he got no decision against Binghamton in a 9-5 Indian loss. Minnick made his first relief appearance two days later against Williamsport, pitching two innings of shutout ball. He started, completed, and won his next three games. On May 12 he shut out Binghamton, 5-0, on two hits. On May 16 he allowed Wilkes-Barre ten hits but only a single run, while Reading scored ten. And on May 24 he beat Albany, 5-2. In his next appearance he worked one shutout inning against Albany in the second game of a Reading sweep. Minnick finished off May with a 10-3 complete game victory at home against Albany in which Roger Maris hit three homers.

Minnick was even better in June. He completed and won every game he started. Don beat Schenectady, 9-5, in the second game of a Reading split on the fourth. In another second-game win, he beat Wilkes-Barre on the eleventh, 6-5. On the seventeenth he beat Williamsport, 4-1, before ending the month with a 7-5 win at Elmira.

He matched June's win total in July, but also suffered his first loss. He started the month with a no decision against Binghamton, a game that Reading won 8-5. On the Fourth of July he pitched a seven-inning complete game against Johnstown, a team that had relocated from Wilkes-Barre in the middle of the season, winning, 5-4. He pitched a scoreless inning in relief against Allentown on the seventh, then shut out Schenectady, 8-0, on the ninth, behind Maris's seven RBIs. On the fifteenth, he went all the way to

Dennis G. Dillon *is a baseball researcher living in Reading, Pennsylvania.*

beat Albany, 6-4, with the help of a grand slam by Bob Johnson (not the Indian Bob Johnson who played in the big show). Two days later he blanked Schenectady during a 1-1/3-inning relief stint. On the nineteenth he beat Albany again, 6-4. After an eight-hit shutout of Allentown on the twenty-third, he took his first loss, 6-5, to Johnstown on the twenty-seventh.

Minnick seemed to tire in August and September. He was 3-2 and 1-1. On August 2 he beat Elmira despite giving up seven runs in 8-2/3 innings, winning, 9-7. On the seventh he went only four innings and lost his second game, 10-6, to Elmira. He started against the Eastern League All-Star team on August 9, a game Reading won, 6-5. The starting lineup for the All Stars was: 1B Neal Hartweck, Allentown; 2B Marty Devlin, Elmira; 3B Milt Graff, Williamsport; SS Larry Curry, Elmira; OF Zeke Bella, and Sam Seplizio, Binghamton; Emil Plasko, Williamsport; C Johnny Blanchard, Binghamton, and P Jim Coates, Binghamton.

Tired or not, Minnick completed the year with five straight complete games, the first being a 9-1 drubbing of Johnstown on the fifteenth. He lost, 2-0, to Allentown on the twenty-first, then beat Schenectady and future Phillie Henry Mason, 7-1, on the twenty-seventh.

Schenectady and Mason returned the favor and beat him on September 1, 6-5. In Minnick's last start of the season three days later he got his twentieth win, 6-5, in eleven innings over Albany.

In the postseason, Don beat Schenectady's future Phil Don Cardwell, 4-3, in the playoffs. Over the course of the regular season, he was 12-0 at home. He was 11-0 at the end of June, 16-1 at the end of July, and 19-3 on the last day of August. His remarkable 20-4 is the only 20-win season in the history of Reading's Eastern League entries.

Don Minnick's major league career consisted of two appearances, both for the 1957 Washington Senators. The first occurred on September 23 against the Boston Red Sox. In this game Ted Williams ran his consecutive on-base streak to 16 by singling in the first, walking his next three times, and getting hit by a pitch before leaving in the eighth. Minnick entered the game in the fifth and issued the walk that extended the streak to 15. Williams was the only runner Minnick allowed. Also in this game future Hall of Famer Harmon Killebrew hit one of his seven minor league career pinch-hit homers. The game was Roy Sievers Night in Washington and was attended by then Vice President Richard Nixon. In Minnick's only other appearance, he started five days later against Baltimore going 7-1/3 innings, walking three, striking out five, and giving up fourteen hits while taking the loss.

Don Minnick's appearances for Reading, 1955

Date		Opp	IP	H	BB	K	W	L	
4-23	Start	Elmira	8	7	1	7	1	0	
4-29	Start	@Williamsport	9	4	1	4	1	0	CG SH
5-4	Start	Binghamton	6.3	8	0	3	0	0	ND
5-6	Relief	Williamsport	2	0	1	0	0	0	
5-12	Start	@Binghamton	9	2	2	4	1	0	CG SH
5-16	Start	Wilkes-Barre	9	10	1	3	1	0	CG
5-24	Start	@Albany	9	11	5	5	1	0	CG
5-27	Relief	@Schenectady	1	0	0	1	0	0	
5-30	Start	Albany	9	4	0	6	1	0	CG
6-4	Start	Schenectady	9	9	1	8	1	0	CG
6-14	Start	@Wilkes-Barre	11	10	2	5	1	0	CG
6-17	Start	@Williamsport	9	6	3	3	1	0	CG
6-23	Start	Elmira	9	6	0	5	1	0	CG
6-27	Start	@Elmira	9	8	3	6	1	0	CG
7-1	Start	@Binghamton	6	7	4	3	0	0	
7-4	Start	Johnstown	9	7	2	2	1	0	CG
7-7	Relief	Allentown	1	1	0	0	0	0	
7-9	Start	@Schenectady	9	6	3	3	1	0	CG SH
7-15	Start	@Albany	9	9	1	4	1	0	CG
7-16	Relief	Schenectady	1.3	0	0	0	0	0	
7-19	Start	Albany	7.3	8	3	3	1	0	ND
7-23	Start	Allentown	9	8	3	3	1	0	CG
7-27	Start	@Johnstown	8	10	2	2	0	1	CG
8-2	Start	Elmira	8.6	12	2	6	1	0	
8-7	Start	@Elmira	4	7	2	3	0	1	
8-9	Start	All Stars	2	2	1	1	0	0	ND
8-15	Start	Johnstown	9	5	0	1	1	0	CG
8-21	Start	@Allentown	6	8	0	1	0	1	CG
8-27	Start	Schenectady	9	6	4	3	1	0	CG
9-1	Start	@Schenectady	8	9	2	3	0	1	CG
9-4	Start	Albany	11	11	3	4	1	0	CG
Totals			224.6	203	52	102	20	4	
Home Totals			107.6	99	18	52	12	0	
Road Totals			117	104	34	50	8	4	

A Tale of Two Seasons

Veale in 1971 and Henke in 1987

Jamie Selko

It was the best of a bad season, it was the worst of a good season.

This is the tale, not of seven castaways stranded on a tropic isle, but of two pitchers. One went 6-0, the other, 0-6, and therein lies the story...

The year: 1971.
The team: the Pirates.
The man: Bob Veale.

Going into the '71 season, big (6' 5-1/2") Bob Veale had been one of the National League's premier power pitchers for the preceding seven seasons. His career ERA at the time was 2.95. He had been named to two All-Star teams. He had pitched no fewer than 200 innings and had never struck out fewer than 170 batters during that seven year stretch—indeed, in four of those seasons, he had had over 200 Ks. He was only the third National League pitcher with at least 200 innings pitched to average more than one strikeout an inning in a season when, in 1965, he whiffed 276 in 266 IPs. Over the course of his career up to that point, he had averaged eight strikeouts per nine innings. In 1968, he had the misfortune to go 13-14 despite a 2.06 ERA. His luck was about to change.

On May 10, Veale came in against the Dodgers with one out in the sixth and the Pirates trailing, 4-3. He closed out the seventh, and then the Bucs scored eight runs in the eighth. Relieved by Mudcat

Grant who held the Dodgers scoreless the rest of the way, Veale was credited with the win.

His line score: 1-2/3 IP, 1 H, 0 R, 0 ER, 0 BB, 3 K.

On June 8, he came in in relief of Nellie Briles against the Cubs with the score tied, 3-3. He gave up a hit, allowing the go-ahead run to score, then pitched fairly well until two were out in the fifth, when Dave Giusti relieved him. Giusti went 4-1/3 without allowing the Cubs to score. Did I mention that while Veale was on the mound the Pirates scored six runs (including a RBI single by Bob himself)? Win: Veale.

His line score: 2-1/3 IP, 1 H, 0 R, 0 ER, 1 BB, 1 K.

On June 28, Veale came in against the Phils with the Pirates behind, 7-5. When he left the mound, the Phils had expanded their lead to 9-5—but the Pirates scored four in the top of the seventh and Giusti held the Phils scoreless the rest of the way. Veale was given credit for the Bucs' 10-9 win.

His line score: 2 IP, 3 H, 2 R, 2 ER, 0 BB, 2 K.

On July 20, Veale relieved Steve Blass in the second with the Pirates down, 1-0. Bob surrendered two runs in the inning. He gave up another in the fourth. In the bottom of the fourth, the Pirates scored five (with Veale getting another RBI single) to take a 6-5 lead. Veale gave up two more runs in the fifth, and left trailing, 7-6. The Pirates scored two in the bottom of the fifth and hung on for the win, which

Jamie Selko *lives in Eugen, Oregon.*

was credited to Veale. It was his longest stint of the year.

His line score: 4 IP, 6 H, 5 R, 4 ER, 3 BB, 0 K.

On July 29, Veale relieved Blass again, this time in the fourth with his team down, 4-0. The Bucs scored one in the fifth and, after Bob left for a pinch hitter, six more in the sixth. Final score, 10-6 Pittsburgh. W-Veale.

His line score: 1-2/3 IP, 3 H, 0 R, 0 ER, 0 BB, 1 K.

On August 3, he relieved Blass yet again, this time in the seventh with the Bucs trailing, 5-4. After he retired the two batters he faced, the Pirates scored six runs in the top of the eighth to win, 10-6, with Veale once again getting the decision.

His line score: 2/3 IP, 0 H, 0 R, 0 ER, 0 BB, 0 K.

In his six victories, Big Bob pitched 12-1/3 innings, gave up 14 hits and seven runs, six of them earned, walked four, and struck out six. His ERA was 4.39. In his other 31 appearances that year, he was 0-0 with 45 hits, 31 runs, 30 earned runs, 20 walks and 34 strikeouts in 34 innings, with an ERA of 7.96. He didn't pitch particularly well in the games he won, but his mates scored **33** runs when he was the pitcher of record—an astonishing 24.4 runs per nine innings.

The year: 1987.
The team: the Blue Jays.
The man: Tom Henke.

On May 20, Henke came on in relief of Jimmy Key in the eighth with the Jays trailing the Angels, 4-1. The Jays scored three in the top of the ninth to tie the score. (It should be noted here that at this point of the season, Henke had yet to yield a run. In his eighteen previous appearances he had allowed only 12 baserunners in the 19-1/3 innings he had pitched, fewer than half as many as the strikeouts he had recorded over that time.) In the tenth, Tom got a popup out on Schoefield, and then allowed a Sayonara blast to Wally Joyner.

His line: 2-1/3 IP, 2 H, 1 R, 1 ER, 0 BB, 5 K.

Henke's next decision came on June 26, when he came in in relief of Bill Musselman, who had relieved Key. Henke took the mound with the bases loaded in the sixth and the score at 4-2, Jays. He promptly gave up a single to Robin Yount that scored Dale Sveum, but he then got out of the inning without further damage. In the eighth he gave up a double to B. J. Surhoff, walked Bill Schroeder, gave up a sacrifice, and then a double to Dale Sveum which scored two. He then whiffed Cecil Fielder, walked Yount intentionally, walked Castillo unintentionally and allowed a single to Cecil Cooper which scored both Yount and Sveum. Nunez relieved and allowed Cooper and Castillo to score, sealing Henke's fate.

His line score: 1-1/3 IP, 4 H, 6 R, 6 ER, 4 BB, 3 K.

Henke quickly followed this less than stellar outing with one almost as bad on June 29. Playing the Yankees, the Jays had come storming back from an 8-3 deficit to take the lead in the seventh. Tom came in in the eighth with Pagliarullo and Henderson on base. He promptly struck out Willie Randolph, but things went downhill from there. Mattingly walked, and Dave Winfield walloped a grand slam. The Blue Jays, unable to score in the ninth, tumbled to an ignominious defeat. L-Henke.

His line score: 1-2/3 IP, 2 H, 2 R, 2 ER, 1 BB, 3 K.

On the third of July (this was a *really* bad week for Henke), Tom came on in relief in the second game of a doubleheader (remember those?) against the Royals. He was relieving Musselman again with the Jays up, 4-2 in the eighth and Frank White on second. He gave up a sacrifice fly to "Bye-Bye" Balboni, but got out of the inning still up, 4-3. In the ninth, he got Eisenreich to fly out, but gave up a single to Beniquez, who was replaced on the base by Willie Wilson who stole second. Tom then struck out Seitzer, and was one out away from the win. He walked George Brett intentionally, then Tartabull unintentionally, loading the bases. A wild pitch scored Wilson and tied the score. Frank White singled, scoring Brett. The Jays go down, 5-4. Henke took the loss.

His line score: 1-1/3 IP, 2 H, 2 R, 2 ER, 3 BB, 1 K.

On August 31, Tom came in relief in the eighth with Toronto ahead of the Angels, 7-6. He gave up the tying run in the ninth, but held the Angels scoreless in the tenth. In the eleventh, things deteriorated quickly. Howe singled to right, Ray sacrificed him to second. Joyner was intentionally walked, setting up a double play. Buckner flied to right, allowing Howe to go to third. Whitt allowed a ball to get by him, scoring Howe. LP-Henke.

His line score: 4 IP, 3 H, 2 R, 2 ER, 2 BB, 1 K.

Against the Yankees on the September 7, Henke relieved Wells with a runner on third (Wells had struck out Lombardi, but Whitt allowed the ball to get by him and Lombardi reached first. Wells then threw a wild pitch. Lombardi went to second, then advanced to third on an Easler fly out). Henke gave up a single to Henderson, which tied the game, 5-5. Tom then pickec Henderson off, ending the inning. In the ninth, Randolph led off with a single, and he stole second on a pitch that struck out Mattingly. Winfield struck out. Pasqua singled to center, scoring Randolph. LP-Henke.

His line score: 1-1/3 IP, 3 H, 1 R, 1 ER, 0 BB, 1 K.

In his six losses, Henke pitched 12 innings and gave up 16 hits, 14 runs (13 earned), walked nine, and struck out 14. His ERA was 9.75. He allowed 12.3 hits and 19.2 baserunners per 9 innings. In games where he had no decision, his stats were 82 IP, 46 H (5.1 per IP), 13 R, 13 ER, 16 BB (only 1.8 per 9 innings), 114 Ks (12.5 per 9 innings), and an ERA of 1.43.

So, there you have it—one pitcher goes 6-0 with an ERA of 7.04, another goes 0-6 with an ERA of 2.49. As Joe Garagiola used to say, "Baseball is a funny game," and as I never tire of telling my children—although they doubtless tire of hearing it—"It's better to be lucky than good."

Sherry Magee

Psychopathic slugger

Tom Simon

Back in the Deadball Era, Sherry Magee was called "one of the greatest and most neglected of sluggers," "a born dynamiter with the bat," and "a genuine murderer of the pill." Today we'd call him a five-tool player: he could hit, run, field, throw, and hit with power. We might also call him a psychopath.

For more than a decade Magee was the Philadelphia Phillies' left fielder, clean-up hitter, and greatest star, setting the twentieth-century team record in stolen bases (387) and ranking among the top ten in almost every other offensive category. He was undoubtedly the National League's most valuable player in 1910, and either he or Chalmers Award-winner Johnny Evers deserved the appellation in 1914. That season one Philadelphia writer called Magee "probably the best all-around ball player in the National League," and a Cincinnati reporter went a step further: "To my mind Sherwood Magee is one of the best all-around players the game has ever seen." John J. Ward of *Baseball Magazine* called him "a greater slugger than Cobb, Jackson, Lajoie or any of a score of stars whose names are a synonym for Hit."

Today, however, Magee is best-remembered for his 1911 attack on umpire Bill Finneran, one of the most flagrant ever committed—the recent transgressions of Roberto Alomar and Carl Everett pale in comparison, even though most Deadball Era commentators simply chalked up Magee's actions to fighting spirit. "There was that episode, not forgotten by any means, when

Magee suffered a lengthy vacation for mussing up an umpire," wrote Ed M'Grath in the Boston *Sunday Post* four years after the incident. "That wasn't very nice of Sherwood, but it emphasized his determination to have nothing interfere with his idea of what was coming to his crew."

Irish charm...and temper—The son of an oilfield worker, Sherwood Robert Magee was born on August 6, 1884, in Clarendon, Pennsylvania. "The Irish traits of quick wittedness, a hot temper and an aggressive love of fighting are his by birthright," wrote Ward, who obviously wasn't too concerned about perpetuating ethnic stereotypes. Regarding Magee's off-field personality, one Philadelphia reporter called him "as gentle and good-natured as an old woman. You couldn't find a more sociable and companionable fellow anywhere." Another said that Magee was "a care-free, fun-loving, ever-smiling type." But Ward described him as "a man for whom it is easy to conceive a great liking or a passionate hatred."

As for Sherry's appearance, one reporter called him "dashing." Though he stood only 5-foot-11 and weighed 179 pounds, he was pysically imposing—"husky" and "burly" were adjectives commonly used to describe him. Magee was a crackerjack bowler and basketball player, but football was his favorite sport. He sometimes worked out with the Lafayette College team, and during his years in Philadelphia he spent almost every fall day watching the Penn gridiron squad practice at Franklin Field.

Tom Simon *is chairman of SABR's Deadball Era Committee and a member of Vermont's Gardner-Waterman Chapter.*

Like his Phillies teammate Grover Cleveland Alexander, Magee may have suffered from epilepsy. Hans Lobert mentioned it in *The Glory of Their Times*, and some have surmised that a heavily reported episode in which Magee fell through an open French window on the second floor of his Philadelphia home, supposedly while sleepwalking, was probably an epileptic fit. "Poor soul! Little did they know that the fellow was an epileptic," states an unattributed clipping in Magee's file at the National Baseball Library. "I knew this, and found it out one day while playing against Philadelphia. He fell into a fit and I called one of the Philadelphia players to help me revive him. It was this player who told me the secret. Magee, himself, would never admit that he was an epileptic, and was sensitive about that fact."

As spirited as Evers...and as crabby—After playing for independent teams in eastern Pennsylvania, 19-year-old Sherry Magee jumped directly to the majors, joining the Phillies in the midst of their dismal 1904 season. Philadelphia's strength was its outfield—Shad Barry in left, Roy Thomas in center, and John Titus in right—but an injury to Titus caused Barry to fill his position, opening up left field for Magee. Making his debut in an 8-6 loss to Brooklyn on June 29, the nervous rookie misjudged two fly balls, both of which led to Superba runs, but he hit the ball hard in each of his four at-bats (though he had only one hit to show for it). "Magee overcame his unfamiliarity with the Philadelphia grounds and soon learned to field as became a big leaguer," wrote Ward. Three weeks later, when Titus was able to return to the lineup, Sherry was so firmly entrenched in left field that the Phillies traded Barry to Chicago. Magee batted .277 for the season and led the team with 12 triples despite playing in just 95 games.

Over the next several years Sherry Magee rarely missed a game, establishing himself as one of baseball's young stars. In 1905, his first full season, he was the biggest factor in Philadelphia's gain of 31 victories over the previous year, scoring an even 100 runs, stealing 48 bases, and batting .299 with 24 doubles, 17 triples, and five homers. The next year he was just as good, hitting .282 with 36 doubles, eight triples, and six homers and finishing second in the NL in stolen bases with 55, a modern Phillies record that stood until Juan Samuel swiped 72 in 1984. In 1907 Magee had his best season yet, leading the NL with 85 RBIs and placing second to perennial batting champion Honus Wagner with a .328 mark. Magee's average would have been even higher if he hadn't

been charged with times at bat for his many long flies that scored runners from third base, inspiring Phillies manager Billy Murray to lead the fight for the sacrifice fly rule, which was implemented the following season. The manager was so impressed with his young slugger that he turned down the Chicago Cubs' offer of $12,000 and three players for Magee, said to be the largest ever made for one player. Murray told *The Sporting News* that "no offer of any kind for Magee would be considered."

But as he reached stardom, Sherry also developed a reputation as a troublemaker. "On the ball field Magee is so fussy most of the time that people who do not know him naturally form the opinion from his actions that he is a born grouch," wrote the Philadelphia *Times* after the 1908 season. "That he is one of the most hot-headed players in either big league is admitted; it couldn't be denied, because the records, showing how often he has been suspended for scrapping with the umpires, speak for themselves." Off the field, the young slugger could be just as difficult. The captain of the Phillies during Magee's early years was Kid Gleason, who kept an old leather belt in his locker that he used on young players who misbehaved, and on several occasions Magee literally felt the captain's wrath. Sherry also became known for "crabbing" at teammates. "Magee, like Evers, has an unusual amount of base ball gray matter and spirit," explained one reporter. "This spirit plays for victories and is easily upset when 'bones' are pulled. Both men are continually 'bawling out' their fellow players for bad plays. They just can't help it."

In 1909 Magee slumped to .270 (still 26 points above the league average) and played with "marked indifference," prompting rumors that he would be traded to the New York Giants for holdout slugger Mike Donlin. The Phils refused the deal because of the age difference between the two players (Donlin was six years older), and their patience was rewarded when Magee put together his finest season in 1910. Playing in all 154 games, he broke Wagner's tenure on the batting throne by hitting .331, and also led the NL with career highs in runs (110), RBIs (123), and on-base percentage (.445). He walloped 39 doubles, 17 triples, and six homers to give him a league-leading .507 slugging percentage, and his 49 stolen bases ranked fourth in the league. Still, fans blamed Magee for chasing the Phillies' second-best hitter, center fielder Johnny Bates, out of Philadelphia by "continual crabbing."

The Finneran incident—Sherry was enjoying another banner year in 1911, but his season—and career—were marred by his actions in the third inning of a game in St. Louis on July 10. To set the scene, after sitting atop the NL standings on the Fourth of July, the Phillies were engaged in a tight pennant race with the Giants, Cubs, Pirates, and Cardinals. Years later, Hans Lobert claimed that Magee was suffering from a hangover. He had been ejected the day before, and in the first inning he had protested vehemently when he was called out trying to steal. With the Phils leading, 2-1, Magee came to bat with two runners on base and one out. With two strikes, rookie umpire Bill Finneran called Magee out on what appeared to be a high pitch, prompting Magee to turn away in disgust and throw his bat high in the air. Finneran yanked off his mask and threw Sherry out of the game.

Magee, who had been heading to the bench, turned and attacked the umpire, hitting him flush in the face with his fist. With blood spurting from his face, Finneran fell on his back, apparently unconscious. St.

Sherry Magee

Louis catcher Roger Bresnahan grabbed hold of Magee, and the other umpire, Cy Rigler, and other players hustled him away. When Finneran came to and realized what had happened, he broke away from the group at the plate and tried to reach the Philadelphia bench, only to be intercepted by Phillies players and the police.

After he calmed down, Finneran was removed to a hospital for treatment to his badly-lacerated face. The game continued with Rigler behind the plate, and the Phillies won, 4-2, after which Magee expressed regret for the incident, offering as an excuse that Finneran had called him a vile name. Manager Red Dooin added that the rookie umpire had been too aggressive all season, often bragging about his ability as a fighter and threatening to lick players, including Dooin himself during a late-June series in Boston. On that occasion, only two weeks earlier, Magee had served as peacemaker when Finneran invited Dooin under the stands for a fist fight.

Unsympathetic to the Phillies' pleas, National League President Thomas Lynch, himself a former umpire, announced that Magee had been fined $200 and suspended for the balance of the season—reportedly the most drastic punishment meted out since 1877, when three players were barred for dishonesty. The Phillies appealed to the NL board of directors, arguing that Lynch had been too severe, especially since one regular outfielder, Titus, was already out with an injury and the club was fighting for its first pennant. The directors declined to overturn the suspension, and the Phillies went 13-16 while Magee was out of action, tumbling to fourth place, 6.5 games behind the Cubs.

At that point Lynch issued a statement to Magee: "After very careful consideration of your case, I have decided to lift your suspension temporarily and return you to good standing. This reinstatement will date from the time your club returns home, namely Wednesday, Aug. 16, and it will depend solely on your good behavior whether or not this reinstatement shall be permanent. I trust you will see to it that it is."

Injuries...and an attitude adjustment—Magee remained hot through the rest of the 1911 season, hitting seven of his 15 home runs after his reinstatement. But in the following year's city series against the Athletics he was hit by a pitch during batting practice that broke his right wrist and forearm, putting him out for the first month of the season. Magee was scarcely back when he went out again following an outfield collision with Dode Paskert. (The Phillies'

left and center fielders collided off the field, as well, and even their families got into it one afternoon: Paskert hit a home run into the left-field bleachers, and as he rounded third, Magee's two sons booed so loud that Dode heard them, causing a run-in with Magee when he reached the bench.) Overcoming his injuries to bat .306 in both 1912 and 1913, Sherry combined with Gavy Cravath to give the Phillies what Ward called "the greatest 'team' of extra-base specialists in existence."

Despite all he had accomplished in his decade with the Phillies, Magee remained unpopular with the fans of the City of Brotherly Love. "For five years, prior to 1914, the local fans have roasted Sherwood Magee," wrote a Philadelphia reporter. "They cheered his long swats as all fans do, but still they shouted for his release." According to that reporter, "it is a cinch that no ball player ever played as brilliantly on the home field under such adverse circumstances." Ward agreed, attributing Magee's lack of popularity to the generally held belief that he was "a man who played for his own personal record and not for the good of the team."

That all changed, however, when Magee was named captain of the Phillies in 1914. "When he was given the captaincy everyone looked at affairs from a different viewpoint," said one veteran teammate. "Now he could talk all he liked and there would be no resentment, for that was all a part of his job. And it gave the added stimulus to Magee that made him the greatest teamworker we had."

After opening the season at his usual position in left field, Sherry demanded an opportunity to play shortstop in mid-May when it became apparent that none of the players attempting to replace the departed Mickey Doolan was adequate. "I can't do any worse than some of the men that have been in there," he told manager Dooin. (That comment may have instigated his fight with 23-year-old shortstop Milt Reed, who reportedly "draped the great Magee over the clubhouse pool table.") Before the Phils acquired Jack Martin in July, Magee played 39 games at Doolan's old spot, performing surprisingly well for a career outfielder. With characteristic immodesty, he even declared himself among the best shortstops in the business. "Others were more conservative in their estimate of his ability," wrote one reporter, who nonetheless acknowledged that he was not the worst of Doolan's replacements.

That September, "Cap" Magee wrote an article in the Philadelphia *Public Ledger* describing his (mis)adventures at shortstop. "I pulled a play in Brooklyn one day which I am sure never happened before on any ball field," he wrote. "I ran over past second, picked up a grounder and threw to first. The ball hit the runner on the leg and bounded into right field. I was on my way there, so I kept right on going and recovered the ball. Did anybody ever hear of a shortstop recovering his own wild throw to first before?" Making plays like that, Magee had to withstand a lot of kidding from rival players—and sometimes their profanity. "One day I dug up a low throw with my gloved hand and slapped the ball on Heine Zimmerman," Sherry wrote. "'You lucky dog' and a column or two of language I wouldn't dare put down was my reward for getting the Dutchman. Of course, if Doolan had done it that would have been different."

Due to injuries to other players, Magee also played a significant number of games at second base, center field, and first base in 1914. "In spite of the constant shifting of position on a hopelessly demoralized team, he proved himself the most valuable batsman in the league," wrote Ward. Magee batted .314 (sixzth in the NL) and led the league in hits (171), doubles (39), RBIs (103), and slugging percentage (.509). After that kind of season, he was shocked when the Phillies passed him over and appointed Pat Moran manager to succeed Dooin. Magee negotiated half-heartedly with the Federal League's Baltimore Terrapins, whose players included Doolan and several other former Phillies, but what he really wanted was to be traded to a winning team. "This great ball player has been hitched to losing teams for so long that with each season the desire to be with a champion has grown stronger," wrote one reporter.

Be careful what you wish for—On December 26, 1914, Magee thought he had received a belated Christmas present when the Phillies dealt him to the world champion Boston Braves for cash and two players to be named later. The trade had its critics in both cities. Braves manager George Stallings, who already had one crab on his hands in Evers, now had to contend with a second one in Magee. He became further dismayed when one of the Boston players in the deal turned out to be Possum Whitted, a hustling center fielder who had been one of his favorites. And in Philadelphia, one reporter wrote, "Just when Magee becomes popular with the fans, and is playing the game of his life, the club makes another mistake by permitting him to go to a rival club." But some Philadelphians had long believed that Magee was the "jinx" that had been following the Phillies, and they were happy to see him go. What happened to Sherry

in 1915—when the Phillies won their first-ever pennant—would lend evidence to their suspicions.

Reporting to spring training in Macon, Georgia, Magee was in a Braves uniform no more than fifteen minutes when he stepped in a hole while shagging a flyball. He fell and injured his shoulder. Weeks later, when it failed to improve, he finally saw a doctor and learned that his collarbone was broken. Magee was only thirty but would never again be the same player. He had batted over .300 three years in succession and had hit 15 homers in 1914, but in 1915 he batted just .280 with only two homers. Sherry was even worse in 1916, batting a meager .241. In his 1948 team history, *The Boston Braves*, Harold Kaese wrote, "An injured shoulder bothered Magee, but probably not so much as the loss of Baker Bowl's handy fences."

Magee's detractors have long pointed out his park-inflated hitting statistics. True enough, Baker Bowl was the best hitters' park of the Deadball Era, with its tin 40-foot right field fence only 272 feet from home plate. Still, as a righthanded hitter, Magee did not benefit nearly as much as lefties. Before 1910, when the left field bleachers were built, Baker Bowl measured 390 feet down the left field line; thereafter it was still a legitimate 335 feet. Magee hit only 42 of his lifetime 83 homers at Baker Bowl. Compare that to a contemporary lefthanded hitter like Fred Luderus, who hit 62 of his 84 in that bandbox. Baker Bowl's tiny dimensions also explain Magee's apparent lack of fielding range: with the short right field, many righthanded hitters tried to go the other way. When he moved in 1915 to cavernous Braves Field, with dimensions of 402 feet down the lines and 550 to straightaway center, Magee, playing center field, handled a league-leading 2.68 total chances per game.

The 1917 Boston Braves resembled an all-star team, circa 1912. Among the Braves enjoying their last (or nearly last) hurrahs were Johnny Evers, Larry Doyle, and the three Eds: Konetchy, Reulbach, and Walsh. Then there was Magee, who again performed poorly for Boston—in 72 games he batted .256 with only one homer—but turned around his career when the Cincinnati Reds picked him up on waivers in August. Filling in for the injured Greasy Neale, Magee batted .321 over the rest of the season. His revitalization continued during the war-shortened 1918 season, after which he worked as a foreman in a Philadelphia shipyard. Magee batted .298 and drove in a league-leading 76 runs, becoming the only non-Hall of Famer to lead the league in RBIs four times.

The next season, pneumonia forced Magee out of action for two months, causing him to lose his regular position to rookie Pat Duncan. Though he batted a career-low .215, Sherry finally realized his long-held ambition of playing for a pennant winning team. Appearing twice as a pinch hitter in the 1919 World Series, he picked up one hit and was released after Cincinnati's victory, marking the end of his sixteen-year career as a major league player.

Umpire-baiter turned umpire—Though he had skipped the minors on his way up, Magee played seven years in the bushes on his way down, six of them in the American Association. His best full season came with Minneapolis in 1922, when he batted .358 in 257 at-bats, and set a record that August by reaching base in 20 consecutive pinch-hitting appearances. During the streak Sherry hit two home runs and a single, drew 11 walks, and was hit by four pitched balls, but what made it truly amazing is that he had a broken thumb at the time, which is why he was out of the regular lineup. Three years later he was hitting .464 in 28 at-bats when Milwaukee released him in June after losing 16 of 18 games. In desperation, Magee begged for work from his last major league employer, Reds owner Garry Herrmann. His letter remains on file at the National Baseball Library:

> I think I could be of some use to your club as the fans were always for me there and maybe I could improve the hitting of some of the players. I have turned out some one every year for [Milwaukee owner Otto] Borchert.... My Wife was sick all Winter so I am about down. [Former Milwaukee teammate Chuck] Dressen [then playing for the Reds] can tell you about my ability with that bat. Maybe I can help pep up your club on the coaching lines also. You know I never drank Whiskey and don't to-day and have a lot more sense than I had there before.

But when no job from Herrmann was forthcoming, Magee signed on as player-coach with Jack Dunn's Baltimore Orioles. He held on for one more season, finally retiring as an active player at the age of 42.

Unlike many players of his era, Sherry had no trade to fall back on; for years he had spent the winter with his in-laws in Fulton, New York, "living a life of ease and pleasure from the close of one season to the opening of another." He was ill-prepared for the next phase of his life, but an inspiration had come to him while presiding over exhibition games at the Orioles' 1926 training camp: he would become an umpire.

In 1927 Magee served as an arbiter in the New York-Penn League. His work attracted so much positive comment that he was named to the National League staff for the coming season by John Heydler, who had been an assistant to President Lynch at the time of the Finneran incident in 1911. Picking up on the irony of umpire-baiter turned umpire, many veteran reporters expected Magee to be a disaster. "His appointment at the time brought a reflective smile to the fans and players that recalled his ancient feuds with the umpires," wrote one scribe after the 1928 season, "but Sherry surprised the old-timers by his cool decisions on the field, the manner in which he ran his ball games and the cleverness of his work." Heydler commented that Magee had made good in his first year and was destined to become one of the game's leading umpires.

An untimely demise—Sherry spent the 1928-29 offseason at his Philadelphia home at 1152 North 65th Street, working as the overseer of a large string of restaurants. In early March he came home from work complaining of a headache and fever. A physician diagnosed that he was suffering from pneumonia, the same disease that had plagued him in 1919. His condition worsened over the ensuing week. At the age of 44, Sherry Magee died at 8:45 p.m. on March 13, 1929, with his wife, Eda, and three grown children at his bedside. He is buried in the Arlington Cemetery in Drexel Hill. The obituary that went out over the AP wire described Magee as "one of baseball's most colorful figures," "one of the greatest natural batsmen in the game," and "a master in judging fly balls, a fine base runner and full of so-called 'inside baseball.'"

Hall of Fame voters virtually ignored Magee, casting only eleven combined votes for him in the eight elections of 1937-51, and he has received no serious consideration from the Veterans Committee. Some have attributed his lack of support to his erroneous inclusion on a list of ineligible players in the 1969 edition of *The Baseball Encyclopedia* (the list should have included Lee Magee, a contemporary NL outfielder who was no relation). More likely explanations are his failure to play a significant role on any championship team and his lack of any organized lobbying effort. Sherry Magee's twenty-first-century devotees can take some solace, however: he was the highest ranking non-Hall of Famer—aside from Joe Jackson, of course—on the Deadball Honor Roll, as selected by SABR's Deadball Era Committee in 2001.

Baseball Seppuku?

The role of the bases-loading intentional walk in the 1999 playoffs

Chris DeRosa

At the ballpark, when the home team loads the bases, people stand up and cheer. You don't see many fans slapping their heads, saying, "Rats, now there's a force at every base. I wish the bases weren't loaded." Yet in a surprising number of 1999's postseason games, the team in the field chose to load the bases on purpose with an intentional walk.

The intentional walk has been under siege for the last twenty years, both from baseball researchers and managers of the Earl Weaver school. Most recently, David F. Riggs looked at what happened in the plate appearances following World Series intentional walks. ["The Intentional Walk," *BRJ* 1999, p. 108.] He concluded that handing out free passes was akin to inserting Ted Williams into the opponent's lineup.

Worse, the outcome of a free pass is not confined to what the next hitter does; it can also set up a big inning. When a team issues an intentional walk, it is betting that it will win a particular match-up, and in order to bring that match-up about, it places itself in a situation where there is greater potential to give up multiple runs. Loading the bases on purpose is a particularly dangerous form of the intentional walk gamble because it permits the pitcher no margin of error. If the pitcher gets behind in the count, the batter knows he has to come in to him, and can sit on a strike.

Despite the dangers, this move proved quite popular in the 1999 postseason. I would have guessed it happened eight or nine times. Would you believe fifteen? Fifteen times a playoff team issued a Bases Loading Intentional Base on Balls (BLIBB), accounting for 39 percent of all postseason intentional walks (38).

Intuitively, it seems like this move fails nine times out of ten. As a fan, I cringe when my team loads them up on purpose, but perhaps that is because the failures are more memorable than the successes. Let's see how the fifteen postseason gambles worked out in 1999:

ALDS: Yankees vs. Rangers

In Game 1, with the Yanks leading, 3-0, in the bottom of the fifth, men on second and third with two out, Texas gave Darryl Strawberry an *intentional walk to load the bases*. The Rangers escaped when Jorge Posada lined out (1999 Postseason BLIBB Performance Record: 1-0).

NLDS: Braves vs. Astros

In Game 1, with Houston leading, 1-0, in the top of the fifth, the Braves faced Carl Everett with men on second and third and one out. Everett received an *intentional walk to load the bases*. It worked out when the next hitter, Ken Caminiti, bounced into a double play. In the top of the ninth, the Braves were still trailing by a run when Jeff Bagwell came to the plate with first and third and one out. Bagwell got the game's second *intentional walk to load the bases*. Everett hit a sacrifice fly and Caminiti followed with a three-run homer. The walk may have been irrelevant to the sac fly, but it can hardly be called a success, seeing

Chris DeRosa is an historian living in Long Branch, New Jersey

that Bagwell came around to score (BLIBB: 2-1).

In Game 3, with the series tied and the score knotted, 3-3, Bagwell again came up with first and third and one out. The Braves responded with another *intentional walk to load the bases*. This time it worked out when Caminiti fanned and Matt Mieske flew out (BLIBB 3-1).

ALDS: Red Sox vs. Indians

This series' epic Game 5 should long be remembered as a showcase of just how pivotal these intentional walks can be. With the series tied and Cleveland leading, 5-3, in the top of the third, second and third with one out, Nomar Garciaparra came to the plate and received an *intentional walk to load the bases*. Troy O'Leary cleared the bases with a grand slam (BLIBB 3-2).

Later, Cleveland rallied to tie the score, 8-8, and in the top of the seventh, man on second with one out, again gave Nomar a free pass to face O'Leary. Although this did not load the bases, O'Leary punished them again with a three-run blast. The two walks to Garciaparra arguably wrecked Cleveland's season and cost skipper Mike Hargrove his job.

ALDS: Mets vs. Diamondbacks

In Game 3, with the series tied and the Mets leading, 4-2, in the bottom of the sixth, second and third with one out, Buck Showalter decided to deal with Edgardo Alfonso via an *intentional walk to load the bases*. John Olerud promptly followed with a two-run single, then Roger Cedeño knocked in Alfonso, and Darryl Hamilton drove in Olerud and Cedeño, and the game was out of hand (BLIBB 3-3).

In Game 4, with the score tied, 3-3, and two outs in the bottom of the eighth, the D-Backs gave Daryl Hamilton an *intentional walk to load the bases*, after which Rey Ordoñez struck out (BLIBB 4-3).

ALCS: Yankees vs. Red Sox

In Game 2, with New York leading, 3-2, in the top of the eighth, men on second and third and one out, Joe Torre ordered reliever Allen Watson to give pinch hitter Lou Merloni an *intentional walk to load the bases*. Then Ramiro Mendoza came in, struck out pinch hitter Butch Huskey and got Jose Offerman to fly out to Bernie Williams, and Yankee Stadium exhaled (BLIBB 5-3).

In Game 4, with the Yanks leading the series, 2-1, the Red Sox trailed by a run in the top of the eighth with one away and Chili Davis at the plate. The Sox waved Davis to first with an *intentional walk to load the*

bases in order to face Scott Brosius. They were rewarded when Brosius popped out and Chad Curtis fanned. The next inning, with New York ahead, 5-2, with second and third and one out, the Sox gambled again by giving Tino Martinez an *intentional walk to load the bases*. Ricky Ledee capitalized with a grand slam, putting the game out of reach (BLIBB 6-4).

NLCS: Braves vs. Mets

In Game 5, a titanic fifteen inning affair, there were six intentional walks (!) but only one to load the bases. The Mets gave free passes to Chipper Jones (twice), Eddie Perez, Brian Jordan, and Gerald Williams. In the bottom of the fifteenth, the Braves got into the act. Leading by one run with one out, they walked John Olerud to get to Todd Pratt. Unlike the previous five, this one was an *intentional walk to load the bases*. Pratt squeezed out an unintentional walk to tie the game, and Robin Ventura hit it out of the park to win it. Pratt began celebrating before Ventura reached second, thereby reducing the grand slam to a grand single (BLIBB 6-5).

In Game 6, with Atlanta leading the series, 3-2, and the game, 5-3, in the bottom of the sixth with men on second and third and one out, the Mets gave an *intentional walk to load the bases* to the original Brian Hunter. Walt Weiss postponed the decision with a comebacker, but then Jose Hernandez singled to left to drive in two runs (BLIBB 6-6).

This game was just getting started. The Mets kept fighting and tied the score, 9-9. In the bottom of the eleventh, fireballing Armando Benitez was finally out of gas and New York summoned Kenny Rogers to pitch. With one out and a man on third, Mets manager Bobby Valentine ordered Chipper Jones to first base (in the NL East race, Jones had slain the Mets almost single-handedly). Brian Jordan then came to the plate with men on first and third and the Mets' whole misbegotten odyssey of a season on the line. Valentine ordered an *intentional walk to load the bases*. Back-to-back free passes to juice the bags! Rogers then issued Andruw Jones an unintentional walk to lose the game and end the series (BLIBB 6-7).

Superficially, there seemed to be little advantage in pitching to Andruw Jones (.275 BA, .365 OBP, .483 SA) instead of Brian Jordan (.283, .346, .483); however, Jordan had a better record against left-handers. To gain this platoon advantage, though, the Mets had to put Kenny Rogers into a bases-loaded jam with the pennant in the balance.

World Series: Yankees vs. Braves

In Game 1, with the Yankees up, 4-1, in the top of the eighth, men on second and third and none out, Bobby Cox bypassed Bernie Williams with an *intentional walk to load the bases*. John Rocker then struck out Tino Martinez and Jorge Posada, but walked Jim Leyritz before fanning Scott Brosius. In this case, the walk didn't lead to a blowout inning, but the Yankees still scored, and scored only because the bags were full. I'll call that a no-decision (BLIBB 6-7-1).

In Game 4, Williams came to the plate with no score in the bottom of the third, men on first and third with one out. Determined not to let Bernie beat him, Cox called once more for an *intentional walk to load the bases*. Martinez foiled the plan with a two-run single, Strawberry went down on strikes, then Posada drove in Williams to punctuate the inning (Final 1999 Postseason BLIBB Performance Record: 6-8-1).

Damage Assessment—The bases-loading intentional walk did not in fact fail "nine times out of ten" in this small sample from the 1999 playoffs. In fifteen tries, the walk-issuing team came away unscathed six times. Nine times the team at bat scored, and seven times it scored multiple runs. Among the big innings were such memorable self-inflicted wounds as the Indians' loading the bases for Troy O'Leary's grand slam, which put Cleveland in the hole in Game 5 of the ALDS; the Braves' setting up Todd Pratt's fifteenth inning game-tying walk which preceded Ventura's game-winning long shot in Game 5 of the NLCS; and the Mets' returning the favor with their BLIBBs to Hunter and Jordan in the sixth and eleventh innings of the terminal Game 6.

It is important to keep in mind that before a bases-loading intentional walk can occur, there have to be two men on (although the Mets did walk *two* batters to load the bases in NLCS Game 6). In fifteen second-and-third and first-and-third situations, the team in the field is most likely going to yield some runs no matter what it chooses to do. It is possible to compare how many runs scored after the fifteen BLIBBs to how many runs we might expect to have score based on situational averages. To get the expected runs for each situation, I used the averages compiled over the past five seasons by STATS, Inc.

To be clear, on the chart, the "Actual Runs" are the actual number of runs that scored after the BLIBB. The "Expected Runs" are for the situation before the BLIBB. The "Net Runs" is the theoretical increase or decrease in runs allowed as a result of the move.

All bases-loaded situations expect to yield more runs than any situation without the bags loaded and the same number of outs. Obviously the defensive manager knows that, in general, it is not preferable to

1999 Postseason BLIBBs: Actual Runs and Expected Runs

Series	Team	G/In	Runners	Outs	Actual Runs	Exp. Runs	Net Runs
1. ALDS	CLE	5/3rd	2&3	1	4	1.42	2.58
2. ALDS	TEX	1/5th	2&3	1	0	1.42	-1.42
3. NLDS	ARI	3/6th	2&3	2	5	1.42	3.58
4. NLDS	ARI	4/8th	1&2	2	0	0.47	-0.47
5. NLDS	ATL	1/5th	2&3	1	0	1.42	-1.42
6. NLDS	ATL	1/9th	1&3	1	4	1.20	2.80
7. NLDS	ATL	3/7th	1&3	1	0	1.20	-1.20
8. ALCS	NYA	2/8th	2&3	1	0	1.42	-1.42
9. ALCS	BOS	4/8th	2&3	1	0	1.42	-1.42
10. ALCS	BOS	4/9th	2&3	1	4	1.42	2.58
11. NLCS	ATL	5/15th	2&3	1	2	1.42	0.58
12. NLCS	NYN	6/6th	2&3	1	2	1.42	0.58
13. NLCS	NYN	6/11th	1&3	1	1	1.20	-0.20
14. WS	ATL	1/8th	2&3	0	1	2.05	-1.05
15. WS	ATL	4/3rd	1&3	1	3	1.20	1.80

load the bases. The question is how they do when they go *against* the odds.

From the fifteen pre-BLIBB situations, we might reasonably have expected 20.1 runs to score. After issuing the walks, 26 runs scored, a 29 percent increase over the expected scoring. Of course in terms of total runs, the extent of the damage in Cases 11 and 13 is contained by the fact that they involved game-ending plays. On the chart, Case 13 (Rogers walks Jordan) looks like a success, but believe me, it was not. In Case 11, had Ventura circled the bases, 29 runs would have scored after BLIBBs, an increase of 44 percent.

Of the fifteen bases-loading intentional walks, nine were issued while the team was behind, two while ahead, and four while tied. The walk-issuing team won only two of the twelve games above.

The bases-loading intentional walk proved an unreliable weapon for 1999's postseason managers. It would take further research, however, to determine if in a larger sample the move tended to convert potential big innings into actual big innings with the same efficiency.

The funny thing about this move being in vogue now is that the frequency of intentional walks overall, long stable, is in sharp decline. In 1975, the average NL team gave out 66 free passes and AL teams averaged 45. In 1980, it was 66 in the NL and 46 in the AL. In 1985 it was 65 in the NL and 40 in the AL. Five years later in 1990, it was 66 in the NL and 42 in the AL. Look, however, at what happened to intentional walks during the hard-hitting '90s: in 1996, the NL average was 52 and the AL average was 44. In 1997, it fell to 45 (NL) and 39 (AL). In '98 it fell again to 40 (NL) and 30 (AL), before leveling off in 1999 (42 for the NL, 31 for the AL).

Managers are likely changing their habits in direct response to the surge in scoring. When almost anyone can hit it out of the park, it makes less sense to put runners on for free. At the same time, when there are runners on second and third with one out, they seem to be saying, "This is probably going to be a big inning anyway, so I'll just take a shot with one good match-up." In the 1999 playoffs, the gamble paid off less than half the time.

Bill Stewart

The late Bill Stewart was a fine, hustling umpire who called them in the National League for 22 years. Bill was a chunky 5-foot-6 180, ran a game well, took no nonsense, and had the respect of the players. Stewart was also the first American ref in big-time hockey, serving in the NHL during baseball's off-season. He even took off his skates in 1938 to coach Chicago. The Black Hawks won the Stanley Cup, but the following year Bill was back on the ice as a ref.

The native of Fitchburg, Mass., lived in Boston most of his life. Stewart pitched and played some outfield in the Cape Cod, New England, Tri-State, Eastern, International Leagues and the American Association. When America entered World War I, the first pro baseball player to enlist was Bill Stewart. Hank Gowdy, the old catcher, was the first major leaguer.

A freak accident killed Stewart's major league dream. A White Sox farmhand, he took a winter job as a census taker in Boston. He knocked on a door on the third floor and was taken by surprise when it opened outward, toward him. He jumped back and clutched a bannister, which gave way. He fell two stories into a stairwell. He injured his back and wrenched his pitching arm. It never fully came back.

Bill coached college baseball, hockey, and football before going into umpiring in 1930. As Boston University's baseball coach, he pulled a black-haired Irish kid off third base to replace his injured catchers. Mickey Cochrane was on his way as one of the great receivers in history.

Bill was signed by the National League in 1933. He was assigned to the World Series in 1937, 1943, 1948, and 1953, retired after the 1954 season. He served on the major league rules committee for several years after that.

He is best known, unfortunately, for one controversial play in the '48 Series between the Braves and the Indians. In Game 1 at Boston on October 6, Bob Feller and Johnny Sain were locked in a brilliant scoreless mound duel in the bottom of the eighth. Feller, who allowed only one hit and whose control had been superb, walked Brave catcher Bill Salkeld to open the inning. Boston manager Billy Southworth put another catcher, Phil Masi, in as a runner for Salkeld. Outfielder Mike McCormick rolled a perfect sacrifice bunt to the left of Feller, who threw him out as Masi moved to second.

Feller intentionally walked Eddie Stanky, who was run for by Sibby Sisti. Sain then flied out to short right for out number two, as the runners held. With the dangerous Tommy Holmes at bat, Feller and manager-shortstop Lou Boudreau tried to work their timed pickoff play. On a set count, Boudreau broke for the bag and Feller whirled and made a perfect throw. Masi dove back head first. It was a bang-bang play. Stewart called Masi safe and Boudreau blew his top, but quickly gained his composure. When play resumed, Holmes lined a single between third baseman Ken Keltner and the bag, scoring Masi. The Indians did not score in the ninth, so that was the ball game. It was a tough loss for Feller who allowed only two hits, and although the Tribe went on to win the Series in six games, the great righthander never notched a World Series win. Photographs later showed Boudreau laying the tag on Masi before he had reached the base—but Stewart, of course had not had the benefit of stop-action photography.

That play at second is one of those well-remembered World Series moments, and it's a pity that Stewart is best known today for that one blown call. But then, the great American League umpire Nestor Chylak said it best about the men in blue. "Umping is the only profession," said Nestor, "where you have to be perfect when you start and improve thereafter!"

Bill Stewart, a fine man and solid manager, was 73 when he died February 19, 1964, in Jamaica Plain, Mass.

—Tom Knight

Juan Marichal: An Opening Day Dandy

Giants' ace pitched six complete games in ten season starters

Jay Roberts

In the nearly 120-year history of the New York and San Francisco Giants, several of the club's pitchers have distinguished themselves on Opening Days. "Smiling" Mickey Welch won the franchise opener in 1883, followed by three more first day victories. In 1902, Christy Mathewson's shutout of Philadelphia snapped the Giants' losing streak of nine consecutive lid lifters (an Opening Day record). Red Ames pitched well in his four outings, including taking a no-hitter into the tenth before eventually losing to Brooklyn in thirteen.

In his prime, Carl Hubbell yielded only six runs in three outings. For shutting out the Dodgers in the San Francisco inaugural at Seals Stadium in 1958, Ruben Gomez gets an honorable mention. More recently, John Burkett can claim back-to-back wins, including an 8-0 shutout of the Pirates in front of 58,077—the Giants' largest Opening Day crowd—in 1994.

The Giants' greatest Opening Day pitcher, though, is Juan Marichal. His ten starts, six wins, six complete games, two shutouts and ten strikeouts in one game are all Opening Day franchise records. He lasted at least eight innings eight times and had only one bad outing. His ERA was a phenomenal 1.73.

Here is a brief description of Marichal's ten Opening Day games, as well as an explanation of why he missed the season starters in 1963 and 1970. A statistical summary is provided at the end of the article.

Jay Roberts, *a lifelong Giants fan, writes about them at his website,* The Giants Journal. *He and his wife live in Alexandria, Virginia.*

Tuesday, April 10, 1962.
Milwaukee at San Francisco.

Juan Marichal opened his big league career at Candlestick Park by tossing a one-hitter against the Phillies in the summer of 1960. His 2.66 ERA led the Giants' talented staff that year, but the effort was not enough to earn Opening Day honors in 1961. Marichal experienced a bit of a "sophomore jinx" in 1961 with an ERA of 3.89, but that figure did not seem to worry skipper Alvin Dark. In the spring of 1962, he wisely gave the Dominican Republic native both permission to fly home to get married and the season-starting honors.

In what could be considered his debut as the Giants' ace, the twenty-four-year-old bridegroom responded in front of 39,177 at sunny Candlestick. Marichal was occasionally wild, but worked his way out of jams three times. "All day I work the corners," he told reporters afterwards.

The Giants reached Braves veteran Warren Spahn early. Willie Mays cracked the first pitch he saw over the fence, then Marichal helped his own cause—a double and run scored in the third to give the Giants a 2-0 lead, and a single in the fourth that knocked in two. He took a one-hitter into the ninth and completed the game with a three-hit, ten strikeout, 6-0 shutout.

Tuesday, April 9, 1963.
San Francisco at Houston.

The Giants won the National League pennant in

1962. Marichal had the team's best ERA, but Jack Sanford got the run support, the wins (24, including 16 in a row) and the subsequent privilege to open the 1963 campaign. Sanford and the Giants beat the Astros, 9-2, in Houston. Marichal pitched the next day, giving up four earned runs and lasting only two innings in a game the Giants won, 8-7.

Tuesday, April 14, 1964.
Milwaukee at San Francisco.

With a league-leading 25 wins in 1963, including a no-hitter and an epic 16-inning win over Spahn and the Braves, Marichal was well on his way to becoming one of the best pitchers in baseball. On Opening Day in San Francisco in 1964, he once again faced Spahn and the Braves. In front of 42,894, the largest crowd yet to see a regular season game at the 'Stick, Marichal gave up four early runs, three unearned.

With the Giants down, 4-2, Mays, an Opening Day standout in his own right, came to the rescue. In the third inning he clouted a two-run homer to tie the game. In the eighth Willie hit a solo shot to give the Giants a 6-4 lead. Orlando Cepeda and Tom Haller followed with home runs and Marichal, who settled down after the third, went the distance. The win was San Francisco's sixth opening day victory against only one loss since their move west.

Monday, April 12, 1965.
San Francisco at Pittsburgh.

28,189 at Forbes Field witnessed an extra-inning duel between the craftsman Marichal and the flame-thrower Bob Veale. Marichal retired the first ten Pirates he faced, yielded just five hits and one walk, allowed no one past second base in regulation, struck out nine and issued one free pass. The Giants put up threats in the first and fourth, but Veale shut the door both times. The tall righty gave up just three hits, struck out ten, walked one and retired the last nineteen Giants he faced. Both teams backed up their pitchers with brilliant defense and showed the fans "at least a dozen sparkling gems with the glove."

In the top of the tenth, Veale set the Giants down. Bob Bailey then spoiled Marichal's attempt to go 3-for-3 in openers. The young infielder deposited a curve ball from the Giants' ace into the trees beyond the left field fence, sending Number 27 quickly off the mound, and the crowd into a frenzy.

Tuesday, April 12, 1966.
Chicago at San Francisco.

Back in his favorite park, Marichal gave Giants fans

what they were coming to expect on Opening Day at Candlestick. He retired the first eighteen Cubbies and went on to give up one lone unearned run in the seventh. "His control was exceptional for this time of the year," Giants' catcher Tom Haller said. "I was surprised because he reported so late for spring training."

The Giants broke open a scoreless game in the fourth. Mays hit a circuit shot to get things rolling. Singles by Jim Ray Hart, Jesus Alou, Haller, and Marichal, and a double by Hal Lanier put the game out of reach. The 9-1 win brought Marichal's Opening Day record at Candlestick to 3-0, and the victory was his fourth straight Opening Day complete game.

Tuesday, April 11, 1967.
San Francisco at St. Louis.

The '67 opener in the nation's heartland matched up two of the National League's greatest franchises, two teams with excellent chances to win the pennant and, arguably, the two best pitchers in the game. Marichal was coming off a brilliant 25-6 campaign that included ten wins in a row and an appearance on the cover of *Time* magazine.

The Cardinals, who went on to win 101 games and the World Series, launched a 14-hit assault against Marichal. Although he lasted seven innings, the acrobatic righty gave up six runs. Meanwhile, Bob Gibson completely shut down the Giant machine. He struck out the first five, scattered five hits, walked none and fanned an Opening Day record-tying thirteen batters. St Louis's 6-0 win proved to be Marichal's only bad Opening Day outing.

Wednesday, April 10, 1968.
New York at San Francisco.

The Giants three-game Opening Day home win streak was in serious jeopardy against the Mets in 1968. In what would prove to be his last Opening Day start at home, the Dominican Dandy gave up four early runs, including a three-run homer to Ron Swoboda. He settled back down after the shaky third and shut the Mets out for five more innings.

With his team down, 4-2, Marichal was removed for a pinch hitter in the bottom of the eighth. Giants' reliever Fred Linzy did his job in the top of the ninth, giving San Francisco one last chance.

Seaver yielded an infield single to Mays who then scored on Hart's single to left. Mets' reliever Danny Frisella came on and could not overcome the Giants' Opening Day magic at the 'Stick. A single by shortstop Nate Oliver moved Hart over to second. Jesus Alou then laced a double into the left field corner, scoring Hart with the tying run and Oliver the winner when shortstop Bud Harrelson's relay throw home was high. The come-from-behind win ran San Francisco's Opening Day record to 6-1 at home and kept Marichal undefeated in Candlestick starters.

Monday, April 7, 1969.
San Francisco at Atlanta.

Exciting finishes characterized the Giants' openers in 1965, 1968, and again in 1969. The "Surprise Braves," who would end up sending San Francisco to a frustrating fifth straight second-place finish, hosted the Giants at Atlanta-Fulton County Stadium. Marichal, who had minor foot surgery during the off-season, gave up a run in the second and two more in the third. In the middle three frames, he shut the Braves out.

With a Giant on third in the top of the seventh, and San Francisco down, 3-2, skipper Clyde King lifted his ace (Marichal's earliest Opening Day departure) for a pinch hitter. King's strategy may have raised a few eyebrows, but it worked. Bob Burda's pinch hit scored Lanier from third. Two runs later, the Giants were ahead, 5-4.

Fred Linzy retired the side in the eighth and took the Giants' one-run lead into the bottom of the ninth. But to the delight of those in the crowd who had remained, light-hitting but speedy Sonny Jackson knocked a triple over the head of Mays in center field. The shot drove in Clete Boyer from second to tie the game. Mike Lum followed with a squibber past the Giants' drawn-in infield, giving Atlanta the thrilling come-from-behind victory.

Tuesday, April 7, 1970.
Houston at San Francisco.

Conspiracy theorists would have a field day with the tribulation Marichal went through in the spring of 1970. First he fell ill with the flu during the team's spring training trip in Japan. Then his trainer, showing no sympathy, simply reminded him he had to pitch the next day. A few days later, Marichal reacted poorly to a shot of penicillin. After telling him, "Oh, no, you don't have a reaction," another doctor in Phoenix gave him a second dose of the medicine. That injection landed Marichal in St. Luke's hospital in San Francisco and prevented him from trying to improve his Opening Day home record to 4-0.

At Candlestick, a somewhat disappointing (and surely disappointed) crowd of 30,333 watched Gaylord Perry give up seven runs in seven innings to the Astros. San Francisco, winner of its previous four openers at home, lost, 8-5. Marichal was out of action until April 25, when he returned to Candlestick to pitch five scoreless innings against the Expos in a contest the Giants lost, 7-3.

Tuesday, April 6, 1971.
San Francisco at San Diego.

1971 turned out to be a comeback season for both the Giants and their ace. Marichal was coming off a year of chronic arthritis, back pain, and an ERA that soared to 4.12. The Giants were aging and were not among the favorites to win the National League West.

Marichal, who would win three key games down the stretch of the division race and the clincher on the last day of the season in San Diego, sent the Giants off to a great start in '71 with his forty-seventh career shutout. In front of a record crowd of 34,554 in San Diego, he scattered four hits and allowed no one past second base. Mays hit career homer number 629 in the first inning and the Giants went on to win, 4-0. After the game, Marichal told reporters, "There's nothing better than something like this."

Saturday, April 15, 1972.
San Francisco at Houston.

"Few fans, lots of booing," one headline said. In the spring of 1972, the enthusiastic articles about the magic and aura of Opening Day were replaced with depressing news. The thirteen-day strike was disappointing to fans and the sparse first day crowds reflected their anger. But interestingly enough, 23,021, one of the largest crowds that day, showed up at the Astrodome for the delayed season opener.

With one out and the game tied at zero in the fifth, the Astros loaded the bases. Marichal was in trouble and had to face the speedy Cesar Cedeno. The high-kicking righty came in with a slider. Cedeno hit the ball sharply to shortstop Chris Speier who quickly threw to Tito Fuentes covering at second. The Giants' second baseman fired to Willie McCovey at first, nailing Cedeno in the nick of time. Marichal led the Giant cheers with a reach towards the heavens. "The double play ball...that was the whole ball game," he told reporters after the game.

In the top of the sixth, McCovey crashed a two-run homer to give San Francisco a 2-0 lead. Marichal continued to retire batters and helped his own cause with a double and run scored in the eighth. In the eighth inning, skipper Charlie Fox inserted relief specialist Jerry Johnson to close out his starter's effort and the righty did just that. The victory pushed San

Francisco's Opening Day record to 10-5 and Marichal's to 5-2.

Thursday, April 5, 1973.
San Francisco at Cincinnati.

In terms of how historians would one day regard Marichal's Opening Day record, his season starter in 1973 proved to be pivotal. Up to that point, he could claim no victories against any team that went on to win 90 or more games. The better teams, like the '65 Pirates and the '66 Cardinals, had defeated him.

Going into the '73 opener, a sixth Opening Day victory did not seem likely for Marichal. His record had fallen to 6-16 in 1972, due in part to continued back problems. During the off-season he underwent spinal surgery. And in the traditional season opener in Cincinnati, the thirty-five-year-old veteran had to deal with not only cold weather, but a lineup that featured Pete Rose, Joe Morgan, Tony Perez, and Johnny Bench and a Reds team that would go on to win the National League West division by 14-1/2 games.

Marichal fell behind, 1-0, in the second inning, breaking his Opening Day consecutive scoreless inning streak at 21. The Giants responded with a run in the fifth, only to watch the Reds rally in the bottom half of the frame. With one out, Cincy ignited the home crowd of 51,569 by putting runners on first and second. Marichal came in with a slider to Bobby Tolan, who hit a weak popup to shortstop Chris Speier. He then got slugger Johnny Bench to ground into an inning-ending double play.

In the seventh inning, with the score still tied at one, the Giants took control of the contest. A key moment in the uprising came with one on and one out. Starter Don Gullet walked Marichal, a .325 hitter in 26 Opening Day at bats. Chris Speier and Bobby Bonds then cracked timely hits off the tiring Gullet, and San Francisco forged a 4-1 lead. In what would prove to be his last Opening Day start, Marichal completed the game in a blaze of glory by retiring the final thirteen Cincinnati batters. The victory was his third straight Opening Day win on the road. In those three contests, he gave up just one run.

Epilogue—The nagging injuries and medical problems that plagued Juan Marichal throughout much of his sixteen-year career began to take their toll during the 1973 season. He became increasingly ineffective, and owner Horace Stoneham sold him to the Boston Red Sox at the end of the season. His departure was one of the final acts of the Giants' first era in San Francisco. During the fourteen years Marichal had been on the ball club, the Giants had been involved in a pennant race eight times. Their average record from 1962 through 1973 was 89-73.

In 1974, the first year without Marichal, Opening Day attendance at Candlestick Park was only 17,527. The season's average attendance (7,027) is the record low for the Candlestick Era. During the next ten years, Opening Day honors went to seven different pitchers. The Giants won only one at Candlestick and lost a team-record five in a row from 1980 to 1984.

Marichal pitched in eleven games with the Red Sox in 1974, two with the Dodgers in 1975, then retired from the game at age thirty-seven. His name will probably always be associated with the John Roseboro incident in August of 1965 and the Cy Young awards that eluded him.

What isn't well known about Juan Antonio Marichal is his Opening Day record. Like the man himself, that record is a dandy: Wins, 6; Losses, 2; No-decisions, 2; Innings, 83; Hits, 65; Runs, 20; Earned Runs, 16; Walks, 19; Strikeouts, 57; ERA, 1.73.

Giants' Opening Day Records Held by Marichal
Most Starts, 10; Most Wins, 6; Most Complete Games, 6; Nine-inning Shutouts, 2 (1962, 1971); Most Strikeouts, 10 in 1962; (Tied) Fewest Hits Allowed, 3 (1962 and in 1966).

Sources:

Atlanta *Journal.*

Cincinnati *Enquirer.*

Houston *Post.*

Pittsburgh *Post-Gazette.*

New York *Times.*

San Francisco *Chronicle.*

Washington *Post.*

The Sporting News.

Baseball Weekly.

Dickey, Glen. *San Francisco Giants: 40 Years.*

Einstein, Charles. *Juan Marichal, A Pitcher's Story.*

Kerr, Don. *Opening Day: All Major League Baseball Season Opening Games, by Team, 1876-1998.*

Mandel, Mike. *An Oral History of the San Francisco Giants.*

Peters, Nick. *San Francisco Giants Almanac.*

Schott, Tom and Nick Peters. *The Giants Encyclopedia.*

Total Baseball. Sixth Edition.

Silent John Gillespie's Forgotten Home Run Record

Pitcher hit four homers in a game

Michael J. Bielawa with Frank J. Williams

Let's face it, in whatever quarters folks ponder baseball, be it in schoolyards or saloons, certain names come to mind. Babe Ruth. Hank Aaron. Bonds. McGwire. Sosa. Naturally. They are our home run heroes. And we all have our favorite home run memories. From the World Series telekinesis of Fisk willing his long hit fair in '75 to Gibson's hobbled jog in '88, baseball fans worship the home run. I remember dancing around my own living room late one rainy autumn night, the phone ringing off the hook with delighted friends, when Robin Ventura beat the Braves with his fifteenth-inning grand slam turned single. The home run unites us. The homer, long ball, dinger. It's Americana. It's part of our vernacular. When something is tops or best or wonderful we term it a "home run."

Pitchers, of course, are more noted for giving up long balls than hitting them. Branca, Terry, Stallard, Moore, Williams. They do, though, sometimes tag one deep. Occasionally more than one. Actually, lots of pitchers have belted two home runs in one professional game. Back in 1886 Guy Hecker of the American Association Louisville club hit three, and Jim Tobin of the 1942 Boston Braves did the same— a rare bright spot for that awful team. But John

Gillespie, pitching for the 1923 Eastern League Bridgeport (Connecticut) Americans, slammed four, count 'em, four, home runs in one game, a unique pitcher's accomplishment that was promptly forgotten—until Bob McConnell came along. McConnell is a founder of SABR and the chair of its Minor League Committee. Some time ago, while he was researching old newspaper accounts for his *Minor League Home Run Record Book*, he discovered Gillespie's feat in a Springfield, Massachusetts, newspaper. Surprised, he contacted Bridgeport resident and fellow SABRite, Frank Williams, and asked him to confirm the game in local dailies. John Gillespie's record began to emerge.

Pitcher John Patrick Gillespie was born on February 25, 1900 in Oakland, California. Nicknamed "Duke" and "Silent John," he played pro ball for eight years, including one season with the Cincinnati Reds in 1922. Silent John appeared in 31 games that year and finished with a record of 3-3. He batted .133 and hit no home runs. That offensive ineptitude would all change the following season with Bridgeport. On August 9, 1923, against the Ponies at Springfield, Silent John accomplished something no professional pitcher before or since has matched.

Gillespie's Springfield counterpart was Gary Fortune, an outstanding minor league pitcher having a fine (22-12) season. But the day belonged to Gillespie. Silent John pitched nine innings and went five for five at the plate with four home runs, five RBIs, and a single. His fourth round-tripper was a

Michael Bielawa *is fascinated with the history of Connecticut's minor leagues and is the author of* From FarField to Newfield: The Baseball Dream of Orator Jim O'Rourke (1999). *His baseball poetry has appeared in numerous publications. Around the time pitchers and catchers report each February he faithfully reports to Mardi Gras. When not in New Orleans you can find him at Shea Stadium. He would like to acknowledge Frank Williams for his incredible research and support.*

leadoff homer in the top of the tenth that broke a 9-9 tie and secured Bridgeport's victory and his win. George Abrams came on to pitch the bottom of the tenth for the Americans and was credited with the save.

The following day's Bridgeport *Telegram* reported, "Johnny Gillespie, burly Bridgeport pitcher, slugged his way into baseball's hall of fame today at League Park in Springfield. Four times his lusty drives soared over the left field fence for home runs. The Americans hurler made it a perfect day hammering out a single which gave him a total of 17 bases, an Eastern League record. Incidentally, Bridgeport trimmed the Ponies 10 to 9 in a real diamond thriller."

The *Telegram* article continued, "There was nothing fluky about Gillespie's belts. His first, in the third inning, was a high loft which just cleared the fence. His second opened the sixth inning. His third came in the 8th with one runner on base and his fourth was clouted when he appeared at the plate in the tenth, first man up. Each of these was a husky sock and each cleared the barrier by a good margin."

Seasons came and went. Gillespie tallied a total of six career homers. Eventually he returned to his home state and died in Vallejo, California, just ten days shy of his fifty-fourth birthday. The roaring twenties, Ruth's era, gave way to the Great Depression and then World War II. Then that other human tragedy, television, pretty much tore minor league ball apart. Silent John's feat faded from baseball's memory, finally resurrected by good SABR sleuthing. SABR's Frank Williams, a good hometown boy, states, "Gillespie's record will probably last forever and it will always remain a Bridgeport record." Aaron, Ruth, Sosa, Bonds, and McGwire. We all have our favorite home run memories. Now John Gillespie can once again be one of them.

Beans Reardon

Back in 1969, twenty years after he retired as a great and colorful National League umpire, my dear friend "Beans" Reardon was asked about the possibility of replacing umpires with "electric eyes" or some other gadgets in the future. He replied, "It will never happen, because when you do that you've taken away all the alibis. Who can the manager blame losses on? Who can pitchers and hitters blame their troubles on? Believe me, the umpire will always be with us."

John Edward Reardon was born in New England of Irish parents but was raised in Southern California. He played ball only as a boy. He tackled umpiring at the age of sixteen and with the kind of eyes he had, this first attempt labeled him for life as a chosen man for the job.

His debut was at Boyle Heights in Los Angeles. Before joining the National League staff in 1926, he operated in the War Service League, the Movie League, the Copper League, the Arizona League, the Western Canada League and the Pacific Coast League. Veteran umpire Hank O'Day recommended him for a big league job.

Reardon's unusual nickname dates from his brief playing career. He was trying out for the ballclub representing the Southern Pacific Car shops in L.A. The team captain asked him where he was from. "Taunton, Mass.," retorted Reardon. "I get it, a bean-eater," said the captain.

That day the new player came to bat with the bases full. "Come on, Beans," yelled the captain, "let's see you knock it a mile." Young Reardon promptly knocked a ball over the left-field fence, and after that the boys all called him Beans. (His Christmas cards were always imprinted "Mr. and Mrs. John E. Reardon.)

Spending winters in Los Angeles, Beans got to know Mae West and was in a few of her hits of the '30s. Beans was a good businessman. He had a successful beer distributorship for years, and he eventually sold it to Frank Sinatra for a cool million.

During his long career as an umpire he worked his share of All Star Games and World Series. His final Series was in 1949, when the Yankees beat Brooklyn in five games. Beans always said that no one ever saw a major league game until they saw one in Ebbets Field. When Beans was honored on the TV show "This Is Your Life," host Ralph Edwards had Hilda Chester, the lady with the cow-bell, represent the Brooklyn fans. Incidentally, in August, 1926, when Babe Herman doubled into a double play with Herman, pitcher Dazzy Vance, and second baseman Chick Fewster all hanging onto third, the umpire at the base was Beans.

Beans was very fond of Gene Autry and had a season box at the Angels ballpark in Anaheim. The last time I saw him was sitting in that box in 1981. He was 83 years old. He rarely went to Dodger Stadium. He told me when he did go he always paid for his tickets. He said, "I don't want to be obligated to Walter O'Malley."

Beans Reardon was 86 when he died in Long Beach, California, July 31, 1984.

—Tom Knight

Sandlot Baseball:
The Way the Kids Like It

Who's the game for, anyway?

Paul McCary

Sandlot baseball has given way to the organized variety nearly everywhere. And that's a shame. Real uniforms, real fields, real umpires, and real fans sitting in the stands look and feel like a large advancement over the ragtag sandlot scene. But it's a real step backward as a life experience for children. It's not hard to understand the richness of the sandlot experience.

Equal teams, every game—Kids instinctively know that the only way to have fun playing a team sport is if the teams are somewhat equal in talent. So they always divide themselves up that way when left on their own. Adults forget this. They commandeer Little League teams, engineer tryouts and scout the local talent as if they were general managers. Their goal is to field the strongest team possible. Result: some teams lose almost every game while some others win almost every game. The players get false signals about their talent level (even good players on bad teams get tired of losing every game) and the games are less fun. Sandlot kids understand this principle so well that they will modify the teams if one player has to leave early or if new players show up halfway through the game. Team formation is the subject of informal negotiation among the children, not the result of manipulation by adults living out their own Dan Duquette dreams.

The role of rules—Kids also understand that rules need to be flexible to serve the higher goal of having fun. So anything left of that rock near shortstop is foul and invisible runners abound. If someone thinks up a good new rule during the game, it is quickly embraced and adopted. Try that in Little League.

Disputed calls—Close plays are always the subject of shouting regardless of the level at which the game is played. But on the sandlot, interesting things happen. First, there is a loud negotiation session. Then, after a while, either the biggest kid or a kid with a reputation for fairness will settle the argument. Players who argue every call are ignored. Sometimes teams alternate winning close calls. And once the argument is over, it's over. You'll never hear sandlot players complaining about a bad call on the way home.

The schedule—Sandlot games are spontaneous. Kids play when they want to. A game can start with two kids on each team (anything left of second base is either foul or an out) and expand as additional players show up, with a new player sometimes having to recruit another so teams stay even.

Here again, some negotiation skills are involved, but the goal remains having fun playing and trying to win an exciting game. By contrast, the long season and formal schedule of organized baseball intrudes on other activities like weekend trips with family or friends. Sandlot players may be late for dinner, but they never miss out on camping trips.

Paul McCary *is a Hartford, Connecticut, attorney who played one year of Little League baseball. A version of this article appeared in the Hartford Courant.*

No fans—Playing in front of fans, even well meaning and well-behaved family and friends, introduces a level of pressure that most kids don't like and shouldn't have to worry about. On the sandlot, dropping a fly, crying if you get hit in the face by the ball, or criticizing another player all quickly recede into insignificance and are forgotten. Not so when thirty adults have seen your mistake.

These comparisons do not rely on any of the well documented horror stories of organized baseball. And they are not limited to baseball. The same could be said about football, basketball or any other team sports. The point is that kids approach sports and games differently than adults do. We make a mistake when we superimpose adult values and structures on all of our children's activities.

Pedro in the Pantheon

Dominant dominance

Dayn Perry

Baseball's here and now is most notable for its almost uncouth levels of offense. Records fall and lose their luster. Benchmarks of yore are swatted into obsolescence. The time span of the typical game is more of the Cecil B. DeMille variety than of the Woody Allen. It's a tumult, to be sure.

Almost overlooked in all this is an improbably scrawny Boston righthander who plies his trade as though a man out of time. Indeed, Pedro Martinez's numbers for the 2000 season look as though they were culled from 1968: 18-6, 1.74 ERA, 217 innings, 128 hits, 32 walks, 284 strikeouts. That's fine mound work in any era, but it's particularly eye popping in today's game, when runs are anything but dear. If we place his efforts in the context of time and place, we're led by the hand to an inevitable question: Was Pedro Martinez's performance in 2000 the greatest ever?

None of us is thunderstruck by the idea that Martinez is the greatest pitcher of today, but can we justly call his work last season the greatest ever? Should we ask this question of a player whose ERA for the year in question was not in the top 100 of all time? Yes we can, and yes we should.

ERA, among traditional pitching measures, passes muster reasonably well, but, as is the case with any unadjusted, non-normalized metric, it can be only so instructive. To gain a sensible remove, we must consider that the American League ERA for 2000—4.91—is the third highest of the twentieth century. This should surprise no one who watched a day's worth of scores roll across a ticker at night and was struck by the, well, footballlishness of them. To put Martinez's ERA in perspective, we need to adjust it to take league performance into account, along with the moods of Fenway, where he made 13 of his 29 starts. The best tool for this is a statistic called ERA+, which is nothing more than a ratio of the park-adjusted league ERA to the park-adjusted ERA of the individual pitcher, with the decimal dropped for ease of expression. One important thing to note is that ERA+ is inversely proportional to ERA; a low ERA yields a high ERA+. Therefore, the higher Martinez's ERA+, the more impressive is his season. ERA+ is scaled so that a value of 100 means dead average: the pitcher's ERA+ is the same as the league's park-adjusted ERA.

Pedro Martinez's ERA+ for 2000 is 292—185 percent superior to the league average. This is the best ERA+ of the twentieth century (being a purist of the calendar, I'm counting 2000 as part of the twentieth century). Relative to league performance, Pedro Martinez's ERA is the best of the past hundred years. The last and lone hurler to better Pedro's mark was Tim Keefe in 1880 with an ERA+ of 294 (and an ERA of 0.86). Conditions in that era were so different from those of today that it is impossible to usefully compare the two stunningly dominant seasons.

Yes, Martinez's season in 2000 was dominance unabated. The signposts are everywhere. In terms of

Dayn Perry, *a native Mississippian now living in Austin, Texas, is a baseball writer for ESPN Insider.*

keeping the opponents off the basepaths, Pedro was unchallenged in history. His combined walks and hits per nine innings was 6.636—the lowest ever. And this number is a straight measurement, not normalized to a league or an era. Despite working in one of the hitter-friendly eras in baseball history, Martinez's was stingier with baserunners than every other pitcher, from every other era. But there's more.

His raw ERA of 1.74 led the American League by a healthy margin. Just how healthy? Roger Clemens finished second, but his ERA of 3.70 was closer to that of Rolando Arrojo, owner of the thirty-eighth best American League ERA, than it was to Pedro's. In fact, taking a cue from ERA+, if we form a ratio of Clemens's second-best ERA to Martinez's loop-topping mark, we find that the resultant figure of 213 is the highest ever. No ERA league leader in the annals of the game has been so far ahead of his runner-up.

We also find that Martinez led the American League in a bevy of pitching categories in 2000: ERA (1.74), shutouts (four), strikeouts (284), opponents' on-base percentage (.213), opponents' slugging percentage (.259), fewest hits allowed per nine innings (5.31), fewest home runs allowed per nine innings (0.71), average versus lefthanded batters (.150), average versus righthanded batters (.184), average allowed with runners in scoring position (.133), strikeout-to-walk ratio (8.88) and quality starts (25). That .213 opponents' on-base percentage is the lowest of the twentieth century. Yet there is still more that etches his season in sharper relief.

Pedro's opponents' batting average of .167 trumps the previous gold standard, .168, set by Luis Tiant in, appropriately, "the year of the pitcher," 1968. Martinez's 8.88 strikeout-to-walk ratio is the second lowest of the century, behind only Bret Saberhagen's mark of 11.0 from his unheralded 1994 season. But if we look at the more enlightening proportion of strikeouts to walks plus hits, we find that Pedro's mark of 1.78 is easily the greatest ever.

He also thrived in what should otherwise be troubling circumstances for a pitcher: he was 12-1 on the road, with a 1.66 ERA, a .190 on-base percentage, and a .213 opponents' slugging percentage allowed.

His 18-6 record is somewhat underwhelming. However, Martinez's ERA in those six losses was 2.44. If you ignore the small sample size, that ERA—taken only from games he lost—would have led the majors. If we take the park-adjusted league ERA and form a ratio this time to Pedro's park-adjusted ERA from this past season's losses, the yield is an ERA+ that would still rank in the top thirty of all time. Even in games he lost, he dwelt in rarefied air.

So did Pedro Martinez craft the greatest season of pitching ever? That the question can even be asked speaks volumes. A better query might be: How exactly is it that Martinez can perform at such unassailable level and not win an MVP in one of the last two seasons? It's a farce and it bespeaks of the flaws of the award and our dreary, modern predilection toward offense. Even when we have recognized his excellence, we've given short shrift to a man who is pitching with the force of history.

Mike Donlin, Movie Actor

Roll 'em!

Rob Edelman

Scores of professional ballplayers have made their way from the big leagues to the big screen. A few, including Chuck Connors, Bob Uecker, and John Beradino (who played for the Browns, Indians, and Pirates as Johnny Berardino), became successful actors or media personalities. Some, notably Babe Ruth, appeared in movies as themselves, or as thinly veiled versions of themselves. Still others have been extras or bit players in comedies, action-adventures, dramas—and baseball films. But one ballplayer was the first to regularly be listed in film credits as well as box scores. He is Michael Joseph "Turkey Mike" Donlin, who played in the big leagues between 1899 and 1914.

In his overview of Donlin's career, which appeared in *The Baseball Research Journal* last year, Michael Betzold cites the ballplayer-turned-actor's screen work in the final paragraphs. Additionally, in my 1994 book *Great Baseball Films*, I devote a chapter to Donlin as a vaudevillian and movie actor. However, given his status as a pioneer ballplayer-turned-screen performer, Donlin's celluloid career is worthy of further scrutiny.

Make no mistake, Mike Donlin was no movie star. Nor was he movie star material. While not homely, he was not handsome; his voice was ordinary sounding; his demeanor was less than charismatic. In most of his films, he was a supporting actor and, occasionally, even an uncredited bit player. He may have worked with such pantheon directors as John Ford, William A. Wellman, and Josef von Sternberg. He may have had roles in several bona-fide classics, including *The General* and *Beggars of Life*, released respectively in 1927 and 1928. He may have been employed by the A-list film studios. And he may have appeared in films starring screen legends from Jean Arthur, Wallace Beery, and Louise Brooks to Will Rogers and Mae West. Yet just as often, his directors, co-stars, and films are long-forgotten, and his studios are strictly poverty row.

Furthermore, even when Donlin earned billing, most of his screen roles were nondescript. Rarely was he a key supporting player. His characters either added background color and atmosphere or served to move the story along.

Quite a few of Donlin's early screen appearances are in films that no longer exist. Such is the case with his debut feature: *Right Off the Bat*, released in 1915, a baseball drama in which he starred as himself. It was his only celluloid leading role.

Happily, his next screen appearance came in a film that still may be viewed. It is *Raffles, the Amateur Cracksman*, released in 1917, in which Donlin appears in a supporting role as Crawshay, a stick-up man. He shares several minutes of screen time in the company of two celebrated actors: John Barrymore, the film's star, who is cast as the title character, a gentleman thief; and an astonishingly young Frank Morgan,

Rob Edelman *is the author of* Great Baseball Films *and* Baseball on the Web. *With his wife, Audrey Kupferberg, he has written* Meet the Mertzes, *a double biography of* I Love Lucy's *Vivian Vance and William Frawley. Their latest book is a biography of Walter Matthau, to be published in 2002.*

twenty-two years before playing his most celebrated screen role, the title character in *The Wizard of Oz*. After appearing onscreen, Donlin's Crawshay points a gun at Barrymore's Raffles and Morgan's Bunny Manders. His intention is to pilfer some gems, which are referred to in the intertitles as "sparklers" and "dem jewels," but is easily manipulated by the crafty Raffles.

Donlin's friendship with Barrymore led to his being cast in the film, as well as in *The Sea Beast*, a Barrymore swashbuckler released in 1926. In his 1944 biography, *Good Night, Sweet Prince*, Gene Fowler noted that Barrymore had "all sorts of friends," among them Donlin, Jack Dempsey, Winston Churchill, and Albert Einstein. "It pleased [Barrymore] when any of these faces could be seen on his set or in his dressing-room," Fowler added.

Raffles, the Amateur Cracksman and *The Sea Beast* are of course silent films, as are more than half of Donlin's fifty-odd screen credits. Among his "talkies," or early sound films, is *Hot Curves*, a 1930 baseball comedy in which he plays a gruff scout who signs frenetic, double-talking train concessionaire Benny Goldberg (Benny Rubin) to a contract. The scout utters a line that might have been ad-libbed by Donlin, who played for the New York Giants for several seasons. It sounds like "I hope McGraw'll be sold," but the scout actually is referring to "McGrew," his team's skipper. The storyline in *Hot Curves* reportedly was inspired by the real-life signing of Andy Cohen by Giants manager John McGraw. Cohen, like the fictional Benny Goldberg, was Jewish, and their respective inkings were intended to lure Jewish fans to the ballpark. (By the way, fifteen years earlier, McGraw had appeared on-screen with Donlin in *Right Off the Bat*.)

In *The Tip-Off*, a 1931 gangster comedy-drama, Donlin is sixth-billed as Swanky Jones, a boxing trainer and pool room habitue who is as equally harsh in demeanor as the scout in *Hot Curves*. While the role mostly is nondescript in relation to anything that occurs onscreen, *The Tip-Off* does allow Donlin to share screen time with Ginger Rogers, then a Hollywood starlet.

In some of his sound films, Donlin (who died in 1933) appears uncredited. In order to note his presence in a number of them, you have to stumble across him while watching the film. One such appearance is in *Picture Snatcher*, a 1933 James Cagney crime drama. *The American Film Institute Catalog, Feature Films, 1931-1940*, perhaps the definitive published reference of film credits for that decade, lists the bit players who

appear in *Picture Snatcher*, cast in such roles as "fireman," "head keeper," "journalism student," and even "sick reporter" and "reporter outside prison." None is Mike Donlin. Yet there he is, unmistakable in one brief shot. He is seen in a pool hall, and he speaks the following words into a telephone: "No, Mr. McLean, he ain't been around here in over a week." After a brief pause, he adds, "Yeah, I'll tell him."

What may be Donlin's most memorable screen appearance is equally fleeting. In one sequence in *Riley the Cop*, a 1928 comedy-drama directed by John Ford, a bunch of kids are playing baseball on an inner-city street. The title character (J. Farrell MacDonald) arrives on the scene to reprimand the lads and break up their game, yet the boyish Riley is quickly convinced to join the kids in their play. He picks up a bat, and clumsily swings and misses at the first pitch tossed his way, in the process falling to the pavement. The cop does connect on his next swing, lifting a pop fly that crashes through a storefront window, necessitating the kids—and Riley—to commence scattering.

After Riley's swing-and-miss, Ford includes an all-too-quick shot of Donlin looking on and smiling, with a cigarette dangling from his lips.

While he is not billed on screen, various film references list the actor-ballplayer as playing "Crook." Thus, the implication is that Donlin's character is amused because he is eluding the law while Riley is indulging in a child's game.

Yet given his background, the sequence— intentional or not— serves as an homage to Donlin's past, and a wink-of-the-eye to anyone who recognizes him as an ex-major leaguer.

Mike Donlin Filmography

Right Off the Bat (1915), All Feature Booking Agency. Dir: Hugh Reticker. Cast: John J. McGraw, Claire Mersereau, Rita Ross Donlin. Donlin plays himself.

Raffles, the Amateur Cracksman (1917), States Rights. Dir: George Irving. Cast: John Barrymore, Frederick Perry, Frank Morgan, Evelyn Brent. Donlin plays Crawshay.

Jack Spurlock, Prodigal (1918), Fox. Dir: Carl Harbaugh. Cast: George Walsh, Dan Mason, Ruth Taylor. Donlin plays Foreman.

Brave and Bold (1918), Fox. Dir: Carl Harbaugh. Cast: George Walsh, Francis X. Conlon, Regina Quinn. Donlin's role is undetermined.

The Unchastened Woman (1918), George Kleine System. Dir: William Humphrey. Cast: Grace Valentine, Mildred Manning, Catherine Tower. Donlin plays O'Brien.

Railroaded (1923), Universal. Dir: Edmund Mortimer. Cast: Herbert Rawlinson, Esther Ralston. Donlin plays Corton.

Woman-Proof (1923), Paramount. Dir: Alfred E. Green. Cast: Thomas Meighan, Lila Lee, Louise Dresser, Mary Astor. Donlin plays Foreman.

The Unknown Purple (1923), Truart. Dir: Roland West. Cast: Henry B.

Walthall, Alice Lake, Stuart Holmes. Donlin plays Burton.

Flaming Barriers (1924), Paramount. Dir: George Melford. Cast: Jacqueline Logan, Antonio Moreno. Donlin's role in undetermined.

The Trouble Shooter (1924), Fox. Dir: Jack Conway. Cast: Tom Mix, Kathleen Key, Frank Currier. Donlin plays Chet Connors (also credited as Chet Conners).

Hit and Run (1924), Universal. Dir: Edward Sedgwick. Cast: Hoot Gibson, Marion Harlan, Cyril Ring. Donlin plays Red McCarthy.

Oh, Doctor! (1925), Universal. Dir: Harry A. Pollard. Cast: Reginald Denny, Mary Astor, Otis Harlan. Donlin plays Buzz Titus.

Fifth Avenue Models (1925), Universal. Dir: Svend Gade. Cast: Mary Philbin, Norman Kerry, Josef Swickard, Jean Hersholt. Donlin plays Crook's Henchman.

The Primrose Path (1925), Arrow. Dir: Harry O. Hoyt. Cast: Wallace MacDonald, Clara Bow, Arline Pretty, Stuart Holmes. Donlin plays Federal Officer Parker.

The Unnamed Woman (1925), Arrow. Dir: Harry O. Hoyt. Cast: Katherine MacDonald, Herbert Rawlinson, Wanda Hawley. Donlin plays Chauffeur.

The Sea Beast (1926), Warner Bros. Dir: Millard Webb. Cast: John Barrymore, Dolores Costello, George O'Hara. Donlin plays Flask.

Her Second Chance (1926), Vitagraph. Dir: Lambert Hillyer. Cast: Anna Q. Nilsson, Huntly Gordon, Charlie Murray. Donlin plays De Vries.

Ella Cinders (1926), First National. Dir: Alfred E. Green. Cast: Colleen Moore, Lloyd Hughes, Vera Lewis, Harry Langdon. Donlin plays Film Studio Gateman.

The Fighting Marine (1926), Pathe. Dir: Spencer Gordon Bennett. Cast: Gene Tunney, Marjorie Gay, Walter Miller. Feature version of 10-reel Pathe serial. Donlin's role is undetermined.

The General (1927), United Artists. Dir: Buster Keaton, Clyde Bruckman. Cast: Buster Keaton, Glen Cavender, Marion Mack, Jim Farley. Donlin plays Union General.

Slide, Kelly, Slide (1927), MGM. Dir: Edward Sedgwick. Cast: William Haines, Sally O'Neil, Harry Carey, Junior Coghlan, Irish Meusel, Bob Meusel, Tony Lazzeri. Donlin plays himself.

Warming Up (1928), Paramount. Dir: Fred Newmeyer. Cast: Richard Dix, Jean Arthur, Claude King, Philo McCullough. Donlin plays Veteran.

Beggars of Life (1928), Paramount. Dir: William A. Wellman. Cast: Wallace Beery, Louise Brooks, Richard Arlen. Donlin plays Bill.

Riley the Cop (1928), Fox. Dir: John Ford. Cast: J. Farrell MacDonald, Louise Fazenda, Nancy Drexel, David Rollins. Donlin plays Crook.

Below the Deadline (1929), Chesterfield. Dir: J. P. McGowan. Cast: Frank Leigh, Barbara Worth, Arthur Rankin. Donlin plays Sandy.

Noisy Neighbors (1929), Pathe. Dir: Charles Reisner. Cast: Eddie Quillan, Alberta Vaughn, Theodore Roberts. Donlin plays Second Son.

Thunderbolt (1929), Paramount. Dir: Josef von Sternberg. Cast: George Bancroft, Fay Wray, Richard Arlen, Tully Marshall. Donlin plays Kentucky Sampson.

Born Reckless (1930), Fox. Dir: John Ford. Cast: Edmund Lowe, Catherine Dale Owen, Warren Hymer, Marguerite Churchill, Lee Tracy. Donlin plays Fingy Moscovitz.

Hot Curves (1930), Tiffany. Dir: Norman Taurog. Cast: Benny Rubin, Rex Lease, Alice Day, Pert Kelton. Donlin plays Scout.

Her Man (1930), Pathe. Dir: Tay Garnett. Cast: Helen Twelvetrees, Marjorie Rambeau, Ricardo Cortez, Phillips Holmes, James Gleason, Thelma Todd. Donlin plays Bartender.

Widow from Chicago (1930), First National. Dir: Edward Cline. Cast: Alice White, Neil Hamilton, Edward G. Robinson, Frank McHugh. Donlin plays Desk Man.

Iron Man (1931), Universal. Dir: Tod Browning. Cast: Lew Ayres, Robert Armstrong, Jean Harlow, John Miljan. Donlin plays McNeill.

Sweepstakes (1931), RKO. Dir: Albert Rogell. Cast: Eddie Quillan, Lew Cody, James Gleason, Marion Nixon. Donlin is listed in *Variety* as playing The Dude, a character credited onscreen to Tom Jackson.

Star Witness (1931), Warner Bros. Dir: William A. Wellman. Cast: Walter Huston, Frances Starr, Grant Mitchell, Sally Blane. Donlin plays Mickey, a Thug.

The Tip-Off (1931), RKO. Dir: Albert Rogell. Cast: Eddie Quillan, Robert Armstrong, Ginger Rogers. Donlin plays Swanky Jones.

The Secret Witness (Terror By Night) (1931), Columbia. Dir: Thornton Freeland. Cast: Una Merkel, William Collier, Jr., ZaSu Pitts. Donlin plays Mike the Speakeasy Proprietor.

Arrowsmith (1931), United Artists. Dir: John Ford. Cast: Ronald Colman, Helen Hayes, Richard Bennett, Clarence Brooks, Myrna Loy. Donlin has a bit part.

Bad Company (1931), RKO. Dir: Tay Garnett. Cast: Helen Twelvetrees, Ricardo Cortez, John Garrick, Paul Hurst, Harry Carey. Donlin has a bit part.

Beast of the City (1932), MGM. Dir: Charles Brabin. Cast: Walter Huston, Jean Harlow, Wallace Ford, Jean Hersholt. Donlin plays Reporter Going to Phone His Stuff.

A Fool's Advice (Meet the Mayor) (1932), Warner Bros. Dir: Ralph Ceder. Cast: Frank Fay, Ruth Hall, Hale Hamilton. Donlin has a bit part.

The Famous Ferguson Case (1932), First National. Dir: Lloyd Bacon. Cast: Joan Blondell, Grant Mitchell, Vivienne Osborne. Donlin plays Photographer.

Madison Square Garden (1932), Paramount. Dir: Harry Joe Brown. Cast: Jack Oakie, Thomas Meighan, Marion Nixon, ZaSu Pitts. Donlin plays himself.

One Way Passage (1932), Warner Bros. Dir: Tay Garnett. Cast: William Powell, Kay Francis, Aline MacMahon, Frank McHugh. Donlin plays Hong Kong Bartender.

She Done Him Wrong (1933), Paramount. Dir: Lowell Sherman. Cast: Mae West, Cary Grant, Owen Moore, Gilbert Roland. Donlin plays Tout.

Doctor Bull (1933), Fox. Dir: John Ford. Cast: Will Rogers, Vera Allen, Marion Nixon, Andy Devine. Donlin plays Lester Dunn.

High Gear (1933), States Rights. Dir: Leigh Jason. Cast: James Murray, Joan Marsh, Jackie Searl. Donlin plays Ed Evans.

Air Hostess (1933), Columbia. Dir: Albert Rogell. Cast: Evalyn Knapp, James Murray, Thelma Todd. Donlin plays Mike.

Picture Snatcher (1933), Warner Bros. Dir: Lloyd Bacon. Cast; James Cagney, Ralph Bellamy, Patricia Ellis. Donlin has a bit part.

Swell-Head (1935), Columbia. Dir: Ben Stoloff. Cast: Wallace Ford, Dickie Moore, Barbara Kent, J. Farrell MacDonald. Donlin plays Brick Baldwin.

Hack Wilson's 191st RBI

A persistent itch finally scratched

Clifford Kachline

As famed radio news commentator Paul Harvey might expound, "And now for the rest of the story." What story? The one detailing the how and the who of the long-overlooked run batted in that, sixty-nine years after Hack Wilson accomplished the feat, boosted his one-season major league RBI record to 191.

It's a story that from start to finish spanned almost twenty-two years and took many twists and turns. It also is a product of the effort of numerous SABR researchers who provided assistance and deserve credit.

It all started in 1977 during my tenure as historian of the Baseball Hall of Fame, when an envelope arrived from *The Sporting News*, where I had earlier been a member of the editorial staff for twenty-four years. Enclosed were two letters. One was dated November 17, 1977, written by staff member Larry Wigge.

> Dear Cliff: We just received this [enclosed] letter from a reader, and since *The Sporting News* boxscores from 1930 did not reveal RBI totals, there was no way to answer the man. I thought maybe you have come across this before, and Mac [Paul MacFarlane, another *TSN* staff member] suggested that you had the official boxes and could check into this.

The enclosed handwritten letter was from a James Braswell, who was living in Chicago at the time.

> Gentlemen: I believe if you check Hack Wilson's record from July 24 thru August 5, inclusive, of 1930, you will find Wilson knocked in at least one run in 11 consecutive games, and should be listed in your Baseball Record Book—along with Mel Ott—as the co-holder of this N.L. record [for consecutive games with an RBI].

After making a quick check, my response to Braswell on November 22 (with a copy to Wigge) advised:

> Wilson's day-by-day record for 1930, as kept by the National League's official statistician, shows that he was credited with RBIs in only 10 of the 11 games during the period you listed. However, an Associated Press boxscore of the game for which he is shown with no RBIs on the official sheet does in fact credit him with a run batted in. I am now attempting to obtain a play-by-play of the game in question…and will be getting back to you.

Exactly one week later a followup letter to Braswell (a carbon again going to Wigge) declared:

> We have received copies of accounts ap-

Clifford Kachline *was a writer and editor with* The Sporting News *for 24 years and historian of the National Baseball Hall of Fame for 14 years before serving as SABR's first executive director from 1983-1985*

pearing in the Chicago *Tribune* and Chicago *Herald-Examiner* of the second game of the July 28, 1930 doubleheader between the Cubs and Cincinnati at Wrigley Field. Both accounts state that Hack Wilson singled home Kiki Cuyler from second base in the third inning. Wilson subsequently moved to third base on an error and scored on Charlie Grimm's single. In summary, the newspaper accounts indicate that Wilson and Grimm should have been credited with one RBI each in this game—rather than Grimm with two and Wilson with none as is shown on the official records. This would then give Wilson a streak of 11 successive games with an RBI. The Official Baseball Records Committee will be meeting next week, and I will arrange to have this matter presented to the group at that time.

The Baseball Records Committee had been founded in Milwaukee during the All-Star Game break in July 1975, prompted by discrepancies between the Elias Bureau's *Book of Baseball Records* and *The Sporting News*'s *Baseball Record Book*, together with the discovery of numerous mistakes in the official records through the years. With the approval of Commissioner Bowie Kuhn and the concurrence of the two league presidents, Joe Reichler of the Commissioner's staff arranged to formally organize such a committee. It originally consisted of ten members, including two from the Commissioner's staff, the two league public relations directors, three from the Baseball Writers' Association, the head of the Elias Sports Bureau, and one representative each from *The Sporting News* and the Baseball Hall of Fame. Later the committee was expanded to fifteen members.

My memorandum on the Wilson RBI matter was presented to the Records Committee at its December 7 session during the 1977 major-minor league meetings in Hawaii. The report included play-by-play-type accounts by Ed Burns in the Chicago *Tribune* and Wayne Otto in the *Herald-Examiner* of the two innings in which the Cubs scored while edging the Reds, 5-3, in the second half of the July 28, 1930, twin-bill. Both clearly stated that Wilson and Grimm each singled in one run in the third inning. (The box score appearing in the Chicago *Herald-Examiner* and the one distributed by Associated Press both show Wilson and Grimm with one run batted in apiece. The Chicago *Tribune* did not include RBIs in its box scores in 1930, while the *Daily News* and *American*

seldom listed them.)

In a letter dated December 16, I informed Braswell:

> Three factors prompted the Committee to defer any action on the [Wilson] findings: 1-Seymour Siwoff [head of the Elias Bureau] pointed out that his *Book of Baseball Records* already shows a longer NL RBI streak (12 games by Paul Waner from June 2-16, 1927), 2-Additional data is still needed on other discrepancies in Wilson's 1930 RBI record, and 3-The group simply ran out of time at this particular session [to pursue the matter further].

The letter also noted six other instances where the daily RBI figures that Braswell listed for Wilson differed from the official records. I asked if he was in a position to check Chicago newspapers for play-by-play accounts of these games. About a week later Braswell provided information on the six games and added: "This has spurred me on to doing a complete analysis of Hack's incredible 1930 RBIs. Needless to say, it will take several months of research, but this is a hobby with me so eventually I will complete it."

More digging...and diggers—Beginning in late December 1977, my involvement in the Baseball Museum's major expansion and total remodeling project increased greatly. As a result, my next contact with Braswell was delayed until the following September. He responded that he had not had a chance to do further research, but hoped to be able to in the future. Unfortunately, this was the last I heard from him. Because of the heightened workload resulting from the Museum expansion/renovation program, I didn't write him again until May 14, 1982, with a followup four weeks later. Neither letter brought a response. Braswell, who had joined SABR in 1978, dropped out after 1983, and all contact with him was lost.

I contacted another SABR member living in the Chicago area—Bob Soderman—in January 1981 to ascertain if he might be willing to assist in the research. Ironically, as it turned out, Soderman had been gathering information for several years for a possible biography of Wilson. He advised that his research and writing had carried him through the 1929 season.

Soderman proved to be a key figure in verifying Hack's 191 RBIs. His background made him an ideal choice. As a young man in the late 1940s, he had been a sportswriter with Chicago's City News Bureau. Later he joined the advertising department of the Jim Beam Distilling Company and eventually became vice president of marketing and advertising for the firm. In that role he developed a relationship with *The Sporting News* by placing Jim Beam ads in what then was known as the Baseball Bible. After retiring from Jim Beam, Soderman became active as a boxing historian and has contributed many articles to boxing publications. In 1980 he helped found the International Boxing Research Organization (IBRO). In addition, he continued as an active baseball researcher and was responsible for discovering a unique record: most consecutive at-bats without a home-run—Tommy Thevenow, 3,347 in the National League, and Ed Foster with 3,278 in the American League.

Another who became involved in the Wilson project during this period was Paul MacFarlane of *The Sporting News*. We had been colleagues for much of my career with that publication. Among his responsibilities as TSN historian/archivist at the time was *Daguerreotypes*, a book containing the lifetime records of the game's greatest players. He was TSN's representative during the last few years of the Official Records Committee and as a consequence of our frequent contacts was aware of the "missing" RBI, and had even changed Wilson's RBI total to 191 in the 1981 edition of *Daguerreotypes*. (A year or two later he changed it back to 190 following Bowie Kuhn's ruling on the 1910 Cobb-Lajoie batting championship dispute.)

By early summer 1982, Soderman's research had uncovered numerous mistakes in RBIs credited to 1930 Cub players. It became obvious that it would be necessary to check every Cub RBI in each game that season if there was to be any possibility of acceptance of a revision of Wilson's total. In a letter dated June 10, 1982, I had asked Soderman whether he'd be willing to do this and reminded him of a day-by-day grid of 1930 Cub RBIs that I had compiled from the official NL records and had sent him. He quickly dug into the assignment full blast. Taking the train or bus from his suburban Mt. Prospect home into the Windy City, he spent days at the Chicago Public Library going through microfilm of four Chicago dailies—*Tribune, Times, Daily News,* and *Herald-Examiner*.

Early in May 1983, during a conversation with MacFarlane, Soderman said his research up to that point led him to believe Hack had three more RBIs—not just one—for a total of 193. However, his "final report" to me and MacFarlane, dated May 30, 1983,

scotched that prospect. The twenty-seven-page document included a summary of each 1930 Cub game that listed the opponent, home or away, and final score; a daily log of Wilson's home runs and RBIs; a game-by-game grid for all twenty-six Cub players who had an RBI, and play-by-play descriptions of Cub scoring in seventeen games where actual or potential RBI discrepancies were found.

The two "dubious" games in which Soderman originally concluded Hack had been deprived of an RBI were those of June 4 at Boston and the second half of an August 19 doubleheader at Wrigley Field which ended in a sixteen-inning, 6-6 tie. In the first instance, the *Tribune's* game account indicated Hack had driven in a run in the fourth inning as well as in the first inning. The play-by-play in the Chicago *Times* refuted this, crediting Riggs Stephenson with both RBIs in the fourth inning.

In the August 19 contest, Soderman's reading of game accounts in two papers originally led him to believe Wilson had driven in Kiki Cuyler in the third inning. As a matter of fact, the Associated Press box score appearing in the New York *Times* and other newspapers did give Hack an RBI. The subsequent discovery of a play-by-play account in the Chicago *Daily News* revealed that, with one out and the Cubs trailing, 4-1, Cuyler scored when Phillies' second baseman Fresco Thompson booted Wilson's grounder for an error. Although Cuyler may have taken off for the plate as soon as the ball was hit, Wilson was not credited with an RBI by the official scorer.

Earlier in the season, another Cub player was deprived of an RBI that seemed warranted. It occurred in the second half of a May 30 morning-afternoon bill against St. Louis at Wrigley Field. With the score tied at 8-8, the bases loaded and one out in the bottom of the tenth inning, Riggs Stephenson smashed a grounder to Cardinal shortstop Sparky Adams. He fired to second baseman Frank Frisch, but Frisch's throw to first attempting to double up Stephenson was off target. Although the winning run scored on the play, the Associated Press and most newspapers listed no RBI for him, and also had no error for Frisch. At the same time, box scores carried a note saying, "One out when winning run scored," thus ignoring the forceout at second base. However, a check of the NL official records revealed the scorer did include that out and also charged Frisch with an error, thus eliminating the possibility of an RBI for Stephenson.

Baseball's official scoring rules in 1930 stated the game summary "shall contain the number of runs batted in by each batsman" but offered no explanation

Why So Many Records Are Wrong

Like Ivory soap, today's major league averages are 99.44 percent pure, that is virtually 100 percent accurate. By contrast early statistics of both the American and National Leagues, especially for the pre-1950 period, are fraught with mistakes.

The reasons are numerous. First, although many of the sportswriters who served as official scorers were diligent and dedicated, some were incompetent and careless. While the official league statisticians supposedly balanced boxscores, they had no way to spot compensating mistakes. It also is obvious that those who entered the figures onto the official sheets sometimes copied them improperly.

Newspapers began barring their baseball writers from serving as official scorers some thirty years ago. The parties who now fill that role are on balance doing a more accurate job.

Another factor was the absence of any cross-checking. Prior to the 1950s few clubs had anyone on their staff who compiled their team's figures. For the past thirty or forty years all clubs have maintained daily updated stats, and there has been constant contact between the clubs and the league statistician to make certain any differences are immediately resolved. Fans of earlier eras paid far less attention to statistics than they do today. Mistakes in the figures weren't readily observed, so there was less pressure to be thorough and accurate.

While we hope that data for most pre-1950 major league games were entered correctly, the ten mistakes found in the so-called Hack Wilson 191st RBI contest are dwarfed by those discovered in another game. The questionable listing of a triple play by the New York Yankees during an 11-inning, 11-10 victory at Boston on September 25, 1929—the day Yankee Manager Miller Huggins died—prompted me to research that game. Not only did the Yankees *not* make a triple play as the official American League statistics proclaim (they had two double plays, each coming with one out), but play-by-play accounts indicate the official records for that game contain *twenty-two* mistakes involving ten players.

In the early 1900s, the final official league averages were listed as having been prepared by each league's president or secretary. Except for an occasional newspaper, few other sources compiled player stats. There was little opportunity for comparison.

In 1912, the American League hired Irwin M. Howe of Chicago to serve as its statistician. He and the Howe News Bureau produced the official AL figures almost every year through 1972. Sports Information Center then purchased the Howe Bureau and handled the AL averages, 1973-1986.

The National League first went outside its own staff in 1923, when Al Munro Elias of New York was appointed league statistician. The Elias Bureau has filled that role ever since. For years both Howe and Elias also compiled averages of the rival league each season to sell to client newspapers. In 1987, the Elias Sports Bureau became the American League's official statistician, and it has handled both leagues the past fifteen years. Elias receives a play-by-play and official scorer's report of each game via fax shortly after the final out. These are checked before being entered on the computer.

Up until the 1950s and 1960s, most major league cities had four or more daily newspapers. Some of them prepared their own boxscores in order to meet deadlines. The wire services—notably Associated Press and United Press—also produced and distributed boxscores. They and the telegraphers for some newspapers tapped out their own play-by-play accounts. This multiplicity of independent sources often resulted in discrepancies, especially in situations where a paper's writer ruled error on a play, unaware the official scorer called it a base hit (or vice versa)—or when the official scorer changed a decision following the game. Differences of this type may well be involved in the question of whether Nap Lajoie had 229 hits or 232 in his banner 1901 season. The American League official team and player stat sheets for 1901 disappeared more than fifty years ago and thus are no longer available as a source against which to check.

Because of the frequency of mistakes in the official records, it has been suggested many times that averages should be recompiled from boxscores. The immensity and expense of such a task have effectively squashed such proposals. Furthermore, as Seymour Siwoff, head of the Elias Sports Bureau, points out: "It would be illogical and impractical to undertake such a project because newspaper boxscores of the same game often differ and even play-by-play accounts sometimes disagree. In most instances there would be no way to reconcile those differences. In cases where the official league statistician's sheets exist, the only logical and practical approach is to limit changes to singular records where mistakes of omission or commission can be readily verified from credible sources."

on how to score RBIs in unusual situations. This seeming oversight was corrected at a meeting of the rules committee on December 12, 1930, when the following definition was adopted: "Runs batted in should include runs scored on safe hits (including home runs), sacrifice hits, infield outs, and when the run is forced over by reason of a batsman becoming a baserunner. With less than two out, if an error is made on a play on which a runner from third would ordinarily score, credit the batsman with a Run Batted In."

Did the last sentence starting "With less than two out ..." represent a new interpretation? The fact that the AP boxscore credited Wilson with an RBI in the August 19 game would indicate that at least some scorers already may have been following that practice. It's possible the league presidents had previously issued instructions covering the situation, although to date no evidence has been found.

An editorial in the December 25, 1930, issue of *The Sporting News* stated:

When the rules makers were revising the code for the future, they discovered to their surprise that no definition had been made in the rules as to what constitutes a run batted in. ... Of course the major league presidents had their own definition and had instructed the official scorers how to record this play which is presumed to be of such importance to batsmen. ... When the new rules make their appearance, the run batted in will be defined and in the future this will help the scorers of all games. It is not a play applying directly to the major leagues, it is for all leagues. ... The run batted in is not a suggestion that is modern. Years ago when Henry Chadwick was fathering baseball, he contended that it should be included in the score and wrote line after line about it. ... It is with us now, and in the future it is hoped that it will be more valuable than it has been in the past.

The arrival of Soderman's "final report" coincided with my assumption of the newly created position of executive director of SABR. The need to devote full time to this endeavor—together with Commissioner Bowie Kuhn's decision two years earlier in the 1910 Cobb-Lajoie batting controversy ("The passage of 70 years, in our judgment, constitutes a certain statute of limitations as to recognizing any changes in the

records with confidence of the accuracy of such changes.")—prompted me to put the Wilson matter aside without even studying and evaluating the results. It would be many years before I pursued it again.

Despite Kuhn's edict, MacFarlane proposed doing a story for *The Sporting News* on the Wilson mess. With the Cobb-Lajoie experience in mind, editor Dick Kaegel turned him down. In an inter-office memo dated August 5, 1983, to MacFarlane, with copies to publisher Dick Waters, several *TSN* staff members and me, Kaegel wrote:

This Hack Wilson RBI research obviously is painstakingly thorough but [there are still] some holes.... Our policy on correcting records—particularly records of this significance—must be to first present the evidence to the Official Records Committee.... When the Kuhn administration ends, perhaps we'll have better luck with a reorganized Records Committee. One of our first steps should be to impress upon the new commissioner the importance of the records committee and renew our suggestion for implementing a research bureau within the commissioner's office (or possibly under the supervision of Elias [Bureau], SABR or even *TSN*).... Obviously because statistics are such an important part of baseball, it is important to have the correct numbers. Hopefully the new commissioner and his people will be more receptive to this concept. Meanwhile, we will continue to list Wilson's RBIs as 190 for 1930.

Unfazed by the rebuff, MacFarlane proceeded to write an article on the subject for the June, 1986, issue of *The Scoreboard News—About the Chicago Cubs*. I did not learn about this piece until ten years later. The 650-word yarn began: "As long as baseball has been played and will be played, there are people who search for the truth in records. Research is less looking for faults as [sic] it is finding an error while looking for something completely non-related."

He then claimed to be the first to find Hack's missing RBI. Completely ignoring Braswell's role, he gave Soderman credit for "painstaking and timeless research [that] proved that I was correct." He also listed the other Cub players whose RBI figures Soderman had found to be incorrect, with their revised totals. (Further study resulted in a subsequent revision.)

A sidebar inserted next to MacFarlane's story by *Scoreboard News* editors pointed out the possibility that Wilson may have been deprived of another RBI, which would have made his total 192. The sidebar cited the 1978 biography of Wilson written by Robert S. Boone and Gerald Grunska. In it, Clyde Sukeforth, a catcher with Cincinnati in 1930, was quoted as saying Hack should have had 57 home runs that season instead of 56. According to Sukeforth, one day when he was sitting in the bullpen in Redland Field, Hack "hit one...way up in the seats...so hard that it hit the screen and bounced back [onto the field]." Sukeforth said the umpires, apparently not realizing it had cleared the fence, ruled the ball in play and Hack thus was deprived of a home run and RBI. "Of course, we weren't going to say anything," Sukeforth was quoted as saying.

A somewhat similar version appeared in "The Fans Speak Out" section of the August, 2001, edition of *Baseball Digest*. According to the writer, then living in Wroclaw, Poland, Wilson allegedly hit a drive into the seats with a runner aboard, but the ball bounced back on the field and Hack wound up with a double instead of a two-run homer. Sukeforth supposedly told Wilson about the incident in 1933, when both were with the Dodgers.

Unfortunately, no newspaper reference has been found to confirm Sukeforth's recollection. As a matter of fact, Sukeforth was the Reds' catcher in eight of the eleven games played against the Cubs at Redland Field that season. In one of the eight, the first half of a July 6 doubleheader, the Cincinnati *Enquirer* stated Wilson smashed homer No. 24 "into the right field seats, which is Hack's favorite spot on this field," and then in the second game drove a ball over right fielder Harry Heilmann's head that "hit close to the top of the screen (but) Hack was held to a single on account of preceding baserunners" [English on second and Cuyler on first], who "feared Heilmann was going to catch the ball." English scored on the hit, but Cuyler was thrown out at the plate and "Hack had to be satisfied with probably the longest single ever made on the [Cincinnati] grounds."

Of the three 1930 Chicago-at-Cincinnati games when Sukeforth conceivably could have been sitting in the bullpen, Wilson had only one hit—a triple on July 9. Accounts in Cincinnati newspapers indicated there was nothing unusual about the hit.

Reawakening—For me, the Wilson dispute remained dormant until SABR's 1996 annual convention in Kansas City. After sitting in on the SABR Records Committee meeting, I mentioned the Wilson matter to committee chairman Lyle Spatz. He immediately

expressed deep interest. Another who did was Dave Smith, head of Retrosheet, the group whose goal has been to locate play-by-play accounts of every major league game ever played.

This prompted me to dig out the files and resume evaluating the research that had been done. I looked closely at Soderman's "final report" of 1983, and contacted him directly. His further research clarified matters and led to a few revisions of the figures he had originally provided (and which MacFarlane had listed in *The Scoreboard News* story).

At the 1997 Louisville convention, Spatz asked me to make a presentation on the Wilson matter at the SABR Records Committee meeting. Although a few details still remained to be untangled, the members in attendance seemed convinced that 191 should be accepted. With the assistance of Spatz and another committee member, Joe Dittmar, who on visits to Washington checked accounts in newspapers in the Library of Congress, we tied up the remaining loose ends.

The next significant step in the process was to compile: (1) a box score of the second game of the July 28, 1930, Reds-Cubs doubleheader (in which Wilson's RBI was "missed") from the data shown in the NL official records; (2) another from the play-by-play account; and (3) compare the two results with the box scores that appeared in the four Chicago newspapers.

There was, incidentally, an obvious mistake in the play-by-play carried in the Chicago *Daily News*. With one out in the Reds' final at-bat, the account stated: "Lucas batted for Ford and singled to left. Callaghan batted for Ford and singled to left." After tapping out the last sentence, the Western Union operator obviously realized his mistake and followed with "Callaghan batted for Durocher and singled to right, Lucas stopping at second."

The process revealed that besides the Grimm-Wilson RBI mixup, the official records for this one game include eight other mistakes. A box score comprised of figures taken from the official National League player and team sheets is shown on the next page.

Based upon the play-by-play in the Chicago *Daily News* and the box scores appearing in various newspapers, the official NL data contain the following mistakes: 1–Wilson had 1 RBI (instead of 0); 2–Grimm had 1 RBI (not 2); 3–Blair had 4 assists (not 3); 4–Chicago had 13 assists (not 12); 5–Gooch had 4 AB (instead of 3); 6–Cincinnati had 34 AB (not 33); 7–Ford had 0 hits (not 1); Callaghan had 1 hit (not 0); 8–Cincinnati had 6 LOB (not 5); 10–Bush faced 36 batters (not 35). Following are the figures from the official National League records:

Cincinnati	AB	R	H	2B	3B	HR	RBI	PO	A	E	BB	HP	SO	SB
Walker, lf	4	0	1	0	0	0	0	1	0	0	0	0	0	0
Swanson, cf	4	0	2	0	0	0	0	1	0	0	0	0	0	0
Stripp, 1b	4	0	0	0	0	0	0	8	1	0	0	0	0	0
Cuccinello, 3b	3	0	0	0	0	0	0	1	0	0	1	0	1	0
Heilmann, rf	3	1	1	0	0	1	1	0	0	0	1	0	1	0
Ford, 2b	3	0	1	0	0	0	0	0	4	0	0	0	0	0
Lucas, ph	1	0	1	0	0	0	0	0	0	0	0	0	0	0
Durocher, ss	3	0	0	0	0	0	0	3	7	1	0	0	0	0
Callaghan, ph	1	0	0	0	0	0	0	0	0	0	0	0	0	0
Gooch, c	3	1	1	0	1	0	0	10	1	0	0	0	0	0
May, p	1	0	0	0	0	0	0	0	0	0	0	0	0	0
Johnson, p	1	0	0	0	0	0	0	0	0	0	0	0	0	0
Crawford, ph	1	1	1	0	0	0	1	0	0	0	0	0	0	0
Ash, p	0	0	0	0	0	0	0	0	0	0	0	0	0	0
Sukeforth, ph	1	0	0	0	0	0	0	0	0	0	0	0	0	0
Totals	33	3	8	0	1	1	2	24	13	1	2	0	2	0

Chicago	AB	R	H	2B	3B	HR	RBI	PO	A	E	BB	HP	SO	SB
Blair, 2b	4	1	2	0	0	0	0	3	3	1	0	0	1	0
English, 3b	3	2	2	1	0	0	0	2	0	0	1	0	0	0
Cuyler, rf	2	1	2	1	0	0	3	0	0	0	1	1	0	1
Wilson, cf	4	1	1	0	0	0	0	4	0	0	0	0	1	0
D. Taylor, lf	4	0	0	0	0	0	0	2	0	0	0	0	1	0
Grimm, 1b	4	0	1	0	0	0	2	12	0	0	0	0	2	0
J. Taylor, c	4	0	0	0	0	0	0	4	1	0	0	0	2	0
Beck, ss	2	0	0	0	0	0	0	2	3	0	2	0	0	0
Bush, p	3	0	0	0	0	0	0	0	3	0	0	0	2	0
Totals	30	5	8	2	0	0	5	27	12	1	3	2	9	1

LOB–Cincinnati 5, Chicago 6.

DP–Cincinnati 2 (Stripp 2, Ford 1, Durocher 2); Chicago 1 (J. Taylor 1, Beck 1).

Cincinnati	BFP	IP	H	R	ER	BB	SO	HB
May	15	2	7	5	5	1	4	0
Johnson	17	5	1	0	0	2	4	2
Ash	3	1	0	0	0	0	1	0

Chicago	BFP	IP	H	R	ER	BB	SO	HB
Bush	35	9	8	3	2	2	2	0

Balancing boxscore:

    Cincinnati 3 R, 27 PO, 6 LOB = 36

    Cincinnati 34 AB, 2 BB, 0 HB/SH = 36

    Chicago 5 R, 24 PO, 6 LOB = 35

    Chicago 30 AB, 3 BB, 2 HB/SH = 35

When I presented this report at the SABR Records Committee meeting during the 1998 convention in San Francisco, the unanimous feeling was that enough evidence had been developed to justify changing Wilson's total. Soon after my return home from the convention, an enterprising young journalist named Owen S. Good heard about it while chatting with a staff member of the Baseball Hall of Fame Library. Good, who at the time was employed by *The Daily Star* of nearby Oneonta, promptly called and said he'd like to interview me for a story on the subject. At the time, Cleveland's Manny Ramirez was on pace to threaten Wilson's record just as Juan Gonzalez of Texas had been at the All-Star break a year earlier.

Under the headline "WILSON'S LOST RBI HAS HISTORIANS BOTHERED," Good's 1,200-word article appeared at the top of the first sports page of the July 15, 1998, edition of the Oneonta paper. It quickly caught the attention of the Associated Press, which proceeded to send out a brief item to its clients throughout the country. Because of my long friendship with Seymour Siwoff, head of the Elias Bureau, I immediately called to inform him how the publicity developed. His reaction was that he would need to see play-by-plays of all 1930 Cub games before he could consider supporting a change in Wilson's RBI record.

Siwoff subsequently contacted Retrosheet's Dave Smith. Retrosheet already had complete play-by-plays of 107 of the Cubs' 1930 games and partial accounts of eighteen others. Smith forwarded them to Siwoff, and the Elias Bureau staff began its own study. In December Smith advised that he had sent Siwoff a short note saying "it seems inescapable that Hack's correct total for 1930 is really 191."

Most of the games for which play-by-plays were still lacking involved the second half of Sunday or holiday doubleheaders. In the 1930s it was not unusual for large metropolitan newspapers to publish several editions every day. While the earliest Monday editions usually carried play-by-play accounts of the Sunday games, subsequent editions often replaced them with other sports news, and the files maintained by local historical associations as well as the newspapers themselves usually contain only the later editions.

At this juncture, two other SABR members made significant contributions to finalizing the research effort. They were David Stephan of Culver City, California, and Walt Wilson of Chicago. Stephan, a mathematician who has his own consulting business, asked Wilson to search Chicago newspapers for the remaining play-by-plays. Having heard about the dispute, Walt had already worked up his own compilation of Wilson's 1930 RBIs, and had arranged

Run Batted In Rule

The evolution of the runs-batted-in rule has never been fully documented. Henry Chadwick, the first well-known baseball writer, is said to have originally come up with the concept of such a statistic as far back as 1879, but major league baseball did not officially accept it until some forty years later.

Prior to the 1891 season, baseball's governing board adopted "a new and most important rule" that specified the summary of al games should include "the number of runs batted in by base hits by each batsman." The proviso apparently proved unpopular. Not only did the National League and American Association averages of 1891 fail to contain any RBI data, but the rule was eliminated the following winter.

In 1907 Ernest J. Lanigan, then a baseball writer with the New York Press, suggested to the paper's sports editor, Jim Price, the idea of compiling and publishing RBI data. The proposal was enthusiastically accepted, and Lanigan worked up runs batted in figures for players in both leagues from 1907 through 1919, starting with the Press and later moving on to the Tribune, World, and finally the New York Sun.

Runs batted in became an official statistic starting in 1920, but the scoring rules from then through 1930 simply stated: "The summary shall include…the number of runs batted in by each batter," and provided no specifics whatsoever. While the league presidents or the Baseball Writers' Association itself may have issued some scoring instructions during that period covering unusual circumstances, no such interpretations have yet been located.

Baseball's rules committee finally rectified the situation in December, 1930, by adopting a description of a run batted in that is essentially the same as that in effect today. The only significant change became effective 1939 when it was specified that no RBI should be credited when a runner scores as the batter grounds into a double play. That later was expanded to include situations where an error was charged on the second part of a potential double play.

for his friend Eddie Gold to distribute copies at the 1998 SABR Records Committee meeting. (An article by Walt that includes Hack's game-by-game RBI production of 1930 appeared in last year's Baseball Research Journal.)

Walt's efforts, over the next eight or nine months, in digging up most of the missing play-by-plays proved to be a clinching factor. Three other SABR members who assisted in this phase were Mark Stangl of St. Louis, Bill Hugo of Cincinnati, and Denis Repp of Pittsburgh. Stangl was able to dig up data on several Cub games played in St. Louis. Hugo checked out Cub games in Cincinnati and found nothing to corroborate Sukeforth's reference to a phantom homer by Wilson. Repp provided a play-by-play from the Pittsburgh Post Gazette of the Cubs' August 3 game in Pittsburgh.

For the record, the list of mistakes in 1930 NL official RBI statistics of Cub players is presented below. It should be emphasized that it would be unfair to change the season totals for the players involved—other than Wilson's record 191—without performing similar research on the entire league, as well as for other seasons. The revised totals of those affected follow, with the original figure in parentheses: Wilson 191 (190), Cuyler 134 (no change), Hartnett 124 (122), Stephenson 69 (68), Grimm 64 (66), English 62 (59), Blair 55 (59), D. Taylor 36 (37), Beck 35 (34), Kelly 53 as a Red and Cub (not 54), Hornsby 17 (18), and Bush 6 (7).

It is worth noting that of the thirteen games in which RBI mistakes were found, all except the last two were played in Chicago. Following are the Cub RBI errata by date, with the correct figure shown first and the number credited by the league statistician in parentheses:

June 23–Cuyler 2 (3), Bush 2 (3), Stephenson 4 (3), Blair 4 (2), Hartnett 1 (2), Grimm 1 (2), Beck 1 (0); July 28 (2nd game)–Wilson 1 (0), Grimm 1 (2); August 1–English 1 (2), Hartnett 3 (2); August 2– Blair 0 (1); August 10 (2nd game)–English 1 (0), Cuyler 4 (3), Blair 1 (3); August 14–Blair 0 (1); August 16 (1st game)–Cuyler 2 (3), D. Taylor 1 (0); August 22–Hartnett 5 (4), Kelly 1 (2); August 24–D. Taylor 0 (2), Hartnett 2 (1); August 29–English 2 (1), Blair 0 (1); August 30–English 2 (0), Blair 0 (2); September 6–Hornsby 2 (3), Blair 1 (0); September 12–Cuyler 3 (2).

Official recognition—The wheels of justice often move slowly. This time, though, the Elias Bureau was simultaneously concerned about a possible mistake in one of the Babe Ruth records that was being threatened. This contributed to quick consideration of the evidence in the Wilson case.

My first inkling that a change in Wilson's 1930 RBI total was going to be officially recognized came on June 17, 1999. Jerome Holtzman, recently named major league baseball's official historian following his retirement as a sportswriter for the Chicago *Tribune*, and a longtime friend, called to inform me of the decision. He requested some background information for use in a press release.

The story was given to the media on June 22, the second day of the SABR convention in Scottsdale, Arizona. "I am sensitive to the historical significance that accompanies the correction of such a prestigious record, especially after so many years have passed," Commissioner Bud Selig declared, "but it is important to get it right." The same news release also disclosed that extensive research by the Elias Bureau had discovered six additional walks for Babe Ruth, boosting his record career total to 2,062. The pressure to accept that discovery was driven by the fact that Rickey Henderson was approaching the record, which he exceeced early in the 2001 season.

A week following the official approval of Wilson's 191st RBI, Holtzman posted a story on www.majorleaguebaseball.com explaining why the record was corrected after sixty-nine years and pointing out that "a mystery [still] remains: Where is James Braswell?" He had been living at 1334 W. George Street in Chicago back in the late 1970s and early '80s. Telephone calls made by David Stephan to the current resident of that address and also to several neighbors failed to develop any leads. A check of telephone listings on the internet revealed there are more than 150 men named James Braswell in the U.S. Calls to those shown as living in Illinois and seven nearby states failed to locate the *real* James Braswell.

At the 2001 SABR convention, Holtzman told Records Committee members that about six months after Wilson's record was officially approved, he received a call out of the blue from Braswell, who mentioned he had been attending Northwestern at the time. Unfortunately, Holtzman had no recollection of the location from which Braswell called, and officials at Northwestern were unable to find any record of him. And so, as Holtzman noted in his 1999 article on the internet, "the only missing piece of the puzzle is the whereabouts of James Braswell, the hero of the story."

Even Paul Harvey almost certainly would be intrigued by the story.

37 innings to finish one game

The Cubs' 1930 season was marked by a number of noteworthy events besides Hack Wilson's record 191 runs batted in. As an example, the Cubs and Phillies required 37 innings over four different dates to complete one game, Walt Wilson has pointed out.

On May 5, the finale of a four-game series between the two clubs at Wrigley Field was wiped out after one inning by rain. The contest was rescheduled as the second half of a doubleheader on August 16. That game ended in an 11-inning, 3-3 tie halted by darkness.

Three days later, again at Wrigley, the next attempt to make up the game as the second part of a twin-bill saw the two clubs battle to a 16-inning, 6-6 tie before darkness again intervened.

The schedules of both teams called for an open date on August 20. The Phillies, due to head to St. Louis, agreed to stay over in Chicago for another attempt to reach a decision that afternoon, and the tortuous trail finally came to end with Philadelphia winning, 10-8, in a nine-inning encounter that was highlighted by five home runs.

—Cliff Kachline

From One Ump to Two

The players realized that the game had outgrown the one-umpire system by 1890; it took twenty years for the major leagues to catch up

John Schwartz

When professional baseball began, one umpire was assigned to each game. By the 1911 season, both major leagues had adopted the two-umpire system. The transition between the one-umpire system and the use of two officials per game was at times abrupt, at times gradual. It took three tries for the double-umpire system to become established.

To track the changeover, I examined every box score in the transition period, 1889-1911, and in a few seasons before and after, and recorded the names of the umpires. I divided the number of umpires' names (U) by the number of total games (TG). This number was multiplied by a figure I refer to as "league size" (LS) which is the number of games that could take place at the same time (four for an eight-team league, six for a twelve-team league). The result takes into account both long-term and short-term umps, permanent staff and temporary fill-ins, and yields the average number of umpires working on a day when all a league's teams were in action. The accompanying table sets forth the results.

Through 1889, the one-umpire system was in use. Two umps worked some games in 1888, and even more in 1889. The ratio never reaches 4.5, though, let alone 8.

The 1890 season saw the first season-long use of the double-umpire system. This season was fraught with

Number of Umpires per League, 1888-1912						
Yr	Lg	U/TG LS AU		Lg	U/TG LS AU	
1888	NL	572/544 x 4 = 4.21		AA	571/550 x 4 = 4.15	
1889	NL	592/531 x 4 = 4.46		AA	615/559 x 4 = 4.40	
1890	NL	595/539 x 4 = 4.42		AA	575/540 x 4 = 4.26	
1891	NL	595/532 x 4 = 4.31		AA	566/559 x 4 = 4.05	
1892	NL	940/921 x 6 = 6.112		1890 PL	1065/531 x 4 = 8.01	
1893	NL	803/785 x 6 = 6.14				
1894	NL	856/799 x 6 = 6.43				
1895	NL	929/799 x 6 = 6.98				
1896	NL	887/792 x 6 = 6.72				
1897	NL	917/811 x 6 = 6.78				
1898	NL	1781/921 x 6 = 11.60				
1899	NL	1799/923 x 6 = 11.69				
1900	NL	581/569 x 4 = 4.08				
1901	NL	635/561 x 4 = 4.53		AL	664/549 x 4 = 4.84	
1902	NL	667/564 x 4 = 4.73		AL	691/553 x 4 = 5.00	
1903	NL	664/560 x 4 = 4.74		AL	633/554 x 4 = 4.57	
1904	NL	829/623 x 4 = 5.32		AL	841/626 x 4 = 5.37	
1905	NL	752/620 x 4 = 4.85		AL	811/617 x 4 = 5.26	
1906	NL	888/615 x 4 = 5.78		AL	836/613 x 4 = 5.46	
1907	NL	906/616 x 4 = 5.88		AL	916/617 x 4 = 5.95	
1908	NL	864/622 x 4 = 5.56		AL	938/622 x 4 = 6.04	
1909	NL	1067/621 x 4 = 6.87		AL	1187/620 x 4 = 7.66	
1910	NL	1234/621 x 4 = 7.95		AL	1147/628 x 4 = 7.31	
1911	NL	1243/624 x 4 = 7.97		AL	1212/614 x 4 = 7.90	
1912	NL	1222/614 x 4 = 7.96		AL	1233/619 x 4 = 7.97	

John Schwartz *is a Medicaid/Food Stamps examiner for the Monroe County Department of Social Services in Rochester, New York. He has been a SABR member for over twenty years and enjoys haunting local libraries to compile data like "games umpired," available in box scores but as yet unpublished.*

irony. The best players and umpiring were in the Players' League, the only league that adopted the two-ump system, yet the "World's Series" was played between the champions the National League and American Association, the second- and third-best leagues (another irony: it ended in a tie). As the Fifth Edition of *Total Baseball* states (page 2,390): "Leave it to the players to understand the importance of having at least two umpires on the field of play."

When the Players' League folded, the NL and the AA threw the baby out with the bathwater. In 1891, the one-umpire system was back in both leagues. The AA collapsed after the 1891 season, and a twelve-team "League-Association" was formed; in effect, an enlarged National League. For the first three seasons of the twelve-team NL, the one-umpire system remained in effect, but the number of umpires was increasing. By 1895, and through the 1897 season, the league employed seven men for every six games, providing a little (very little) extra coverage.

The 1890s are generally recognized as the peak years for umpire abuse. Owners undermined umpire authority by paying fines for players umpires tried to discipline. Owners, while giving lip service to efforts to eliminate rowdyism, pandered to anti-umpire sentiment because they felt umpire baiting would increase their profits.

The National League adopted the double-umpire system in 1898. The experiment lasted two seasons. When the league contracted to eight teams in 1900, it once again regressed to the one-umpire system.

Ban Johnson declared his American League "major" in 1901, and both the AL and NL had five-man staffs available for every four games. This continued in the NL until 1905, and the AL until 1906. From 1906 through 1908, the NL had a six-man staff. The AL went to six for 1907 and 1908. In 1909, the National League moved up to a seven-man staff, and the American had eight men, in effect, two men per game.

In 1910, the NL went to the double-umpire system, never to regress. The AL slipped back to seven umpires. In 1911, both leagues had eight-man staffs. The players realized that the game had outgrown the one-umpire system by 1890; it took twenty years for the major leagues to catch up.

This state of affairs would continue until 1921 in the American League and 1923 in the National League, when umpiring staffs again began to increase. A summary of the transition to two-man umpiring crews:

American Association
1882-1891	1 per game

Players' League
1890	2 per game

National League
1876-1894	1 per game
1895-1897	7 for every 6 games
1898-1899	2 per game
1900	1 per game
1901-1905	5 for every 4 games
1906-1908	6 for every 4 games
1909 (first half)	2 per game
1909 (second half)	6 for every 4 games
1910	2 per game

American League
1901-1906	5 for every 4 games
1907-1908	6 for every 4 games
1909	2 per game
1910	7 for every 4 games
1911	2 per game

Ump tales

The World Series of 1888 was ten games long, but the New York Giants of the National League had won six of the first eight games. The umpires were John Kelly of the NL and John Gaffney of the American Association. The ninth and tenth games, which would not affect the outcome of the Series, were played in St. Louis. Kelly did not bother to stay around, and Gaffney worked them by himself.

In 1889, the umpires chosen to work the New York NL-Brooklyn AA World Series were Gaffney and Tom Lynch, of the NL. Lynch staged a holdout for more money, so the first game was worked by Gaffney and Bob Ferguson, both AA umpires. Lynch came to terms, and he and Gaffney worked the rest of the games.

During the 1910 season, Jack Sheridan, senior American League umpire (he was on the staff in 1900, before the AL was a major league) resigned in June, but returned in late August. When he came back he was strictly a base umpire, yet he was chosen to work the World Series that year. It is the only time in World Series history since 4 umps were assigned to games that one of the four did not take a turn calling balls and strikes.

—J.S.

Yankee Stadium and Home Park Advantage

It's not the size, it's the location close to home

Ron Selter

Yankee Stadium, from its opening April 18, 1923, has had the reputation of being a good park for lefthanded batters and a sad place for righthanded batters. The fact that two of the greatest hitters of all time were lefthanded batting Yankees (Ruth and Gehrig) has contributed to this impression of Yankee Stadium as a happy hunting ground for lefty hitters. Anyone familiar with the configuration of the park, before its renovation in 1974-75, knows that the left field and left center field areas, known as Death Valley, made Yankee Stadium very tough on righthanded batters. It is also a fact that the home run data shows that lefthanded Yankee batters have consistently hit more homers at the Stadium than on the road.[1]

In the select world of SABR researchers, the superior road performance of Lou Gehrig has become a well-known mystery. Why did Gehrig hit .351 on the road as opposed to .329 at home?[2] Home/road batting average data for Lou, six other well-known lefthanded Yankee batters, and four righthanded batters are shown at the right.

The general question concerning lefthanded batters remains: Was Yankee Stadium, compared with the other AL parks, 1923-73, a better hitter's park as measured by batting average? A more specific research question is: To what extent can the comparative sizes of the AL ballparks in this era be used to explain the Home/road batting performances of Yankee lefthanded and righthanded hitters.

I used the following approach. I determined the average fence distances for left field, center field, and right field in Yankee Stadium during the tenure of each of the batters below. For the same time periods, I determined the average fence distances of each field of each of the batters' road ballparks. I then derived a weighted average composite outfield distances by weighting the fields. For Ruth, I used actual 1927 data on the distribution of hits and putouts: 13 percent LF, 24 percent CF, 63 percent RF. I also used the 1927

Player	Yankee Stadium Years*	Home BA	Road BA
LH Batters			
Yogi Berra	1946-62	.286	.283
Earle Combs	1925-25	.326	.324
Bill Dickey	1929-43, 1946	.309	.316
Lou Gehrig	1925-38	.329	.351
Tommy Henrich	1937-42, 1946-50	.281	.283
Charlie Keller	1939-43, 1945-49	.278	.294
Babe Ruth	1923-34	.349	.345
RH Batters			
Joe DiMaggio	1936-42, 1946-51	.315	.333
Joe Gordon	1938-42, 1946	.257	.284
Elston Howard	1955-66	.274	.283
Tony Lazzeri	1926-37	.291	.294
Composite		.2995	.30

*Excludes seasons of limited service

Ron Selter *is an economist with the space program. A SABR member since 1989, he has done research in the minor leagues and ballparks. He presented "Evolution of Yankee Stadium" at the 2001 National Convention in Milaukee.*

data for Gehrig, "who did not pull the ball as much as Ruth."[3] Results were: 19 percent LF, 33 percent CF, 48 percent RF).[4] For all other lefthanded batters, I used the distribution 50 percent RF, 25 percent CF, 25 percent RF. For the righthanded hitters, I assumed 50 percent LF, 25 percent CF, 25 percent RF).

I computed the average park size by weighting equally each season of a player's Yankee career (excluding noticeably less-than-full seasons like Gehrig's 1924 and 1939). The average for the road ballparks for each player was the unweighted average of the road ballpark's average distances. For Cleveland, I derived a composite of League Park and Municipal Stadium based on the number of Yankee games at each park for each season when both parks were in use (1932-1946). I adjusted the average road park size for the elevation difference between New York and the average elevation of the road parks. This reduced the road average park size by 0.5 percent. As an illustration, the park size data (in feet before elevation adjustment) for Babe Ruth are shown below:

Babe Ruth 1923-34

City-Park	LF	CF	RF	Wt. Average
NY-Yankee	399	446	346	376.9
BOS-Fenway	339	436	389	394
CHI-Comiskey	379	432	381	393
CLE-League	393	411	308	
Municipal	399	450	399	
Composite	394	416	320	353
DET-Navin	359	428	367	381
PHL-Shibe	347	422	346	364
STL-Sportsman's	371	410	327	353
WAS-Griffith	399	420	368	384

Road Average: 374.3

Elevation Adjusted: 372.4

Home-Road Park Size Differential: 4.5

Relative Park Size Differential: -1.2 percent

Note: Percentage change calculated by dividing differential by average of Home+Road park size.

Based on a study of National League home and road batting average against Philadelphia pitching in the in the 1930s (presented at SABR 30), I estimated the park size batting average coefficient to be –1.046. Thus a park with ten percent deeper fences would, all other factors held constant, reduce batting average by 10.46 percent. I used this coefficient to estimate road batting average for the differential park sizes. For each

batter listed above, I used the home average in conjunction with the park size differential to predict road average. This procedure has implicit in it the assumption (only temporary) that only park size affects the relationship between home and road batting averages.

Player LH Batters	Yankee Stadium Years * (Used for Park Size)	Predicted Road BA	Actual Road BA	Variance Percent
Yogi Berra	1946-62	.295	.283	+4.2
Earle Combs	1925-35	.339	.324	+4.6
Bill Dickey	1929-43, 1946	.309	.316	+1.9
Lou Gehrig	1925-38	.344	.351	-2.0
Tommy Henrich	1937-42, 1946-50	.292	.283	+3.2
Charlie Keller	1939-43, 1945-49	.290	.294	-1.4
Babe Ruth	1923-34	.353	.345	+2.3
Composite LH		.3174	.3137	+1.2
RH Batters				
Joe DiMaggio	1936-42, 1946-51	.333	.333	0
Joe Gordon	1938-42, 1946	.271	.284	-4.9
Elston Howard	1955-66	.290	.283	+2.5
Tony Lazzeri	1926-37	.309	.294	+5.0
Composite RH		.301	.299	+0.6
All Above		.3115	.3082	+1.1

*Excludes seasons of limited service

As measured by batting average, Yankee Stadium in the 1923-66 era was not a hitters park for either righthanded or lefthanded batters. The use of park size as an explanatory variable over-corrects in the estimation of road batting average. This suggests there is an inherent home park advantage even for identical home and road park sizes. The data show an unexplained variance of +1.2 percent for lefthanded batters and +0.6 percent for righthanded batters. This unexplained variance may reflect non-quantified park differences, such as hitting background or prevailing winds. However, I believe that the unexplained variance, which averages +1.1 percent, is inherent home park advantage. It translates to three points of batting average.

1. Berra, Combs, Dickey, Gehrig, Henrich, Keller and Ruth, all lefthanded batting Yankees, had more home runs at home than on the road. *Home Run Encyclopedia*, by Bob McConnell and David Vincent.

2. "Home Park Effects on Performance in the American League", by Pete Palmer, *Baseball Research Journal*, 1978.

3. Ibid.

4. Retrosheet data supplied by SABR's David Vincent.

Whatever Happened to Charley Jones?

Colorful gamer just fades away

Bob McConnell

Charley Jones was one of the stars in the early days of the major leagues. He was the career leader in home runs at the end of the 1877 season and he continued to be the career leader through 1884. In addition, Charley was a colorful character who managed to get his name in the newspapers. Yet his date and place of death are unknown. The late baseball historian, Lee Allen, spent a great deal of time researching biographical information on players. Charley Jones was one of his special projects. However, he drew a blank on Charley's death data.

The SABR Biographical Research Committee prides itself on digging up (pardon the expression) death data on obscure players, but it also has drawn a blank on Jones. The Committee lists a *Mystery of the Month* in each of its reports and from time to time the reports include a *Top 20 Most Wanted List*. Jones was the mystery player in the March, 1991, report. He was number 18 on the *Most Wanted List* in May, 1992, and he moved up to number three on the March, 1994, report.

Charley was born Benjamin Wesley Rippay on April 30, 1850 on a farm in Alamance County, North Carolina. He was the third of six children of Abel, a farmer, and Delilah. Several publications have spelled the family name Rippy and several have used an April 3 date of birth.

In the early 1860s, possibly after the death of his parents, Charley moved to either Princeton, Indiana, or Cincinnati to live with Reuben Jones, who was ei-

ther his uncle or his grandfather. Charley took his relative's surname and became Charles Wesley Jones. Biographical Committee chairman Bill Carle had a great comment on the name change: "In order to make future baseball researchers' lives more complicated, Rippay decided to change his name to Jones. Why couldn't his uncle have a name like Abbaticchio?"

Jones began his baseball career with a club in Evansville, Indiana in the early 1870s. He made several unsuccessful attempts to hook on with National Association clubs. One source credits him with playing for Association clubs in Baltimore in 1873 and 1874. However, Charles Weaver, a member of SABR's Biographical Committee has recently determined that this was a different Jones. Finally, he joined the Association club in Keokuk in 1875. The club folded in June. Charley then received a one-game tryout with the Hartford club in late June in a game at St. Louis.

Jones joined the Cincinnati club in the newly formed National League in 1876. He made his mark early. In the seventh inning of a game on May 2, he hit the second home run in league history. (Ross Barnes hit one in the fifth inning of the same game to win the honor of hitting the first homer.) Jones had a decent year, hitting .286, and he was runner-up in home runs with four.

Jones returned to Cincinnati in 1877. After a poor start, the club ran into financial trouble and it was announced that it would disband. William Hulbert,

Bob McConnell *is one of the original sixteen members of SABR.*

Dapper Charley Jones

year. He hit .313, was runner-up in triples with 10, third in homers with two and fourth in RBIs with 38.

Cincinnati moved up in the standings in 1878 to finish second. Jones had another good year, hitting .310, second in home runs, fourth in RBIs, and tied for second in triples.

Jones went to Boston in 1879 where he had a career year. He led the league in runs with 85, home runs with nine and RBIs with 62, while batting .315. On June 10 the following year against Buffalo, Charley hit two home runs in the eighth inning—the first time that this feat had ever been accomplished.

Late in that 1880 season, Jones got involved in a salary dispute with Boston club president Arthur Soden. Though he was batting .300, the club claimed that his play had been unsatisfactory and that his conduct was unacceptable. It refused to pay Jones his August salary. When he protested, he was suspended, fined $100 for poor play and insubordination, and finally expelled from the league. Although there was some indication that Jones's fondness for alcohol was a contributing factor in his feud with the front office, he was not the only player involved in a salary dispute with the Boston club that year.

Jones never played in the National League again. He made several appeals to the league, but highhanded officials refused to hear them. In 1881, he sued the Boston Base Ball Association in the Common Pleas Court of Cleveland. He asked for $378 on his 1880 salary. He obtained a favorable judgment and collected by levying on Boston's share of gate receipts at Cleveland during the 1881 season.

president of the Chicago club, sent an agent to Cincinnati to sign Jones and teammate Jimmy Hallinan. Jones then played in two games for Chicago. In the meantime, a new group with financial backing took over the Cincinnati club. The league ordered Jones to return to Cincinnati, and Chicago reluctantly returned him. Charley wound up having a pretty good

In the meantime, Jones operated a laundry in Cincinnati and played with the outlaw Portsmouth, Ohio, club. In November, 1881, he signed with Cincinnati of the newly organized American Association. However, the new league decided to honor the National League blacklist and Jones was never asked to report to the Cincinnati club. He sued Cincinnati for his 1882 salary, but lost in a bitter trial in which his alleged alcohol problem was an issue. He continued to play for the Portsmouth club.

In 1883, the National League voted to reinstate most of its blacklisted players, including Jones. He then joined the Cincinnati American Association club. He hit .294 and was runner-up in homers with ten. In 1884, he hit .314 and was runner-up in runs with 117.

Jones was still in Cincinnati in 1885 and 1886, hitting .322 and .270 respectively. There is an interesting story about Charley from sometime after the 1885 season. He began running around with a woman from Newport, Kentucky, named Ollie Smith. One day, Ollie and Charley were sitting in a Cincinnati saloon when they spied Charley's wife walking up and down in front of the place. The pair boldly walked outside and tried to board a streetcar. Mrs. Jones spotted them and screamed, "Catch him! Hold that man and woman!" She caught up with them and threw the contents of a package into their faces. The weapon was cayenne pepper and it scored a bullseye in Charley's eyes, temporarily blinding him. That strange injury practically ended his career. He played a while longer, but it was all downhill. Maybe this story had a happy ending. Charley and Ollie were secretly married on July 1, 1886, in Cincinnati. Charley used his birth name of Rippay and Ollie used her maiden name of Horton. However, it didn't take long for the word to get out. They had a son, born in 1887. Charley also had at least one daughter.

Jones opened the 1887 season with Cincinnati, but was sold to the New York Mets on July 9 for about $1,100. This was the highest price paid for an outfielder up to that time. It was reported in the newspapers that Cincinnati's puppy mascot did not go to New York in the deal. It seems that Charley had been the puppy's favorite player ever since the day that Charley filled him up with beer. Jones's first game with his new team was at Cincinnati and the fans cheered for him every time he came to bat.

New York let Jones go after 1887. He hooked on with Kansas City for 1888, but played in his last game on April 26 before being released. Manager Dave Rowe said Charley was bothered by a foot injury from the previous season. Jones then negotiated with Jersey City of the Central League, but the deal fell through. He never did play in the minor leagues.

Jones was one of the most colorful players in an era that had plenty of them. In spite of his fondness for John Barleycorn, he had a reputation as a gamer. He was very popular with the fans, especially in Cincinnati. When he came to bat, the cry from the stands was, "Home run, Jones." Children followed him in the streets and shouted his name. The Cincinnati *Enquirer*, as well as other newspapers, always gave him a good press. He was something of a dandy and his extensive wardrobe led to such colorful nicknames as The Knight of the Limitless Linen. A Cincinnati clothing store gave him all the new suits he needed as an advertising gimmick. Charley often said that he hated baseball, but played it in the summer so that he could hunt and fish in the winter in his native North Carolina. He was considered a great outdoorsman. He had a mania for collecting guns and he had an arsenal of weapons dating back to the Civil War.

After his playing career ended, Jones returned to Portsmouth, where he served with the Ohio State Militia and later as sheriff of Portsmouth County. He moved to New York City sometime in the 1890s and became an inspector of elections. He returned to baseball briefly in 1896 as an umpire in the Atlantic Association.

In 1906, well-known sportswriter Tim Murnane bumped into Jones at a bicycle race in New York City. Murnane said that Jones was connected with Billy Muldoon's "sanitary farm" in upstate New York and had been given the week off to help with the bike race.

On August 28, 1909 *Sporting Life* ran the following article, datelined August 20: "Friends of Charley Jones, who was famous as the left fielder of the old Bostons and Cincinnati Reds, and one of the greatest batsmen in his day, have arranged a benefit for him to be held at South Beach, Staten Island, on Tuesday, August 31. Jones is an invalid and in need of assistance. William Muldoon, the former wrestler, is chairman of the committee in charge of arrangements."

No further mention of the benefit, the illness, or Charley Jones's eventual death has ever turned up, despite the best efforts of SABR's Biographical Research Committee and others. Perhaps a reader of this story will be able to answer the question: Whatever happened to Charley Jones?

Bones of Contention

Wild card competition? Not all that wild.

Stephen Taylor

I come to bury baseball tradition, not to praise it!"
So goes the cry heard throughout the land. And who can argue with such a sentiment? Here we are, seven years into the brave new world of major league baseball's expanded playoff format, and the change from the old two division system has been a roaring success with fans everywhere. The tyranny of the division championship is dead, and the laurel of victory rests upon the brows of the heroes of the wild card movement.

But is this picture accurate? Has the change to an expanded playoff system really fulfilled its promises to baseball fans? Now that seven seasons of the new order have passed, we can begin to meaningfully assess the impact of the expanded playoffs upon major league baseball.

To do this, let's review those aforementioned promises. When the major leagues revised their divisional format and introduced the wild card playoff teams, proponents made two major arguments in its favor. Point One: the expanded playoffs would bring in more money for the leagues through increased broadcast and gate receipts. And Point Two: the expanded playoffs would give more teams a shot at postseason play, thus enhancing competition and bringing more excitement (and paying customers) to the late season playoff races.

Stephen Taylor *is a writer and graphic artist. He lives in the San Francisco Bay Area. Comments about this article can be directed to: bonchat@aol.com. For further info, please visit: members.aol.com/ursapu/ cresxhome.html.*

Point One is a no-brainer. More playoff games played means more television money, more tickets sold, more merchandising—more of every form of revenue generated by postseason play.

But what of Point Two—the idea that the inclusion of three division champs and a wild card team in each league will heighten the competitiveness and excitement of the pennant races? Is that idea valid?

"Sure it is," scoffs the fan of the wild card format. "The expanded playoffs have been great for baseball. Look at the one-game playoffs we've had the last couple of years. Teams are fighting it out down to the last day. How's that for exciting?"

Well, yes indeed, a cursory look at the last few seasons would seem to support that idea. In 1999, the race for the wild card spot in the National League ended with a playoff. Though the American League races have not been quite so dramatic, we have seen several intense, memorable postseason battles between traditional rivals like the Yankees, Indians, Orioles, and Red Sox.

But a big part of the wild card's appeal lies in broader, more wide-open playoff races. With more teams contending, more teams' fans will have a reason to pay attention—and spend money—in September. So the basic question is: Has the realignment created more late-season contenders? Or, to put it another way: Do more fans feel that their team is a contender?

To answer this question, we need to figure out just what a "contender" is. Then we can look back over the history of division play and see just how much impact the wild card format has had on the pennant races. For the sake of a meaningful comparison, we will only examine the pennant races of the divisional era, 1969 through 1999, and we'll toss out the the strike years of 1981 and 1994.

Let's define a contender as any team that is within 7.5 games of a playoff spot on September 1. Why 7.5 games out? Because that is the largest September 1 deficit to be overcome by a playoff team in the divisional era. (Seattle came from 7.5 games behind the Angels in 1995 to force a one game playoff and take the division championship.)

Given this definition of contender status, does the expanded playoff format provide more reason for more fans to stick with their favorite teams through September?

Sure enough, when we examine the standings from the last seven years, we see an increase in the average number of teams in contention per year versus the two division era. From 1969 to 1993, the number of contenders in the American League averaged out to 5.125 contenders per year. For the National League, the figure is almost identical, at 5.042.

By comparison, the average figures for the wild card era are 7.7 teams per year in both leagues.

Those numbers look even better if you compare them against the division races that would have resulted if the leagues had never been realigned.

(For our purposes, the "reconstituted" leagues look as close a possible to the two division alignments— the Central Division teams go back to their former East or West homes, Atlanta is an NL West team, and the expansion teams, Arizona and Tampa Bay, end up in the NL West and AL East respectively. After 1997, as in reality, Milwaukee moves to the National League to maintain balance, though the Brewers become an NL East team in the "reconstituted" order. All teams are assumed to have achieved the same won-lost records as they did in reality.)

When the leagues are "reconstituted" back to their pre-1994 alignments, the comparable average figures are 4.6 contenders per year in the American League and 5.1 contenders per year for the National League during the years 1995–2001.

In absolute terms, the expanded playoffs have meant more teams in contention for the playoffs late in the season.

"Great!" say the wild card partisans. "Thanks for telling us what we already know. Now if you'll excuse us, we have to go wash our 'Chicago Cubs 1998 Wild Card Champion' t-shirts."

Not so fast. Yes, the numbers show an absolute increase in contenders in the wild card era. But, as they say, numbers can be deceiving.

For one thing, part of the increase comes from the very format itself. In fact, realignment alone doubled the number of playoff teams in each league. But that did not translate into more wide-open competition. The number of playoff spots doubled, but the average number of contenders, moving as we have seen from about five to about eight, did not.

And, lest we forget, those numbers are averages. The figures for both leagues in the wild card era were inflated by the first two years of the format. The new order got off with a bang in 1995, with ten contenders in the AL and eleven contenders in the NL. The next year was almost as good: ten AL contenders, nine NL contenders.

But things have calmed down since. For instance, in 1998, the numbers were five AL contenders and six NL contenders—very close to the averages of the two division era. In 1999, there were six contenders, as opposed to five under the theoretical "reconstituted" divisions alignment. Clearly, the pennant races of the last few years have hardly been "wide open."

What's more, 1995 and 1996 were hardly unprecedented. When we look for the highest number of contenders in a single year of the divisional era, the two division days stack up pretty well with the wild card era. The National League's eleven contenders in 1995 do beat the eight teams vying for the playoffs in 1973. But in the American League, where ten contenders jockeyed for the playoffs in 1995 and 1996, that number is matched by the 1987 season. Over the twenty-four years of two division play, the American League produced eight seasons with six or more contenders. All of those seasons compare favorably to recent years of the wild card era.

This relative shortfall of contenders presents another byproduct of the new league format: more "runaway" division champs. A runaway division champ is a team that moves out far ahead of its competitors and never faces a challenge for the division title—for our purposes, they led their division by more than 7.5 games on September 1 (in most cases, the gap was considerably wider).

With two divisions in each league for the twenty-four years from 1969 to 1993 (excluding 1981), there were forty-eight division championships to be won. In each league during the two division era, eleven—23 percent—were taken by runaway champs.

When we move to the last seven years, the numbers shift dramatically. Of the twenty-one division championships in each league from 1995 to 2001, seven AL teams and six NL teams earned the flag as runaway champs. That's a 33 percent runaway rate for each league in the wild card era.

Stack the numbers up against the "reconstituted" divisions and the leap is equally dramatic: 21 percent of the pennant races in each league would have been runaways during the last seven years, and only 13 percent of the division champs (2 teams) would have been so dominant in the American League.

Apparently, the three division setup has helped foster more dominant teams, creating situations where one team gets to rule over its division like some despotic potentate, clutching the division championship in an iron hand and not letting anyone else get near it.

Did someone mention tyranny being dead?

That wild card fan is beginning to get a bit surly. "All right," he says, "maybe it hasn't exactly been what we thought it would be. But the wild card is about more than just who wins in the regular season. It's also about giving a deserving second place team a chance in the playoffs, right? Why don't you talk about that."

Fair enough. Let's look at the playoffs. When we compare the playoffs that were to "the playoffs that would have been," do we see many significant differences? Are there any teams that made a big splash in the playoffs that would have been nowhere to be found under the two division format?

In fact, as of this writing (pre-2001 postseason) of the six World Series champs of the wild card era, two would not have been in the playoffs without the three division format: the 1996 and 2000 New York Yankees. The '96 Yanks would have finished a healthy 7.5 games behind the Cleveland Indians in the old American League East. As it was, the Yankees won the American League East and went on to give Wade Boggs a chance to ride a horse in Yankee Stadium. The 2000 Yankees had only the *fifth* best record in the American League when they won their third straight title. Whether or not this is a good thing depends on where you live and who you root for.

Apart from the 1996 and 2000 Yankees, three other teams made it to the Series when they would have been watching at home under the old system: the 1997 Cleveland Indians, the 1998 San Diego Padres, and the 2000 New York Mets. Thus, five of twelve pennant winners were rescued by the wild card system, even if they weren't wild card teams themselves. But seven of those twelve would have been playoff teams anyway under the old format—and, presum-

ably, would have won their pennants exactly as they did in the realigned leagues.

By now, the astute fan will have noticed that no mention has been made of the 1997 World Champion Florida Marlins. And with good reason. Though the Marlins remain the only wild card team to win the Series, they weren't really helped by the wild card format. Under the two division setup, they would have wound up National League East champs anyway, four games in front of the New York Mets. (Remember, Atlanta was a National League West team for the entire two division era.) Hence, the Marlins stand as the poster team for how little impact the wild card system has had on the playoffs—the one wild card that won it all would have gotten to the championship series without that second chance.

And we must remember that for all the teams that have been helped by the expanded playoffs, there are teams that have been hurt by them. Instead of being shown the door in three quick first-round sweeps, the Texas Rangers would have had three cracks at the League Championship Series, where it would have taken four games to sweep them away.

The Cubs would have made it to two League Championship Series, in 1995 and 1998, when all of the strongest teams were old National League West rivals. And in 1996, when Montreal and St. Louis finished with identical 88-74 records, the Expos would have had a one-game shot at playing for the championship. Instead they've been buried in obscurity since the days when Marquis Grissom was young. How's that for helping out the small market teams?

Of course, realignment goes beyond the simple fact of who is in the playoffs and who is not. It also affects the postseason results. Cleveland and Atlanta stand out glaringly. They have been dominant teams in the regular season, winning 13 division titles in all. Each team has won its division's championship in every season of the wild card era—ten division championships in all. And what has been the reward for their efforts? Their combined accomplishments: three pennants, and only one World Series victory—when the one (Atlanta) beat the other in 1995.

Is it a good idea to penalize teams that have proven their excellence over the course of a season by placing another layer of playoff hurdles in their paths? Is the wild card's benefit to baseball so great that the sport needs to punish its best teams?

By now that wild card proponent has just about had enough. "Come on!" he cries. "You're missing the point entirely. The fans love the wild card. It gives all the teams something else to shoot for besides the division title."

That argument would be fine, if all the also-ran teams were "shooting for it." But is that what's really happening in baseball today? Look at the impact of the wild card format beyond the playing field. Look at what happens in the off-season, when a team's success or failure is often determined.

The non-contenders tend to remake their teams. The contenders tend to stand pat. For the most part, the teams that lingered at the edge of contention remain static. They don't made the moves that will take them that next step up in the standings.

That wild card proponent has a devilish gleam in his eye. "Aha! Got you!" he cries. "Those teams aren't bringing in any new players because they are the sadsack, poor boy, second class teams. They don't have the money to stock up on All Stars. It doesn't have anything to do with the wild card format."

Ah, yes. Economics. Thanks for bringing it up. Because, in fact, the rich teams-poor teams argument is one of the strong points *against* the wild card format. With a wild card playoff spot available, teams like the A's and Blue Jays can sometimes hang around the upper half of the standings and appear to have a chance at winning it all. Apart from giving the fans in those cities a reason to show up at the ballpark, in a broader context it also gives the appearance of more competitively balanced leagues. Fans can say, "Look how close the A's came, and they didn't need to spend the GNP of Spain in order to win."

Unfortunately, this sort of thinking helps to alleviate any pressure on Major League Baseball to correct its economic imbalance. It plays right to the interests of the wealthiest teams. With a few have-not teams on the brink of contention each year, baseball can hide behind the illusion of competitive balance and do nothing to address the serious economic inequities that hamper so many of its teams. The division championships will remain the province of the few wealthiest teams, while the wild card position becomes a sort of booby prize for the poorer teams—the wealthy teams' version of "Let them eat cake." And even then the poor teams get jobbed, since there are more than three wealthy teams in each league; whichever rich team doesn't land one of the division titles will most often nab the wild card spot anyway. Look at how frequently the American League wild card spot has been the "property" of American League

East teams (five times out of seven). Is this really an increase in competition?

And think about the aforementioned rise in runaway division champions. With three divisions in each league, the major leagues have the potential for six division races to be contested going into the final weeks of the season. Instead, we've seen more teams winning uncontested division titles in the last seven years. Baseball's financial disorder is sapping the realigned leagues of their competitive potential, and robbing the fans of the very thing they were promised: more wide open pennant races.

Taken all together—the less than expected increase in the number of contenders, the rise in runaway division champs, the wild card's mixed-bag impact on playoffs and World Series, the disincentive provided by the wild card toward financial equity—the effect of the expanded playoff format has fallen far short of the goal of Point Two: an increased, broader measure of competition throughout Major League Baseball.

It's no news that baseball's playing field has been tilted toward the wealthier teams. But it may be surprising to see just how much the wild card format bolsters that inequity. Without a league-wide alignment that places a premium on competitiveness within the divisions, a format that requires all teams to spend the money to compete for a division title or languish at the bottom of the standings, there will be no serious incentive for Major League Baseball to clean up the game's economic mess.

"All right already," concedes the browbeaten wild card fan. "You may have a point. Maybe the wild card hasn't been all it was cracked up to be, at least as far as competition is concerned. Maybe it was all shuck and jive, just a sales pitch, when they said it would give more teams a chance to reach the playoffs. But that first argument in its favor still holds, right? Baseball still gets all that extra money from the expanded playoffs. That's got to be good for the health of the game, right? We can trust the owners to take advantage of their increased revenues and do what's best for the game, can't we?"

And they say baseball purists are out of touch!

Sources:

Information for daily standings was taken from the San Francisco *Chronicle* and San Francisco *Examiner*, 1969–1999.

Additional information came from MLB's official site at *majorleaguebaseball.com*; and The Baseball Archive at *www.baseball1.com*.

Hunting for
the First Louisville Slugger

A look at the Browning myth

Bob Bailey

Myth, legend and controversy mix together with history and fact in baseball's churning cauldron of the past. Abner Doubleday's invention of baseball is a myth. Babe Ruth's calling his shot in the 1932 World Series is legendary (and probably a myth). The 1969 Mets World Series win is a fact, however improbable and however much praised as legendary by Met fans.

There are other stories in baseball lore that are probably myths, have grown into legend and then, after much repetition, become treated as fact. Did Mike Kelly really insert himself in the lineup as a pop foul was falling toward his bench? Did Candy Cummings really throw the first curve ball? These and other nineteenth-century tales have little corroborating evidence beyond the original narrator of the story and its endless retelling in popular history.

Louisville baseball has its "historical" tale that I believe has little basis in fact. It is the story of Pete Browning and the turning of the first Louisville Slugger bat.

The story comes down to us, in endless retellings, that early in the 1884 season, Pete Browning was in something of a slump. On this sunny day he had broken his bat. This was a particularly sad event, as we shall see, due to Pete's eccentricities regarding these tools of his trade. When the game ended, seventeen-year-old John A. "Bud" Hillerich hopped out of the stands at Eclipse Park at 28th and Elliott Streets in the west end of Louisville, ran over to Browning,

tugged at his sleeve and offered to make him a new bat in Hillerich's father's wood turning shop. Browning agreed and the two of them made their way to the J. F. Hillerich Job Turning shop on First Street. The teenager and ballplayer worked through the night and crafted a custom-made bat to Browning's specifications. As befits any creation story, Browning pronounced the bat "good" and proceeded to line out three hits the following day to break out of his slump.

It's a nice story. A story with just a hint of plausibility. A story of a boy and ballplayer and a brand name known throughout the baseball world. But there are a few problems. There are no contemporary accounts of this event in any newspaper or other source. This is odd on two accounts.

First, Pete Browning was a hometown hero. Born Louis Rogers Browning in Louisville in 1861, the son of a middle-class merchant, he grew up with such friends as Chicken Wolf and the Reccius boys, John and Phil, who would all be teammates on Louisville's major league team in the 1880s. He picked up the nickname Pete as a child and was a splendid athlete known as a fine runner, ice skater, marble shooter and baseball player. When Louisville landed a team in the fledgling American Association in 1882, a major league rival to the more established National League, Pete was the team's star. He was the American Association batting champ in 1882 and a drawing card in every ballpark he visited. He was also garrulous—a man accessible to the fans and to the press. He was always ready to provide a comment for a reporter and if

Bob Bailey *is a frequent contributor to SABR publications. He lives in Newtown, Pennsylvania, where he is researching ballplayers' burial locations.*

you were buying drinks he was ready to spend some time at the bar with you. So it is unusual that Pete never mentioned this new bat to any of his friends in the press.

Second, Pete was known to have a few strange habits concerning his bats. He believed that each bat had just so many hits in it and when they were exhausted it was time to stop using that club. But he did not discard his bats, he "retired" them. He gave them a name (often of biblical origin) and placed them in the basement of his home. It is said he had over 200 retired bats in his home. So this is not a man who would be shy talking about a special bat.

Throughout Browning's life no mention of this incident, or anything like it, appeared in any of the Louisville papers or in the sporting press around the country. The first mention of Browning in relation to Hillerich occurs in the Sunday insert of the Louisville *Herald* Magazine on September 27, 1914. Written by Bruce Dudley (an interesting character himself, as he moved through the baseball world as a sports editor, Louisville Colonel president and finally president of the American Association), it is titled "Every Knock Is a Boost For the Louisville Slugger Bat." He related the following story:

> Many bats are especially for boys, with rings around them—meaning the bats. These rings represent "home runs." The first one was made by Mr. [Bud] Hillerich for Pete Browning, who always will be remembered in connection with the national pastime...
>
> After a slump, he wandered around the Hillerich plant one day and told Mr. Hillerich the last bat that had been made for him was no good.
>
> "I can't hit a thing with it," he said.
>
> "Well, bring it back and I'll put a home run in it for you," offered Mr. Hillerich.
>
> Mr. Hillerich took the bat, put it into a lathe, and scratched a circle around it. That afternoon Pete poled the promised homer, and ever afterwards his bats were made with rings around them."

This certainly fits with Browning's known superstitions about his bats, but it says nothing about his being the first major leaguer to be a recipient of a Hillerich bat. There is no hint of Bud Hillerich returning to the shop with his hero in tow and working through the night to enter baseball immortality.

In fact, the Dudley article related an entirely differ-

ent story surrounding the first bat. He wrote— presumably after conversations with Bud Hillerich, by this time the head of the company—that young Bud was a good sandlot player in the early 1880s. In 1883 he was a member of the Morning Star team that played in Hillerich's East End neighborhood around Butchertown, and he used a bat turned by his father, J. Frederick Hillerich. The story goes that Bud's cudgel was stolen or misplaced, but was recovered in time for the 1884 season. This was important since his father had decreed that he was too busy to be fooling around making another bat. After all, there were ax handles, bed posts, and butter churns to be made.

With his trusty stick back Bud went off to the field and showed it off to several of his friends, including Gus Weyhing, whom Dudley describes as "just breaking in with the Colonels," but who was actually a minor league player in 1884 before beginning a pitching career in which he won 264 games for nine major league teams. Gus passed the Hillerich bat around to some of his mates including Joe Gerhardt, Tom McLaughlin, and Monk Cline, all Louisville boys and members of the 1884 Colonels squad.

Dudley wrote that Hillerich gave that first bat to Weyhing and that the other players prevailed on J. Fred to make them bats of their own. He agreed after extracting a promise from each of them never to bother him again about bats. Word spread about the quality of the sticks that were first called Hillerich Bats, then Falls City Sluggers, and finally, in 1894, Louisville Sluggers.

If this 1914 story is correct, where does the Browning story come from?

Through the 1920s and much of the 1930s, little was written in the company records or the sporting goods press about the Louisville Slugger bat. In March, 1939 Sam Severance published a recognizable version of the Browning story in *The Sporting Goods Dealer*, a trade publication. Severance's story was that one day in 1884 Browning broke his bat and was directed by a friend to the Hillerich shop to have another fashioned. There he ran into Bud Hillerich, who agreed to turn a bat for him. After working long into the night, Hillerich produced a piece of lumber that satisfied Pete, who took it to the park the next day and pounded out three hits.

We see here elements of the ultimate story coming together. Browning needing a bat, a meeting with Bud Hillerich, a custom-made bat, and a three-hit game. But Severance did not put this tale forward as fact. He called it a "legend around the H&B factory." And Severance should have known: he was the head of marketing for Hillerich & Bradsby at the time.

Not surprisingly, Severance's version of the story is repeated in the *Famous Slugger Yearbook* of 1939. This publication was an annual promotional booklet produced by Hillerich & Bradsby from the late 1920s to 1978. Distributed to sporting goods dealers for their customers, it contained statistics from the prior season, major league records, and ads and promotional pieces about H&B baseball products. In all probability, Severance put the 1939 *Yearbook* together.

It is fascinating to follow the Browning story through the *Yearbook* for the next decade. The story evolved before its readers' eyes. In 1941 the story was told as a quote from seventy-five-year-old Bud Hillerich, still the firm's president. In 1942 the story portrayed young Hillerich as a friend of Browning's. In the 1948 version, Hillerich was not yet acquainted with Browning, but in his desire to meet the star player of his hometown team he approached him after a game with the offer to produce a new bat. The story of Browning breaking his bat and Bud Hillerich "tugging at Browning's sleeve" to offer him the wood turner's services appeared in 1949.

The 1949 version of the Browning tale reappeared in the *Slugger Yearbooks* of 1950, 1954, 1955, and 1959. It was by then virtually the same story we hear today. In 1974, it was put in the mouth of Bud's grandson, Jack Hillerich, who "retold" it in the ninetieth anniversary edition.

But the trail for the first Louisville Slugger bat does not end here. The hunt continues to take various twists and turns. In the corporate files of Hillerich & Bradsby, housed in the Archive Department of the University of Louisville Library, there is a manuscript of an interview with Arlie Latham by Clifford Bloodgood that was published in *Baseball Magazine* in November, 1937. Walter Arlington Latham, seventy-seven years old at the time, contended that the first Louisville Slugger was made for *him*.

Latham, known during his career as "The Freshest Man on Earth," was the third baseman for the American Association St. Louis Browns. He claimed that on a trip to Louisville in 1883 or 1884 he broke his bat and was unable to find another for sale in the entire city. He eventually wandered into the Hillerich wood turning shop near his hotel and made a deal with J. Fred to have Bud turn a new bat for him by game time the next day. In fulfilling that assignment, Hillerich launched the bat-making business. This is so similar to Sam Severance's 1939 version of the story that a suspicious person might wonder if Severance liked the idea of an "advent story" for the Louisville Slugger, but preferred a local hero as the protagonist.

Pete Browning was long gone by the late 1930s, but Bud Hillerich was still around. As the one constant in all the stories he could set the record straight. A refutation or confirmation of the Latham story was not forthcoming. We shouldn't be surprised by this. The Severance story was still over a year away and why should H&B stifle good publicity for their products.

The Latham story now jumps forward thirty-seven years, to a 1974 letter in the Hillerich & Bradsby Archives addressed to Jack McGrath, an H&B marketing executive, from Allen Gibbon of the A. K. Gibbon Lumber Co., of Kansas City, Missouri. After thanking McGrath for some equipment H&B had donated to the local Kiwanis Girls team, Gibbon noted that he had enclosed a copy of the Latham interview with the following note handwritten and signed by Bud Hillerich:

> To my Friend
> Allen K. Gibbons.
> The above is the first, true story of the origin of the Louisville Slugger Base Ball bat. Mr. Latham at age of 82 is still connected in Base Ball, serving at Polo Grounds, N. Y., home of the N. Y. Giants.
> Respectfully
> s/ J. A. Hillerich
> July 17th, 1942.

The Latham story was told again in 1966 for an article by Leslie Lieber in *The Week*.

Where does this leave us? Did Browning break his bat? Did Latham break his bat? Was Browning sent to Hillerich by a friend? Was Gus Weyhing given Bud Hillerich's personal bat? Are any of these stories true?

I discount the Latham story as the tale of a man who had outlived his contemporaries and was not shy about putting himself in the middle of any story. I chalk Bud Hillerich's 1942 note up to good publicity.

The Browning story is clearly the result of Sam Severance's fertile public relations mind borrowing the Latham story of two years earlier and inserting Pete as the main character.

The story that makes the most sense to me is Bruce Dudley's, which makes Gus Weyhing the owner of the first Louisville Slugger. It is the earliest published account, it predates the Latham and Browning tales by over twenty years, and it is the least dramatic and so the most likely.

Stan Musial

1948: A season worth another look

Paul Warburton

No other player in major league history has dominated a season offensively as thoroughly as Stan Musial did when he topped the National League in nine categories in 1948. "Stan the Man" paced the National League in hits (230), doubles (46), triples (18), runs (135), RBIs (131), batting average (.376), total bases (429), on-base percentage (.450), and slugging percentage (.702). He also tagged a career high 39 homers, just one behind the 40 of co-leaders Ralph Kiner and Johnny Mize. His 429 total bases were only 21 behind the NL record of Rogers Hornsby in 1922. Stan was truly "The Man" in the summer of 1948.

During the 1940s and 1950s, Musial was the National League's rival to Ted Williams. While Ted led the American League in batting seven times and slugging nine times, Stan was atop the NL in batting seven times and slugging six times. The most impressive stat in Stan's career is his total bases mark of 6,134, second all-time to home run king Henry Aaron's 6,856. Stan is also fourth all time in hits (3,630), third in doubles (725), tied for nineteenth in triples (177—the most since Paul Waner retired in 1945 with 191), fifth in RBIs (1,951) and seventh in runs scored (1,949). He walloped 475 homers and retired after twenty-two years in 1963 with a batting average of .331. Only Tony Gwynn has retired with a higher batting average since.

Stan rang up this amazing collection of stats with one of the oddest looking batting stances of all time. A lefty, he dug in with his left foot on the back line of the batter's box, and assumed a closed stance with his right foot about twelve inches in front of his left. He took three or four practice swings and followed up with a silly-looking hula wiggle to help him relax. He crouched, stirring his bat like a weapon in a low, slow-moving arc away from his body. As the pitcher let loose with his fling, "The Man" would quickly cock his bat into a steady position, dip his right knee and twist his body away from the pitcher so that he was concentrating at his adversary's delivery out of the corner of his deadly keen eyes. He would then uncoil with an explosion of power. His line drives were bullets.

The package—Musial wasn't just a great hitter; he was the complete package, a hustling ballplayer who came up through the tough St. Louis Cardinals farm system. But for all his accomplishments, Musial has become an overlooked man among baseball's post-World War II greats, and his astonishing 1948 season is seldom mentioned among the great campaigns.

Like Babe Ruth, Musial started out his pro career as a pitcher, with Williamson of the Class D Mountain States League. In 1938 and 1939 his record was a combined 15-8 with an ERA around 4.50. In 1940 the Cardinals sent him to their Daytona Beach team in the Class D Florida State League. The team was managed by former Chicago White Sox pitching star

Paul Warburton is a 1976 graduate of Providence College with a BA in history. While there he took care of the Friars' baseball field and retrieved foul balls during games for spending money.

Dickie Kerr. Under Kerr's tutelage, Stan posted an 18-5 record with a 2.62 ERA.

Kerr also used Musial in the outfield, and Stan responded by hitting .311 with 70 RBIs in 405 at bats. In late August of 1940 he injured the shoulder of his pitching arm attempting to make a diving catch in the outfield. He was never an effective pitcher again.

In 1941 the Cardinals sent him to their Springfield Class C team as an outfielder. Stan pounded the ball for a .379 average with 26 homers and 94 RBIs in 87 games. He was promoted to the Cards' top minor league team, Rochester, in late July. In 54 games, Stan hit .326. When the Red Wings season ended, he received a wire telling him to report to the St. Louis Cardinals. The Cards were in the midst of a fierce pennant race with Leo Durocher's Dodgers. Musial rapped 20 hits in 12 games and batted .426, but Brooklyn edged the Redbirds out for the flag by 2-1/2 games.

In 1942, Stan proved that he was no fluke. He batted .315 as manager Billy Southworth's Cards won 43 of their final 51 games to post 106 victories and overtake the Dodgers by two lengths. There was no stopping the Redbirds as they rolled over the heavily favored Yankees in the World Series in five games. Musial became a superstar in 1943, leading the league in hits (220), doubles (48), triples (20), batting average (.357), and slugging (.562) as the Cards won 105 games and another pennant. In 1944 the Cards won 105 games again for their third straight pennant and then topped the crosstown Browns in the World Series. Stan led the NL in hits (197), runs (112), doubles (51), and slugging (.549). He also hit .347.

Musial spent 1945 in the Navy, where he was assigned to ship repair duty at Pearl Harbor. He returned triumphant in 1946 to lead the Cards to their fourth pennant and third world championship in five years. He paced the NL in hits (228), runs (124), doubles (50), triples (20), batting (.365), and slugging (.587). Musial began the 1947 season in a horrendous slump, and in early May was diagnosed with acute appendicitis. The attending physician in New York recommended immediate surgery. Stan was flown back to St. Louis, where he was examined by team doctor Robert Hyland. Hyland suggested that it might be possible to put off surgery until season's end by freezing the diseased appendix. Stan agreed and was back in the lineup five days later. He came back too fast, however, and on May 19 was hitting a feeble .140. By June 15, he had lifted his average to .203, then turned it all around over the last 104 games. "The Man" smacked the ball at a .469 clip in 315 at bats. He finished the season at .312 with 183 hits, 95 RBIs and 113 runs scored in 149 games. At season's end he underwent surgery on his appendix—and his tonsils.

Stan had played first base for most of 1946 and all of 1947. In spring training 1948, St. Louis manager Eddie Dyer moved him back to the outfield to make room for highly touted prospect Nippy Jones at first base. (In his career he played 1,016 games at first base and 1,890 games in the outfield.)

Sensing the big year—Stan recalled in his autobiography (*Stan Musial: "The Man's" Own Story* as told to Bob Broeg), "From the moment I picked up a bat in 1948, healthy and strong after off-season surgery, I knew this would be it, my big year…I was 27 now, at my athletic peak and healthier than I had been for as long as those low-grade infections had been gnawing at my system. Stronger too, when I picked up a bat and swung it. The bat felt so light that instead of gripping it about an inch up the handle, as I had in the past, I went down to the knob."

On April 20, opening day in St. Louis, the Cards' Murry Dickson scattered ten hits in shutting out Cincinnati, 4-0. In the third inning the Reds' Hank Sauer let a fly ball by Stan fall for a gift RBI double, his only hit on the day. Two days later, Stan stung a single, double and triple against Cincinnati, but the Reds won in the ninth inning, 4-3, when catcher Del Wilber juggled Stan's perfect throw to the plate. On April 24, Stan slashed an RBI triple in Chicago for his 1,000th career hit. St. Louis *Post-Dispatch* sportswriter Bob Broeg teased Stan afterwards, "Look, Banji [short for the ironic nickname Banjo, meaning a weak hitter], if you're going to talk about hits, what about trying for 3,000." Stan had not even considered getting 3,000 hits back then but told Broeg, "That's a long way off. Too many things could happen. Keep reminding me. This is a team game and I play to win, but a fella has to have little incentives. They keep him going when he's tired. They keep him from getting careless when the club is way ahead or far behind. It'll help my concentration."

On April 30, in Cincinnati, Stan had the first of his four five-hit games of 1948. He ripped an RBI single in the first inning. He cranked a two-run homer in the fifth frame. He torched a seven-run rally in the seventh with a double, then capped the uprising with a two-run single. In the ninth inning he doubled again, bringing his average at the end of April up to an even .400. The Cards won, 13-7.

"The Man"—Brooklyn arrived in town on May 4, and home runs by Musial and Enos Slaughter helped top the defending league champion Dodgers, 5-4. Stan ended the game with a sensational tumbling catch with two runners on base.

Musial was always double trouble against the Dodgers. In fact, he received his lasting nickname of "The Man" from Dodger fans during a three-game series at Ebbets Field in 1946. Stan ripped eight hits in 12 at bats in the series. In the final game, writer Broeg had heard Brooklyn fans chanting something whenever Stan came to the plate, but couldn't quite decipher the words. That evening he asked traveling secretary Leo Ward if he knew what the Flatbush fans were saying. Ward told Broeg, "Every time Stan came up they chanted, 'Here comes the man!'" Broeg informed his readers of the chant in his column the next day and one of the most famous nicknames in baseball history was born.

At Ebbets Field in 1948, Stan smashed 25 hits in 48 at bats for a .521 average. The 25 hits consisted of 10 singles, ten doubles, a triple and four home runs. Stan said, "If I could have hit all season at Ebbets Field or the Polo Grounds or, for that matter, if I could have played the 1948 season on the road, I might have hit .400 and ripped the record book apart." In fact, he hit .415 on the road, .334 at home.

The Cards arrived at Ebbets Field for the first time on May 18. Musial singled and doubled off Ralph Branca as St. Louis took the opener, 4-3. The next night before 32,883 fans, they tagged five Brooklyn pitchers for 18 hits in a 13-5 laugher. The Dodgers couldn't get Musial out. "The Man" singled three

Stan the Man in 1942.

times, doubled, tripled, and walked, scoring five runs and knocking in two. In the final game, the Cards routed four Dodger twirlers, 13-4. Musial singled once, doubled twice, and hammered a seventh-inning homer off Hugh Casey. In the series he went 11 for 15.

During the series Durocher's pitchers sent Slaughter to the dirt to avoid a head high pitch, drilled Whitey Kurowski in the back and beaned Del Rice, forcing him out of action. Such incidents were commonplace during Brooklyn-St. Louis battles in the 1940s. Stan did his share of ducking too. In his book, *Nice Guys Finish Last*, Durocher recalled a game in 1948 when his star, Jackie Robinson, was sent sprawling by a Cardinal pitch. Leo's pitcher retaliated by knocking down Musial with two successive pitches, the second one of which hit Stan's bat. He was thrown out while still flat on his back. According to Leo, Stan stopped him on the field a couple of innings later and said, "Hey, Leo, I haven't got the ball out there. I didn't throw at your man." Leo recalled telling Stan, "You're the best player I know on the Cardinals. For every time my men get one, it looks like you're gonna get two." Durocher ended the story by saying, "We never had any more trouble with the Cardinals as far as Mr. Robinson was concerned."

In 1948, however, St. Louis had to be worried about the Boston Braves as well as the Dodgers. Billy Southworth had moved from St. Louis to manage the Braves and he had them playing good ball. On May 21, Warren Spahn beat Harry Brecheen and the Cards, 3-1, despite Musial's eighth-inning homer. The next night the Cards turned the tables and sent

Johnny Sain to the showers on the way to a 6-4 win. St. Louis was in first place by 2-1/2 games. Spahn, Sain and the Braves would not go away, however. They would win their first pennant since 1914 despite Stan's gargantuan year.

Before a Wednesday night crowd of 44,128 at the Polo Grounds on May 26, Stan slugged his eighth and ninth homers, but the Giants exploded for eight runs in the eighth to triumph, 10-7. The Cards lost eight of nine before beating Brooklyn, 4-1, on June 3. Stan bashed a two-run homer in the first inning off Preacher Roe, and Brecheen made it stand up by hurling a four-hitter. From June 15 to June 18, Musial was on fire, lacing ten hits in 11 at bats, including two doubles, a triple and a homer as the Cards beat the Phils twice at Shibe Park, 2-1 and 4-1, then won, 12-8, over the Giants at the Polo Grounds.

On June 22 at Braves Field, Stan tied a National League record with his third five-hit game of the season in a 5-2 win. All five hits were singles, including a bunt. Before he went up to the plate in the ninth with the bases loaded, manager Eddie Dyer jokingly hollered out to him, "Hey boy, we're going to have to send a hitter up for you." Stan did a double take and the Cardinal bench laughed. He then socked Clyde Shoun's first pitch up the middle to drive in two runs and decide the game.

Three days later Musial again tore apart the Dodgers at Ebbets Field, with two singles, a double and his sixteenth homer. The Cards beat Joe Hatten, 6-3. The next night Brooklyn hurler Preacher Roe interrupted a St. Louis clubhouse meeting to tell the Cards that he had finally figured out how to get Musial out. The lefthander born in Ash Flat, Arkansas, revealed his formula. "Walk 'im on foah pitches an pick 'im off first," he drawled before ducking out the door amidst chuckles. The Dodgers did manage to get Musial out three times, but in the seventh inning he homered off Paul Minner as the Cards triumphed, 6-4.

By July 1, Musial had rapped out 101 hits in 252 at-bats for a .401 average. Taking into account his tremendous finish in 1947, he had hit safely 249 times in his last 567 at-bats, for a .439 average over 169 games.

The relatively new phenomenon of night games was not hurting Stan. He was hitting .462 at night, and .437 against lefthanders. Over in the American League, Ted Williams had bashed 92 hits in 229 at bats for a .402 average. On the Fourth of July, the Cards split a doubleheader at Crosley Field in Cincinnati. Musial banged out five singles and a double in ten at bats to raise his average to .405. Nonetheless,

St. Louis went into the All-Star break a full six games behind the Braves.

Top All-Star—The 6-foot-1, 175-pound Musial was flexing his muscles as never before. He slammed his twentieth homer (a career high, though he would average 31 per season for the next ten years) on July 9. Musial was the leading NL All-Star vote getter amassing 1,532,502 votes. At the break his average had shot up to .415. He was called into co-owner Robert Hannegan's office and given a $5,000 raise to $36,000.

Stan delighted a home town All-Star Game crowd of 34,009 at Sportsman's Park with a first-inning two-run homer into the right field pavilion, but the American League won, 5-2. Before he retired in 1963, Stan would hold All-Star records for most games played (22), hits (20), total bases (40), homers (6), and at-bats (60), sporting a cool .333 average. He decided the 1955 midsummer classic in Milwaukee with a twelfth-inning homer off Frank Sullivan.

In Brooklyn the Dodgers had fired Durocher and re-hired Burt Shotton as manager. "Leo the Lip," despised for years by the fans at the Polo Grounds, now was hired by Horace Stoneham to replace their idol, Mel Ott. Durocher's Giants came into St. Louis in late July and the Cards took two of three from them. In the final game Musial capped a six-run Redbird outburst in the seventh inning with a two-run homer that gave his team a 6-5 lead. "Big Jawn" Mize tied the game for the Giants with a solo shot, but the Cards prevailed on Nippy Jones' RBI single in the thirteenth, 7-6.

Southworth's Braves arrived next, and the Cardinals slowed them down by winning three of four to get within five games of the top. Musial went seven for 16 in the series with a double and triple. Encouraged by their recent showing against the Braves, the Cards began a long road trip with a three game set in Brooklyn. Musial was his usual destructive self, with six hits in 12 at-bats, including four doubles, but the red-hot Dodgers won all three to drop the Cards back down to fourth place.

At Braves Field a crowd of 37,071 greeted the Cards on July 30. Musial ignited a five-run rally in the eighth inning with a double as Brecheen bested Sain, 6-2, on the way to a 20-win season. Stan tripled and homered the following afternoon against Spahn, but Sibby Sisti drilled a triple with the bases full in the ninth inning to power the Braves to a dramatic 7-6 victory.

The third stop on the road trip was back at the Polo

Grounds. Durocher's Giants had won seven straight and passed the Dodgers into second place. The Cards were not impressed. In the opener they pulverized Leo's hurlers, 21-5. Musial doubled, homered and scored three times. Two days later the series resumed with the Cards sweeping a doubleheader, 7-2 and 3-0. Musial slammed a two-run homer off Sheldon Jones in the first game and Brecheen outpitched Larry Jansen with a two-hitter in the nightcap.

The Cardinals always seemed to play Durocher's teams tough. Musial explained why in his autobiography: "Leo liked to play the game rough, liked to make it a game of intimidation. His tactics turned us from tabbies into tigers." Stan was the most ferocious St. Louis tiger against the Giants in 1948, tagging their moundsmen for 11 homers. On May 2, 1954, he would belt five home runs and sock a single in a doubleheader against Durocher's eventual world champion Giants.

Pittsburgh's Forbes Field proved to be a chamber of horrors for the Cards in 1948, however. The Pirates came up with four runs in the ninth inning to upend the Redbirds there on August 13, 5-4, despite a triple, two doubles, and a single by Musial. Stan's defense helped beat the Bucs back in St. Louis on August 20. In the first inning he made a sixty-yard sprint and circus catch of a Ralph Kiner blooper with a man on base. In the second inning he made a somersaulting grab of a drive by Danny Murtaugh, then came up throwing to double Ed Stevens off first base. The Cards won, 7-4, and climbed to within a game of first place the following day by drubbing the Bucs, 9-2. "The Pounding Pole," as *The Sporting News* called Stan, singled twice, doubled, knocked in another run and scored two. The win was the Cards' seventeenth in twenty-three games.

Nonetheless, the Braves arrived in St. Louis on August 24 with a 2-1/2-game lead. Musial slugged a two-run homer off Sain in the first inning and made another diving catch of Phil Masi's liner to center in the sixth, but the Braves wore out Cardinal pitching, winning, 9-3. The next night Spahn applied a coat of whitewash, 2-0, and the Cards slid 4-1/2 games out. They weren't ready to fold just yet. Musial rallied his team to a doubleheader sweep of the Giants on August 26, deciding the second game with a two-run ninth-inning homer, 7-5. The Cards then swept another twin bill from the Giants, 5-4 and 7-6, as Stan won the lidlifter with a home run in the thirteenth inning.

Fading pennant hopes—The beginning of the end came on August 29, as the Dodgers came into town and took over first place by sweeping a doubleheader. Musial singled, doubled, and homered in the opener, but the Bums kayoed Brecheen with four runs in the first inning on the way to a 12-7 win before 33,826 fans. In the second game Musial tripled in two runs in the ninth inning to knot the score at 4-4, but Brooklyn got key pinch hits from Pete Reiser and Arky Vaughan in the tenth to win, 6-4. Shotton's Dodgers increased their lead to 1-1/2 games over Boston twenty-four hours later with another doubleheader sweep. Musial played with a wrenched knee, caused when he slipped on the dugout runway before the first game when he was besieged by a crowd of well-wishers and autograph seekers. He went hitless in six at-bats, dropping his average to .377.

Just when Shotton's magic seemed to be working wonders, the Dodgers went into a tailspin, dropping four of five in Chicago and then losing three of four to the Giants back at Ebbets Field. Durocher knocked his old team out of first place on September 3. The fate of the Dodgers and Cards was then sealed on September 6. Pittsburgh swept two from the Cards in the Smoky City, 2-1 and 4-1, while the Braves took two from the Bums in Beantown, 2-1 and 4-0. The next day Stan lined a 3-2 pitch from Fritz Ostermueller into a first-inning triple play in still another loss at Forbes Field.

Boston took a four game bulge over the new second-place team, Pittsburgh. The Braves would never be seriously challenged again, but Musial enjoyed a big September, leading the Cards to a second-place finish. On September 9, he was four for four with a double and triple knocking in two runs and scoring on a double steal as Brecheen blanked the Reds, 4-0. The next day Stan beat the Reds once more, 6-5, with an RBI single in the ninth inning, his 200th hit of the year. In the Cards' last visit to Brooklyn, Stan didn't manage a hit in four at-bats yet highlighted a 4-2 win by taking three hits away from Dodger batsmen with his glove. In the third inning he tumbled to the turf and rolled over to rob Jackie Robinson of a double. In the sixth frame he sprinted over to the exit gate in left center and flung his glove up to make a desperate grab of Pee Wee Reese's drive, stuffing a probable leadoff triple by the Dodger captain in his mitt. Then with two on and two out in the ninth, Brooklyn's Tommy Brown looped a short fly to center for an apparent two-run game-tying hit. But "The Man" raced in, dove hard and snatched the ball off the blades of the grass to preserve the victory.

Stan always took great pride in his fielding, and he

played all three outfield positions in 1948. He told Bob Broeg, "Over the years, I'm proud to say, I had some of my best days defensively when I wasn't hitting. I never said much, but I thought my share about players who would let their chins drag when not hitting so that their fielding was affected, too. If I couldn't beat 'em with my bat, I certainly hoped to try with my glove."

Stan had jammed his left hand making the circus catches but was in the lineup the next day. Dodger rookie Carl Erskine struck him on the right hand with a pitch early in the game, but Stan tied the score at 2-2 with his thirty-sixth homer in the eighth inning. Musial left Brooklyn with injuries to both hands. (Years later Erskine would answer the question of how he pitches to Musial by quipping, "I just throw him my best stuff, then run over to back up third base.")

September 22 at Braves Field was one of those rare days in which the wind was blowing out toward the small right field bleachers, nicknamed "the jury box" by Boston scribes. At the batting cage before the game, Broeg pointed to the flag at the right field foul poll and said to Stan, "A great day for the hitters, Banj." Musial then decided to rip the tape that had been protecting his injured wrists off and attempt to play without it. In the first inning he dumped a single to left off Spahn, punching the ball to the opposite field to lessen the strain on his wrists. In the third, Stan went to left again off Spahn, this time driving the ball over Mike McCormick's head for a double. In the fourth, new Braves' pitcher Charley Barrett tried to puzzle Musial with a changeup. Stan saw it coming and said to himself, "To hell with the wrists!" He pulled the ball into the jury box for a two-run homer. In the seventh, Stan grounded a single between third and short off Clyde Shoun for his fourth hit of the game. Stan was well aware that he needed just one more hit to tie Ty Cobb's major league record of four five-hit games in a season. Braves hurler Al Lyons missed badly with his first two pitches to Stan in the eighth. Lyons' third offering was just a bit outside but Stan hooked it between first and second for a seeing-eye single. In protecting his wrists, Stan had taken the minimum five swings to get his five safeties. In an earlier five-hit day that season, he had knocked out all five hits with two-strike counts.

As October opened, Musial slashed three more hits in a 6-4 win over the Cubs, breaking his previous personal best total of 228 safeties in a season. The next day, Stan broke Rogers Hornsby's single-season team record of 102 extra base hits by ripping his 46th double. The Cards clinched second place by drubbing the Cubs, 9-0.

Baseball's Perfect Knight—In games in which Musial hit safely, the Cards posted a 73-48 record. With a hitless Stan, the Cards were 12-21-1. It was said back then, "As Musial goes, so go the Cardinals." Musial led the NL in every hitting category except home runs. Red Schoendienst remembered, however, that Stan hit a ball at Shibe Park one day that struck the P.A. system above the fence and bounced back on the field. Umpire Frank Dascoli called it a double but Red was sure it should have been ruled a home run. With that homer Stan would have tied Kiner and Mize for the crown and led the league in everything. Stan also had a homer rained out in 1948.

In 1949 the Cardinals battled Brooklyn in another torrid pennant chase down to the last day of the season before missing the flag by a single game. That was St. Louis's last real pennant race for seven years. Musial, though, kept turning in great performances. He led the league in batting in 1950 (.346), 1951 (.355), 1952 (.336), and then again in 1957 (.351) at age 36. He was named *The Sporting News* Player of the Decade in 1956. Along the way he played in 896 consecutive games, establishing a new National Legue record, later broken by the Cubs' Billy Williams in 1969. In 1962, at age forty-one, Stan challenged for his eighth batting crown, finishing at .330. He also tied a major league record by hitting four home runs in succession that year, including three in one game against Casey Stengel's Mets.

Stan the Man was never thrown out of a major league game. He didn't berate writers or sound off in the press. He didn't second-guess his many managers and never got into fisticuffs on the field. Despite his calm demeanor Musial was a man of quiet toughness and stoic endurance. He did not scare easily. In 1953 Rogers Hornsby, then managing the Reds, ordered pitcher Clyde King to knock Musial down. King protested, "Rog, over the years I've gotten Musial out, I guess as good as anybody, and there's no point in knocking him down." But Hornsby was adamant. King then recalled, "Sure enough, I knocked him down. The ball went right up here (under the chin) and the bat went one way and his body went another way. And he hit the next pitch on the roof in right field. Home run! He killed it!"

In 1968, an eight-foot bronze statue of Musial was unveiled in front of the Cardinals' Busch Stadium. The inscription on the statue reads simply, "Here stands baseball's perfect warrior. Here stands baseball's perfect knight." That indeed was "Stan the Man."

1906 Chicago White Sox

A look at an underrated champion

Dave Larson

They were called the "Hitless Wonders." *Chicago Tribune* writer Hugh Fullerton wrote on August 21, 1906, "To those who have not seen the Sox in the wonderful winning streak, it is a wonder how they score so many runs on so few hits. Let them see the Sox take every advantage of misplays and let them see them dash daringly around the bases and invite wild throws. Let them follow the quick accurate work of the fielders and their keen teammates. These wonderful fans will solve for themselves the methods which are winning game after game."

1906 was in the midst of the Deadball Era. Offenses had plummeted from the high scoring 1890s. Just ten years earlier, the Boston Nationals had scored 1,025 runs in 135 games. The National League's batting average in 1897 had been .292, and the average team scored 793 runs. In 1906, with two leagues and sixteen teams, it would have been reasonable to expect even more offense in the face of diluted pitching talent. But in '06, the average National League team hit .244, with an average of 549 runs scored. The American League hit .249 per team, with an average of 562 runs scored.

Several things had happened to help reduce the scoring. In 1900, home plate was changed from a twelve-inch diamond, pointing toward the pitcher, to the present five-sided plate, seventeen inches wide. This did not expand the strike zone, but it did give the umpires a better look as pitches crossed the plate. Walks per team dropped by 17 percent from 1899 to 1901. The National League adopted the modern foul strike rule in 1901. Before this time, foul balls counted as nothing. The American League followed suit in 1903. Strikeouts per team rose 54 percent from 1899 to 1903.

Pitchers were perfecting the use of foreign substances. Twirlers used spit, slippery elm, paraffin, rosin, or anything imaginable to cause the ball to change its course. Balls were rarely taken out of play, and often only two balls were used during a game. Balls hit into the stands were returned to the umpire. Balls with soft sides, cuts, flat spots, were used to the pitcher's advantage. Shutouts per team jumped from 4.2 per team in '97 to 17.6 in '06. The White Sox hurled a record 32 shutouts on the season.

Players were becoming more adept defensively. Errors dropped from an average per team of 335—2.5 per game—in 1897, to 265—1.7 per game in 1906. Sacrifice hits jumped from 94 per team in 1897 to 168 per team in 1906.

Interestingly, stolen bases dropped from an average of 223 per team, in a 134 game season in '97, to 187 per team in 1906, for a 154 game season. Managers were hesitant to steal, potentially losing a valuable baserunner if caught. As the number of runs scored decreased, the value of a single baserunner or run increased.

Deadball Era players bunted for hits, sacrifice bunted, worked delayed and double steals, essayed

Dave Larson *is an operations manager in Orlando, Florida. He was the longtime spring training PA announcer for the Cincinnati Reds. This is his first article for SABR.*

hit-and-runs and bunt-and-runs. The squeeze play was still being perfected. Hitters were more defensive than offensive. They protected the plate, slapped at the ball, and played for one run.

In the field, the prevalence of the bunt required agile and skilled glovesmen at the corners, so the best defensive players usually manned first and third base. Catchers needed to be quick, with accurate arms.

Player-manager Fielder Jones embodied the White Sox. Jones would teach his team to play inside baseball, called by David Anderson in *More Then Merkle*, (University of Nebraska Press, 2000) "A mental game…a form of unrestrained psychological warfare from the first pitch to the last out." Inside baseball was the use of any play or ploy to gain an advantage.

Strong on the mound—The White Sox finished in second place in 1905, on the strength of the AL's best pitching staff. The team finished the season with a 92-60 record, just two games behind Philadelphia. Frank Owen paced the team with a 22-14 record, posting a 2.10 ERA. Nick Altrock finished with a 1.88 ERA and a 21-11 mark. The Sox led the AL with a 1.99 team ERA. Frank Smith won 19 games with a 2.13 ERA. Doc White added 18 victories with a 1.77 ERA. Ed Walsh was still perfecting his new out pitch in 1905. Used sparingly, Walsh had an 8-3 record and a 2.17 ERA.

Jiggs Donahue led the team with a .287 average and 76 RBIs. His RBI total was third best in the AL. Donahue also stole 32 bases. The Sox had a few players who stood out offensively in '05. Frank Isbell, in the role of utility player, hit .296 in 94 games. George Davis hit .278 with 31 stolen bases. Catcher Ed McFarland hit .280 in 80 games. But the Sox had four regulars who hit .201 or less.

Fielder Jones lost 75 percent of his outfield for 1906. He was the sole holdover. Danny Green, Ducky Holmes, and Nixey Callahan were gone. Green was banished to th minors after hitting .243. The thirty-six-year-old Holmes left the team after hitting just .201 to manage in the minors. Callahan left to play with and manage a semipro team he owned in the Chicago area. Callahan had been the most productive of the three, hitting .272 with 26 stolen bases and 43 RBIs.

The Athletics were the favorites going into the 1906 season as they returned virtually the same championship team. First baseman Harry Davis led the A's. Davis paced the American League in '05 in home runs, doubles, runs scored, and RBIs. They also had veterans Socks Seybold and Danny Murphy. The

Ed Walsh

pitching staff had three 20-game winners: Rube Waddell, Eddie Plank, and Andy Coakley. The A's also had a 16-game winner in twenty-two-year-old Chief Bender.

The Tigers, the third-place finishers, returned most of the same team and expected to have nineteen-year-old Ty Cobb for the full season. Cobb would team up with another future Hall of Famer, Sam Crawford. Detroit returned a pair of 22-game winners in George Mullin and Ed Killian. Boston, the fourth-place finisher, returned two of the AL's top starters, Jesse Tannehill and Cy Young. Player-manager Jimmy Collins led the Pilgrims in batting and RBIs.

Cleveland's performance suffered in 1905 as Nap Lajoie played in just 65 games. Lajoie's .329 average would have led the American League had he played more games. Lajoie was the best hitter in the AL and his availability for the full season made the "Naps" stronger. Lajoie, the team's player-manager, would have Elmer Flick in the outfield. Flick led the AL in batting, slugging, and triples in '05. Cleveland had Addie Joss to lead the pitchers.

The Highlanders struggled in 1905 but had two of the league's best twirlers in Jack Chesbro and Al Orth. Chesbro was just one year removed from his 41-victory season. The New Yorkers also had a fine young hitter in Hal Chase, and veterans Wee Willie Keeler and Kid Elberfeld. On paper, only St Louis and Washington didn't look competitive. Going into the 1906 season, the Sox had pitching and defense but little offense.

Position players—The White Sox were a strong defensive team. Jones led the team from center field with George Davis anchoring the infield. Davis, a future Hall of Famer, played shortstop and hit cleanup in 1906. Davis had started his major league career in 1890 with Cleveland. He proved to be an outstanding hitter early, hitting .355 in 1893. Davis hit over .300 for nine straight seasons, 1893-1901, all with New York. He led the National League in RBIs with 134 in 1897. He started his career in the outfield, moving to third base in 1893, and to shortstop in 1898.

Davis quickly became one of the best defenders in the game. *Total Baseball's* runs saved formula says Davis led the National League in that category in 1899 and 1900. According to those statistics, he saved 33 and 43 runs more then the average National League shortstop during those years. NL great Ozzie Smith, in comparison, saved 43 runs above average in his best season.

Davis was a clutch hitter. *Total Baseball's* clutch hitting formula claims Davis led the major leagues in 1906 with an index of 179. This shows that Davis's RBI total was 79 percent higher than expected. Davis led the team with 80 RBIs and 25 doubles. His .277 average was second on the team. Davis, who turned 36 during the season, was the oldest player on the roster. His experience helped anchor both the defense and offense.

The team's leading hitter for average in 1906 was Frank Isbell. Isbell played where he was needed, covering every position during his career. At second base in '06, this career .250 hitter paced the team with a .279 average. He also tied for second on the team with 57 RBIs and had a team-high 37 stolen bases. He hit 18 doubles and a team leading 11 triples. Not known for his power, he did set a World Series record, tagging four doubles in one game. Isbell was the team's weakest defensive player. He made five errors in the World Series.

The team's third baseman was Lee Tannehill, brother of Boston pitcher Jesse Tannehill. In 1906 Lee supplied less offense then any of his teammates with 100 at bats. Tannehill hit .183 with eight doubles, three triples, 33 RBIs, and seven steals. Tannehill was a career .220 hitter. Despite this offensive ineptitude, four different managers kept him in their lineups at shortstop and third base because of his great range and soft hands. *Total Baseball's* formula says Tannehill saved a league high 27 runs above average at third base in '06—in just 99 games. Tannehill led American League third basemen in assists four times and double plays twice. At shortstop in 1903, Tannehill led the league in double plays.

Jiggs Donahue manned first base, and batted .257 with 57 RBIs, 24 extra base hits, and 36 stolen bases. Like Tannehill, he played because of his defense. He led the league in fielding percentage 1905-1907, setting records during 1907 with 1,846 putouts and 1,998 total chances. He once recorded 21 putouts in a nine-inning game. *The National Game*, published in 1911, lists Donahue and Fred Tenney as the best first basemen of the day.

Jiggs was one of the stars of the '06 World Series. He hit a team-high .333, and had the only Sox hit in Game 2, breaking up Ed Reulbach's no-hit bid. Donahue played nine years and had a career batting average of .255.

The team's utility infielder was George Rohe. Rohe played mostly at third base during '06, hitting .256 with 25 RBIs. He was not a power hitter, getting just six extra base hits. Rohe, like most of the infield, excelled on defense, though he was the offensive star in the first two Sox World Series victories. When George Davis missed the first three games, Rohe started at third, with Tannehill moving to short. His heroics were such that when Davis returned to the lineup in Game 4, Rohe stayed at third base, with Tannehill going to the bench. Rohe's .333 average tied Donahue for the best in the Series. Afterwards, owner Charles Comiskey promised, "Whatever George Rohe may do from now on, he's signed for life with me!" Rohe was released after the 1907 season when he hit .214.

The Sox struggled when Billy Sullivan was not catching. During the Jones years, Sullivan was the principal catcher and the White Sox finished no lower than third place. In the years when he missed major portions of the season, the Sox finished over 30 games behind. Like so many other Sox, "Sully" was not in the lineup for his offense. His lifetime average of .212 is second lowest of all players with 3,000 at bats. He hit .214 in 1906 with 24 extra bases, 33 RBIs, with two home runs. But he was one of the finest defensive catchers of the day. Ty Cobb called him the best catcher "to ever wear shoe leather."

"Sully" missed 36 games in 1906, due to food poisoning and a hand injury. While Sullivan was out, the Sox tried four others to fill the spot. Ed McFarland got into seven games, hitting .136. Hub Hart caught 15 games, hitting .162. Frank Roth caught 15 games, hitting .196. Babe Towne, the most successful of the backups, hit .278 in 13 games.

To rebuild the outfield, the Sox brought in two journeymen. Bill O'Neill, a switch hitter, was entrusted with the leadoff spot early in the year, stole 19 bases, but his on-base percentage of .287 was unacceptable. O'Neill totaled just six extra-base hits and batted .248. He would be the team's fourth outfielder by midsummer.

Rube Vinson was purchased from Cleveland. He was the opening day left fielder, but made four errors in four games in the field and was gone after eight games.

On May 9, with the team's record at 8-8, the Sox acquired Ed Hahn. Hahn came to majors with New York at age 30 in 1905, played in 43 games, and hit .319. He started the '06 season hitting .091, though, and the Highlanders released him. Jones inserted him into the leadoff spot. Hahn was the sparkplug the Sox needed. He hit just .227 for the Sox but finished third in the league in walks and led the Sox in runs scored with 80.

Hahn was a sure-handed fielder without great range, who would lead the American League in fielding percentage in 1907. On a team with a pitching staff that induced ground balls, Hahn set a record that year for fewest putouts and chances for a full-time outfielder. Center fielder Jones was a speedy take-charge outfielder, so it is clear that Hahn conceded his manager any fly ball within reach.

Patsy Dougherty joined the team after being claimed off waivers. He had jumped the Highlanders in a contract dispute, hitting .192 at the time. After joining the Sox in late July, he hit .233 the rest of the season. He added 11 stolen bases, driving home 27 runs. He also hit one of the team's seven home runs. Like Fielder Jones, he was a good, fast outfielder, and he finishing just one percentage point behind his league-leading manager in fielding percentage.

Patsy was the first American League player to hit two home runs in a World Series, doing it for Boston in 1903. He was also, after the 1906 Series, the first AL player to appear on two championship teams

The Sox unsuccessfully tried a few other players during the season. Frank Hemphill played 13 games in the outfield and hit .075. Shortstop Lee Quillen played in four games, going three of nine at the plate. Gus Dundon saw action as a backup middle infielder, appearing in 33 games, getting 96 at bats, and batting .136.

Leadership—In 1906 manager Fielder Jones, a lifetime .285 hitter, batted a career low .230, but he finished second in the league in walks. He had 28 extra-base hits including two homers. He also swiped 26 bases. He was considered, offensively and defensively, one of the best outfielders in the game. While he never led a league in any offensive category, he finished second in runs scored twice and second in walks four times. Jones stole 359 bases in his career, finishing in the top ten five times.

Jones took over the managerial role with the White Sox on June 8, 1904. The Sox had been sputtering with a 22-18 mark under Nixey Callahan, who was considered too soft on the players. Jones demanded discipline, and led the Sox to a 67-47 record to finish the season in third place. The Sox would finish no worse than third in the seasons he managed.

Defensively, Fielder lived up to his name. His career fielding percentage is 17 percentage points higher then the league average during his years. In comparison, Tris Speaker, known for his defensive prowess, finished his career with a difference of ten points above the league average. Mixing modern computations with traditional statistics, Jones's range factor is 18 percentage points higher than league averages. He led his league in outfield double plays, fielding percentage, range factor, and putouts, twice each. *The STATS All-Time Baseball Sourcebook* selected Jones as one of the Gold Glove outfielders for the decade from 1901 through 1910.

The ballpark and the pitchers—The Sox played at the 39th Street Grounds (a.k.a. South Side Park), four blocks south of the new Comiskey Park. The ball yard was similar to others of the day with an extremely large outfield. The Sox kept the infield grass long and the ground soft to slow down ground balls. In 1906 the park was very good to the team. The White Sox had a winning percentage of .701 at home, as opposed to .527 on the road. The park helped cut down on home runs and scoring. The White Sox hit just two home runs at the 39th Street Grounds in '06. Their opponents tallied just one. While on the road, the Sox hit five roundtrips, while allowing ten. The Sox scored equally at home and on the road, tallying 275 runs at home compared to 295 on the road.

The large ballpark did help the team's pitching staff. Sox hurlers allowed just 180 runs at home, while giving up 280 on the road. Chicago finished second in the league in ERA with a 2.13 mark. The staff tossed 32 shutouts—a record that still stands. Over a third of the team's victories came from shutouts. The rest of the American League averaged 15 shutouts per team.

Righthander Frank Owen led the staff with 22 wins, appearances with 42, starts with 36, and innings pitched with 293. For the year, Owen had a 2.33 ERA. Owen was a workhorse for three years, 1904-1906, winning 64 games. He would earn just 18 more victories during his career, which ended during the '09 season. He finished with a lifetime 2.55 ERA and an 82-67 record.

Guy "Doc" White was a graduate of Georgetown University, with a degree in dental surgery. He led the league in ERA in 1906, with a 1.52 ERA in 219 innings. White started 24 games, appearing in 28, going 18-6. Ty Cobb, who hit a lifetime .197 against White, called the lefty the toughest pitcher he ever faced. White's mark of 65 innings pitched without issuing a walk was once an AL record. He won thirteen 1-0 shutouts during his career and once held the major league record of tossing 45 consecutive scoreless innings. His lifetime record was 187-156 with a 2.39 ERA. Like his teammates, White was a good fielder. He twice led American League pitchers in fielding percentage. He is certainly one of the best pitchers not in the Hall of Fame.

Future Hall of Famer Ed Walsh emerged as a star in 1906, when he mastered the spitball. Sam Crawford, in *The Glory of Their Times*, described Walsh and what it was like to hit against him, "Great big, strong, good-looking fellow. He threw a spitball—I think that ball disintegrated on the way to the plate and the catcher put it back together again. I swear, when it went past the plate it was just the spit went by." Walsh understood the psychology of the spitter. He would use the spitter to set up his other pitches. The threat of the spitter once got Nap Lajoie to strike out

looking with the bases loaded. Lajoie watched a fastball cut across the heart of the plate while expecting a spitter to dip low and out of the strike zone.

In 1906, "Big Ed" appeared in 41 games, starting 31, and went 17-13 with a 1.88 ERA. Walsh led the league with 10 shutouts and the team with 171 strikeouts. Walsh's lifetime ERA of 1.82 is the lowest in the history of the game.

Walsh's spitter was said to head towards the plate and then "dart two feet down or out." An example of how many ground balls the pitch created comes from Walsh's 1907 season. Walsh set a record for handling 262 chances, registering a total of 227 assists. He tied a record, set by Nick Altrock, for most chances by a pitcher in a game with 13. A comparison between Walsh and Nolan Ryan shows how the game has changed. Ryan, who pitched 27 years, had a career total of 546 assists, or about 20 per season. Walsh had a career total of 1,207 assists. From 1906 to 1912, Walsh averaged 127 assists. STATS lists Walsh as their Gold Glove pitcher of the decade.

The Sox other 20-game winner in 1906 was Nick Altrock, who, like so many of his teammates, was a fine fielder, twice leading American League pitchers in putouts and double plays. Altrock posted a 20-13 record and a 2.06 ERA. He tossed 288 innings, walking just 42 batters, which is just 1.3 walks per nine innings. The lefthander had won a total of 42 games in the two previous seasons. The lefty's 62 wins during that three-year span were 75 percent of his career totals. 1906 was Altrock's last good year. Many of his later appearances came while he was coaching with the Senators. His last appearance, in 1933, was a stunt to give him appearances in five decades. His career record was 83-75 with an ERA of 2.67.

The fifth Sox hurler during 1906 was Roy Patterson. Patterson was signed after he pitched a sandlot team to victory against Comiskey's St. Paul Saints. In 1901, Patterson went 20-16 for the Sox. He won 19 games in 1902 and 15 in 1903. Patterson has the distinction of having won the first ever American League game. He finished his major league career in 1907 with an 81-73 record and a 2.75 ERA.

Patterson showed some of his former brilliance during the 1906 season. He started 18 games, pitched in 21, and posted a 10-7 record with a 2.09 ERA. In 1906 the Sox allowed a league-low 255 bases on balls (1.66 per nine innings), as opposed to the league average 354. Patterson led the Chicago staff, allowing just 1.07 walks per nine innings.

Frank Smith was the sixth pitcher on the staff. Smith pitched in 20 games, starting 13. He went 5-5, with a team-high 3.39 ERA. Despite his two career no-hitters, and his two career 20-win seasons, Smith was not popular. He crossed up his catchers so often that they feared for their safety.

During the season, Jones also gave a few innings work to twenty-one-year-old Lou Fiene. Fiene got into six games, starting two. He had a 1-1 record on the season and a 2.90 ERA. He played in parts of four seasons, compiling a record of 3-8 with a 3.85 ERA.

The pennant race—The Athletics started 1906 strong. They had the league's best record through July. The A's four starters drove the team's early success. The Highlanders settled in as the league's second-best club. Cleveland started strong when Bob Rhodes and Otto Hess proved that Addie Joss wasn't alone on the staff.

The White Sox sat in sixth place at the end of May, improved to fifth in June, and to fourth by the end of July. They caught fire in August. The "Hitless Wonders" won 19 straight games, starting with back-to-back-to-back shutouts by Doc White, Ed Walsh, and Roy Patterson. The streak, which set an American League record, vaulted the Sox from nine games back into first place. The Highlanders and Naps kept pace as the A's fell out of contention.

During the win streak, the Sox scored 97 runs, an average of 5.1 per game—1.4 over their season average. Opponents scored just 31 runs. The Sox beat league leaders New York and Philadelphia for 13 of their 19 wins, defeating Cy Young (twice), Chief Bender, Rube Waddell, Eddie Plank, Jack Chesbro, Al Orth, and Jesse Tannehill. Walsh carried the Sox, winning seven games, four by shutout. One of the keys to the streak was that Jones finally had a set lineup after a season of injuries.

The Highlanders caught and passed the Sox three times in September. But Chicago, who won 21 of their 25 August games, stayed hot. They closed out the season going 22-12 in September and October, finishing three games in front of New York and five in front of Cleveland. Chicago, out of the race at the end of July, battled its way to the pennant. In the National League, the cross-town Cubs, dominant, moved into first place late in May and stayed there.

The Sox started slowly because they were plagued with small, nagging injuries, which at one point forced them to hire the trainer from the University of Chicago. Only one Sox player, Jiggs Donahue, stayed healthy for the entire season.

To win the pennant, the Sox defeated two powerful rivalss that were similar in many ways to the potent cross-town Cubs. The Highlanders, for example, had the two winningest pitchers in the league: Al Orth with 27 and Jack Chesbro with 24. The New Yorkers also finished second in the league in runs scored and batting average. Hal Chase, Willie Keeler, and Kid Elberfeld all hit .300.

The third-place Naps were an even closer match to the Cubs. Cleveland led the league in batting, slugging, and runs scored. It had four .300 hitters, led by Nap Lajoie's .355. Claude Rossman, Bunk Congalton, and Elmer Flick also hit .300. The Naps pitching staff had three 20-game winners and the league's best ERA.

The method—Playing and managing in the Deadball Era, Jones's managerial style was designed to take ruthless advantage of his opponent's mistakes and weaknesses. On defense, the 1906 White Sox were the second-best fielding team in the American League, making 27 fewer errors then the league average. They also allowed the fewest unearned runs in the league. The team was dubbed the "Hitless Wonders" because of their league-worst .230 batting average. The Sox were also last in slugging, 70 points behind the leader.

The Sox did have some punch, as measured in Deadball terms. They finished third in runs scored and also did well in walks (first), hit by pitches (first), stolen bases (third) and sacrifices (first). Nonetheless, this was a team that did more with less. They scored 570 runs and allowed 460. Applying these statistics to a modern formula, *STATS* estimates that the Sox should have had a record of 84-69, rather than their actual 93-58. The team overachieved by nine games.

Again using individual statistics and a modern formula, *Total Baseball* estimates that the 1906 White Sox should have scored a total of 531 runs, a total they surpassed by 39 runs. *Total Baseball*'s modern clutch-hitting index implies that this improvement was largely due to good hitting under pressure. The White Sox had an index of 111, the best in the majors.

Addie Joss, Cleveland Hall of Famer, described playing against Chicago, "The Sox are game to the core. They can stand the gaff with the best of them. They have the spirit and they make the inside play. When you go in the box against Chicago, you know you've got to pitch. That is the greatest secret of their success. They always make the pitcher pitch. Hahn, Dougherty, Jones, and that bunch won't swing at anything unless it's right over the plate. A pitcher who can cut the plate can beat them." Few could.

The Series matchup—On paper, the 1906 World Series was a mismatch. Frank Chance, the Cub first baseman, hit .319 compared to Jiggs Donahue's .257. Cub third baseman Harry Steinfeldt hit .327 to Lee Tannehill's .183. But the White Sox were about to demonstrate that the matchups to be concerned with are pitchers and defense against hitters.

Only one sportswriter, Hugh Fullerton, understood that the White Sox could beat the Cubs. Fullerton's editor refused to run a column before the Series in which he predicted a Sox victory. Fullerton's theory was that the Sox played with brains first, and then feet and hands.

The Sox were 3-1 underdogs going into the World Series. The Cubs led the National League in ERA (1.76), batting average (.262), runs scored, slugging, and stolen bases. They set a never-to-be matched record of 116 victories in a 154-game season. But they had not faced the same strength of opponent as the Sox.

Five teams in the American League had played .500 ball or better in 1906, and only two were truly bad teams. The American League's sixth-place team had a better record then the National's fourth place team. Only three teams in the Senior Circuit played .500 ball or better.

Jones had instilled an aggressive nature into his team. The Sox may have been hitless, but they knew how to manufacture runs. The Sox could scramble for runs whereas the Cubs were used to bashing their way to victory. But the White Sox were unlikely victims for a bashing. The Cubs hadn't faced a pitching staff like that of the Sox. Jones felt that the Cubs were susceptible to lefthanders and spitballers. On the season the Cubs had faced just four lefties who ultimately had double-figure victories and a winning record. Nick Altrock, Doc White, and Ed Walsh were pitchers who fit the bill to defeat the Cubs.

Jones knew that his players, who had just come through a grinding pennant race against two tough clubs, would not be in awe of the team from the West Side. He also felt the Cubs would be overconfident. Cubs' manager Frank Chance proved that by announcing before the Series that "we'll use our second-string pitchers."

Chance was not yet the field general Fielder Jones was. The Cubs' "Peerless Leader" had a great eye for talent but underestimated the Sox. He was known as a hunch manager and one who would fight to force players to do it his way. Jones, on the other hand, was an innovator and a great motivator. He is credited, for example, with creating the motion infield to defend against bunts. He created the "body-twist slide." He carefully and successfully positioned his fielders according to batter, pitcher, and situation.

The National Game mentions a game in which the St. Louis Browns had loaded the bases against Jones's White Sox, with no outs. Jones warmed up all his pitchers and brought in a different one to get each of the next three hitters. The Sox escaped without a run being scored. The article indicates this was the first time this tactic had been used.

The 1906 World Series—The World Series captured Chicago's imagination, and the city almost ground to a halt. The series was to be played on consecutive days, alternating from park to park. Many expected the powerful Cubs to sweep, especially since the Sox would be missing shortstop George Davis, who was out with a sore back. The Cubs won the coin flip for the home field advantage. The Cubs opened the Series with their ace Mordecai "Three-Finger" Brown in West Side Park. Brown dominated the NL, going 26-6 with a 1.04 ERA on the season.

The Sox countered with lefthander Nick Altrock. The two twirlers were perfect through three innings. The bitter October cold added to the batters' troubles. The Sox scored first in the fifth as George Rohe tripled to left. He scored on a comebacker to the mound by Patsy Dougherty when catcher Johnny Kling couldn't handle Brown's throw to the plate. The Sox scored again in the sixth. Altrock walked, was sacrificed to second and tried to score on a Jones single. Altrock was out at the plate with Jones going to second on the play. After moving to third on a passed ball, Jones scored on a single by Frank Isbell.

The Cubs mustered a run in the bottom of the frame, getting two men on, with one scoring after a sacrifice and wild pitch. The Sox held the lead to win, 2-1. Altrock and Brown both tossed great games, each allowing just four hits and one walk. The Sox pitching shut down the Cub offense, while the offense scratched out enough runs to win. Fielder Jones was heard to say, "This should prove the leather is mightier than the wood."

Game 2 moved to the South Side, where Ed Reulbach and Doc White faced off. Reulbach had a strong second season with the Cubs, going 19-4 with a 1.65 ERA. He pitched the biggest game of his career, while White struggled in the cold, gave up three runs in the second, another in the third, and was gone. Frank Owen pitched the final six innings, giving up three more Cub runs.

In classic Sox fashion, they scored in the fifth without a hit. Donahue led off with a walk. After a force out at second on a grounder from Dougherty, Johnny Evers threw wild to first, allowing Dougherty to move to second. With two out, Joe Tinker booted a grounder, allowing the run to score.

Reulbach took a no-hit bid into the seventh inning before Jiggs Donahue slapped a single to center. It was the only Sox hit. The 7-1 victory allowed the scribes to gloat that the Cubs had hit their mark and were ready to finish off the Sox. Future commissioner, Judge Kenesaw Mountain Landis asked Sox fans, "what league is it your team plays in?"

Game 3 move backed to West Side Park, as Ed Walsh took the mound against rookie Jack Pfiester. Pfiester had gone 20-8 with a 1.51 ERA. The Cubs threatened with two hits in the first but a caught stealing took them out of the inning. That would be the only Cub scoring opportunity. Walsh did not allow another hit.

The game was scoreless through five. Pfiester had little trouble with the Sox until the sixth when Lee Tannehill led off with a single. After Walsh walked, Pfeister hit Ed Hahn with a pitch. The lefty bore down with bases loaded, getting Jones to foul out and fanning Isbell. Next up was fill-in Rohe. Kling taunted Rohe, calling him "busher," saying he wouldn't get a pitch to hit. Rohe responded with a triple. Walsh retired nine of the next ten batters to seal the 3-0 victory.

The Sox only had four hits and two walks, but, as they had done all season, found a way to score when needed. The National League's best-hitting team got just two hits and a walk off Walsh, who fanned 12.

Game 4 featured the pitching matchup from Game 1, only this time at the White Sox home field. The Sox were buoyed by the return of George Davis. Altrock pitched a fine game, allowing seven hits, a walk, and a single run. But Three-Finger Brown was better. The future Hall of Famer allowed just two hits and two walks. The Sox got just one runner to third.

The Cubs threatened early but baserunning mistakes took them out of innings. They finally got to Altrock in the seventh. Hahn lost Frank Chance's fly ball in the sun for a single. After being sacrificed to second and third, Chance scored on Tinker's two-out single. The Cubs' 1-0 victory was the fourth for the visitors in four games.

After Game 4, Fielder Jones tongue-lashed his team, especially Isbell. The Sox had just 11 hits in four games. Isbell was 1 for 16 at this point and had committed three errors. Jones himself was just 1 for 15. Yet the Sox had split the first four games. Sox

pitching, with the exception of Game 2, had held the powerful Cubs to 13 hits and two runs.

Ed Walsh was given the start in Game 5, as Jones passed over Doc White. The Cubs countered with the curveballer Reulbach. The Sox scored one in the top of the first, as Isbell doubled home Hahn. The Cubs struck back with three in the bottom of the frame, taking advantage of two errors, including another by Isbell.

The Sox tied the game in the third with two doubles, one being Isbell's second of the game, and a perfect double steal. Reulbach exited. The "Hitless Wonders" exploded in the fourth, scoring four runs on four hits, including three doubles, and two walks. Isbell hit his third double of the game during the rally. Down 7-3, the Cubs got a run back in the fourth on a double steal, with Tinker stealing home. The Sox got that run back in the sixth when Isbell hit his fourth double of the game, scoring on a Rohe single.

Walsh was knocked out of the game in the sixth, when the Cubs scored two on a bases-loaded double by "Wildfire" Schulte. Doc White finished the game for the Sox, saving the 8-6 win. The "Hitless Wonders" scored eight runs on 12 hits, walking four times. The Sox had eight doubles in the game, including Isbell's record four. Jack Pfiester and Orval Overall mopped up for the Cubs after Reulbach was removed.

Chicago was in a state of shock. The upstarts from the South Side had beaten the mighty Cubs three times in their own park. For Game 6, Frank Chance passed over a couple of rested pitchers to throw his ace, Brown, on one day's rest. The Sox countered with White, even though he pitched three innings the day before. Fielder Jones still wanted the lefty against the Cubs.

The Cubs got to White in the first as Solly Hoffman singled, and scored on a double by Schulte. But Brown clearly didn't have his best stuff. He was tagged for three runs in the bottom of the first and knocked from the box in the second, when the Sox scored four more runs. The "Wonders" ripped Brown and reliever Overall for 14 hits and three walks.

George Davis drove in three runs on two hits. Jiggs Donahue drove in three runs, going two for four. White went the distance, scattering seven hits and four walks, as the Cubs stranded nine baserunners. The White Sox won easily, 8-3. The World Series Championship was theirs.

Peter M. Gordon gives a more complete account of the series in the 1990 edition of The Baseball Research Journal. The journal's editor titled Gordon's article "The Greatest World Series Upset of All Time." But was it an upset? Fielder Jones clearly understood what it took to win. He had disciplined his team to win against all odds. The Sox played the same style of ball that they were successful at during the season. The Cubs had their style of play taken away from them.

Chance's team had opportunities during the Series but wasted them with mental errors like baserunning mistakes. Nor could the Cubs take advantage of Sox mistakes or get a timely hit. The White Sox "outhit" the Cubs on the Series, .198 to .196. The Sox pitchers finished the series with an ERA of 1.50, to the Cubs' ERA of 3.40. The White Sox put 55 runners on base via hit or walk, stranding 33.

Doc White

We did not play our game, and that's all there is to it." Chance was right, the Cubs didn't play their game. The Sox didn't let them.

Fielder Jones said of his team, "They were a club that a manager could depend upon. Called the 'Hitless Wonders,' it is true that their batting was light. But they hit at the right time, as you will notice if you look up the record. Every man knew his business. Baseball was at their fingertips. They won games because they were good ballplayers, and a good ballplayer can't be manufactured out of batting averages."

The Cubs were a dominant team of the era, going

The Cubs put 54 men on base via hit or walk, stranding 36. The White Sox had poor defense during the Series, making 15 errors compared to seven for the Cubs. The Sox scored 22 runs in the six games while the Cubs scored 18.

Fielder Jones was a daring, aggressive player and manager. His team possessed the same qualities. The aging Henry Chadwick noted that the White Sox "won on generalship alone." Cubs manager Frank Chance honored the Sox victory, but also said, "There is one thing I will never believe, and that is the White Sox are a better ball club than the Cubs.

to the World Series three times in the next four years, winning two championships. But the White Sox were also a strong team, not by any means a fluke. They averaged 90 wins per season in the Jones years while the first-place American League teams averaged 92. In 1905 and 1908, the Sox lost chances at pennants when the first place teams played fewer games.

The Sox were built to play and win in the Deadball Era. The Sox played inside baseball, and used their talents to the utmost. Fielder Jones also taught the Cubs and Frank Chance a lesson: don't take anything for granted.

Cliff Kachline

Baseball man and SABR pioneer

Bob Obojski

Cliff Kachline has been deeply involved in sports: writing, sports memorabilia, and almost everything else connected with sports—especially baseball—for more than a half century, and through it all he's maintained his boundless energy, youthful high spirits, and keen sense of humor.

In *The Politics of Glory: How the Baseball Hall of Fame Really Works*, Bill James devoted an entire chapter to Kachline's near fourten-year tenure as the Hall of Fame's historian, from 1969 to late 1982.

Kachline, a native of Quakerstown, Pennsylvania (a town of about 7,000, thirty-five miles north of Philadelphia), began his career in 1940 as a $7-a-week printer's apprentice and writer with his hometown weekly. Shortly after taking the job he almost lost his right hand in a printing press accident. Despite winding up with a stiff, slightly-crooked right wrist, he quickly learned to type rapidly and accurately. The following summer he became a full-time correspondent for a nearby daily, the Bethlehem *Globe-Times*. In the fall of 1942, he was named sports editor of *The North Penn Reporter*, a daily in Lansdale.

Early in 1940, *The Sporting News* carried an advertisement promoting the first edition of its new *Baseball Register*. The ad showed the year-by-year stats of two prominent players as they were to appear in the *Register*. Kachline noticed three mistakes in the record of one player—Frank McCormick, the 1939 National League MVP—and dashed off a letter to publisher, J. G. Taylor Spink, in hopes that the errors could be corrected before publication.

Within a matter of days, Spink wrote back to ask if Cliff would be interested in proofreading the entire *Register*. He jumped at the opportunity and soon received a huge package containing galley proofs of the major and minor league career records of 400 players. The book was due to go to press, so he had only a week to check the material.

The following winter, by then recovering from his hand injury, he was again asked by Spink to check the records. Now armed with a copy of *Who's Who in Baseball* and other sources, he spent four weeks at the family's kitchen table with the help of his mother, comparing and reviewing the latest proofs and correcting many errors and typos.

Early in April, 1943, Spink invited the twenty-one-year-old Kachline to come to St. Louis to work full-time on the publication's staff. In those days, *The Sporting News* covered major and minor league baseball only, and nearly all its reference books were baseball oriented.

For nearly a quarter century, Kachline wrote countless features and news articles, credited and uncredited, for TSN, and by the early 1950s his byline began appearing on front page news stories as well as on features on the inside pages. For much of that time, he also edited all of *The Sporting News* stan-

Bob Obojski, *a SABR member since 1974, has written nine books on baseball, and several thousand articles on the diamond game. Among his best known books are:* Bush League: A History of Minor League Baseball *(Macmillan, 1975),* The Rise of Japanese Baseball Power *(Chilton, 1975), and* Baseball's Zaniest Moments *(Sterling, 1999).*

dard reference books, including the annual *Official Baseball Guide*, the *Baseball Dope Book*, *Baseball Register*, *Knotty Problems* and others. These annuals are now collector's items, and it doesn't take the baseball hobbyist long to find out that vintage editions in good shape sell at many, many times their cover price.

The *Official Baseball Guide* represented a prime off-season assignment for him starting in 1948. Spalding and Reach had published guides from the early 1880s through 1939. In 1940 and 1941 they joined forces to produce a single annual. In 1942 *The Sporting News* took over the publication of the annual and has continued to do so to this day. For the first few years, the *TSN* guides rated a bit below the caliber of the old Reach and Spalding annuals, but once Kachline got fully in harness in St. Louis in the late 1940s, the contents were much improved.

TSN guides of that period are now considered classics. The 1954 volume, for example, contains 576 pages, lots of photographs, the official averages of the majors and the thirty-eight minor leagues, and the official playing and scoring rules. The few full-page ads are primarily from sporting goods companies. The price of the publication was $1, but as Kachline noted: "I don't think Taylor Spink was too concerned about making any real profit from the Guides."

In its earliest issues, *TSN* cut down on the space given to obituaries of baseball figures, but under Kachline, the obit section of the guide contained accounts of anyone who played even a single game in the majors. Each year starting in 1947 he collected dozens of interesting and noteworthy filler items to round out the pages, wrote special features, and created a detailed account of the history of the preceding major league season, an account that dominated the forepart of the *TSN* guides.

Kachline was also a stickler for getting his stats straight. For example, when Bob Feller, Cleveland's fireballing righthander, struck out 348 batters in 1946, his accomplishment was thought to be the all-time major league strikeout record for one season, surpassing the 343 K's chalked up by lefthander Rube Waddell of the Philadelphia Athletics in 1904. Kachline, however, researched Waddell's 1904 season boxscore by boxscore, and proved that Waddell had actually fanned 349, a figure that was eventually accepted by the baseball establishment. (Waddell's record was subsequently broken by Sandy Koufax and Nolan Ryan, though he still holds the single-season American League record for a lefthander.)

"You'd be surprised at the number of mistakes that official scorers make when they turn in their scoresheets," Kachline emphasized. "Lots of times they're under deadline pressure to complete those scoresheets, and they don't bother to check out all the key stats."

In 1983, *The Sporting News* received game-by-game breakdowns of Nap Lajoie's 1901 batting record, which two researchers from different parts of the country had compiled from boxscores. For years Lajoie had been listed with 220 hits and a .405 average for that season instead of the .422 with which he was originally credited. One of the researchers came up with 229 hits, the other with 232. Spink turned the matter over to Kachline. Because the official American League statistical compilations no longer existed, this presented a problem similar to that involving the Waddell strikeout total. Since the league's president, Ban Johnson, and statistician were both headquartered in Chicago, Cliff figured the final official 1901 averages would first have been published in Chicago newspapers. He arranged to obtain photocopies; they credited Lajoie with 229 hits and a .422 average. Kachline, with his knowledge of printing, realized that type-set proofs of the averages could easily have had a smudged "9" that was interpreted as a zero, thus explaining the erroneous 220 hits instead of 229.

More recently Kachline was involved in the research of several other records which were in dispute, including Hack Wilson's major league RBI record. (See Cliff's article on page 76.) In 1999 the Commissioner's office formally endorsed the finding that Wilson had 191 RBIs—rather than 190—for the Chicago Cubs in 1930.

The two standard references in recent years—*The Baseball Encyclopedia* and *Total Baseball*—have disagreed on the stats of numerous players. Kachline believes there should be one authority to rule on discrepancies—such as the Official Records Committee that functioned from 1975 through 1982 with the approval of the Commissioner's office.

In the mid-1960s Kachline served a two-year term as president of the St. Louis chapter of the Baseball Writers' Association of America. He was the first *TSN* staff member ever to hold that position. BBWAA officers are usually affiliated with metropolitan dailies based in and around major league cities. He remains an honorary BBWAA member.

On to the Hall of Fame—In May 1967, Kachline left *The Sporting News* after twenty-four years to become public relations director of the newly-formed United Soccer Association, then headquartered in New York

City. The owners of several major league baseball clubs, including Roy Hofheinz, Gabe Paul, and John Allyn, as well as such sports entrepreneurs as Lamar Hunt and Jack Kent Cooke, had teams in the league. Late that year, following a merger with a rival circuit, the league was renamed North American Soccer League. After two seasons, it folded, and Kachline found himself in the job market.

When Lee Allen, historian of the Baseball Hall of Fame, died in May, 1969, Hall president Paul Kerr contacted former baseball Commissioner Ford Frick for his recommendation of someone to fill the position. Frick recommended Kachline, and he occupied the role of Hall of Fame historian for nearly fourteen years before being dismissed at the end of October 1982 in what Bill Madden, prominent New York *Daily News* baseball writer, termed "a surprise move that reeks of in-house politics."

The Hall of Fame historian post wielded considerable influence through the whole baseball community. Because Kachline possessed a strong personality and an encyclopedic knowledge of the sport, he helped to make the position more significant than ever before.

One important and time-consuming chore involved responding to the hundreds upon hundreds of letters and phone calls from fans, visitors, writers, major league clubs, and even former players seeking information.

He developed a booklet that detailed the history of the Hall of Fame, and included historical and statistical information on each member. He also prepared the inscriptions for the bronze plaques of newly-elected HOF inductees. When a major $3,000,000 expansion, renovation and updating of the institution was begun in the mid-1970s, he was given the assignment of coordinating efforts with the design firm and editing the captions of the new exhibits.

The contacts he had developed with many baseball officials during his years at *The Sporting News* proved of immense benefit to the Hall of Fame. During his first year there he realized that many major league teams were storing historically valuable material such as correspondence, contracts, financial records, and old publications, and that this material might eventually be disposed of. He wrote to all twenty-six clubs suggesting that the Hall would be interested in looking over such material and salvaging important items for the Hall of Fame archives.

Dick Wagner, Cincinnati's assistant general manager, was the first to respond. The Reds were preparing to move from old Crosley Field to new Riverfront Stadium later in the season, and Wagner invited Kachline to come to Cincinnati to sift through the storage area under Crosley's stands. After a quick look, he realized he had come across a veritable goldmine of baseball players, both major and minor league. The cards, dating back to 1902 and compiled under the aegis of club president Garry Herrmann, listed the clubs to which the player belonged each year.

Kachline visited many clubs during the next few years, before his involvement in the museum expansion forced him to change his focus. Among his other acquisitions were Yankees' financial ledgers from the 1920s and 1930s, historic documents from the files of the Commissioner's office, and the player card files that the National Association no longer needed when the minor league headquarters were moved from Columbus, Ohio, to Florida.

"With the materials we found on those scavenging expeditions and those donated by various clubs and the Commissioner's office, the Hall of Fame Library grew into an enormous collection of valuable source material, such as team yearbooks, roster guides, World Series programs, World Series films, photographs, old scorecards, documents and similar items," Kachline commented. "And almost all has been liberally used by researchers."

Kachline quickly realized that the number of visitors to the Hall of Fame fell far short of what he felt it should be. Attendance during his first year there (1969) was reported as 191,000. With the approval of the Hall's higher-ups, he worked with Tom Dawson, then director of radio and TV for the Commissioner's office, to arrange for free promos for the Hall on Game of the Week telecasts, and he induced the individual clubs to run the spots, too. The museum's attendance began rising steadily.

Noting that almost no major league club officials ever visited Cooperstown except when their team played in the annual Hall of Fame game, Kachline suggested in 1973 that an attempt be made to get the general managers to hold their annual fall meeting in the so-called "Home of Baseball." At the time the village's only hotel, which like the Hall of Fame was controlled by the Clark family, closed before the World Series ended, but he nevertheless was given the okay to pursue the idea. Through his contacts with Frank Cashen, then with the Baltimore Orioles, a proposal to have the general managers meet in Cooperstown the following year was approved at the GMs' October 1973 session in Scottsdale, Arizona. Unfortunately, when Kachline relayed word of the decision, Hall president Paul Kerr changed his mind about keeping the hotel open a few extra days to accommodate the group. As a result, Cooperstown did not host an official meeting of major league executives until the owners' meeting there in the fall of 1999.

An indication of the respect which baseball officials had for Kachline was exhibited when he was asked to serve as editor of the Official World Series program. Prior to 1974, each World Series team produced its own program. With expansion and the divisional playoffs, there were occasions when eight or more clubs spent considerable time and money preparing a program, only to fail to reach the Series. To eliminate the wasted efforts, it was agreed that the Commissioner's office would handle production of the Series programs. Kachline served as editor from 1974 through 1977 before the Commissioner's office decided to handle the entire project in-house.

Another tribute to Kachline's abilities and dedication came late in 1979. A dozen years after he had left The Sporting News, the publisher called to inquire if he would again write the lengthy Review of the Year that he had made an important feature of the Official Baseball Guide. Chicago writer Jerome Holtzman had handled this assignment during the intervening twelve years but had decided to discontinue doing so. Kachline's accounts appeared in the Guides of 1980 through 1991 before he chose to relinquish the role.

Other significant innovations which Kachline was responsible for during his tenure with the Hall of Fame included the Baseball Today exhibit and having Museum attendants outfitted in distinctive red jackets. "The Museum had attendants available to assist visitors who might have questions, but it was almost impossible to distinguish them from visitors," Kachline said. "On a scavenging trip to St. Louis, I spotted a long rack of red jackets. It turned out the ushers at Cardinal games wore them one season, but complained it was too hot for jackets. The Hall of Fame arranged to buy a dozen or so from the Cardinals." As for the Baseball Today exhibit, the Museum previously had essentially no display devoted to the current teams. The new exhibit featured the uniform, player, manager, and stadium photos, of each major league team and proved to be extremely popular, especially among younger visitors.

Shortly after Kachline's departure from the Hall of Fame in 1982, he sent an open two-page letter addressed "To the Commissioner, league presidents, general managers, PR directors and other interested parties" detailing events that led up to his dismissal. The strongly-worded letter concluded with this statement: "If all of this has you puzzled, you can appreciate my bafflement. After 40 years of close association with baseball–dating from my start with The Sporting News in 1943—developments at the Baseball Hall of Fame have left me wondering whether the best interests of baseball are always being served."

Since Kachline's departure, the title "Hall of Fame historian" has also disappeared. Functions of that office are now spread out among several members of the Hall of Fame staff.

SABR—Early in 1983, Cliff accepted the newly-created position of executive director of the Society for American Baseball Research (SABR). He was one of sixteen baseball aficionados who gathered for the organization's founding meeting in the Hall of Fame Library in August, 1971. By the end of 1982, SABR membership had risen to 1,800 and the Board decided that a full-time paid administrator was required.

In his three years as executive director before retiring, he saw membership climb to 6,200. Prior to Kachline's appointment, founder Bob Davids had written SABR's bimonthly newsletter and edited the annual Baseball Research Journal as well as most other SABR publications. Once Cliff was named administrative head of the organization, Davids turned those writing and editing chores over to him. Many of the early SABR publications are now regarded as baseball classics and rate as prime collector's items among those who specialize in baseball publications.

Cliff and his wife Evelyn, who handled the SABR financial records and membership rolls from 1975 through 1985, own a home on a two-acre property on the outskirts of Cooperstown. Among their prized possessions are four reddish-orange seats from old Sportsman's Park, the one-time home of the St. Louis Cardinals and St. Louis Browns. The Kachlines have two married daughters: Jeri, who lives in suburban Atlanta, Georgia, and has two boys, and Joyce, who resides in central Illinois and has two girls.

Loserville's Crowded Dead Heat

1951's top AL losers set century marks

Dixie Tourangeau

New York Giant Bobby Thomson's one October swing fifty seasons ago will provide much nostalgic talk in 2001. But going unnoticed, to no surprise, during the course of that campaign, an interesting record was unintentionally set by a half dozen American League hurlers. Coincidentally, over in Thomson's Senior Circuit, three other pitchers nearly set an equivalent mark.

Twenty-first century researchers now have the pleasure of sifting through an entire century's worth of complete "modern baseball" statistics, uncovering oddities and investigating the stories behind them. Such is the case of 1951's "small-time losers" in the AL, who unknowingly combined to set a double record. Neither stat has been approached since.

Through the AL's first fifty years, the pitcher(s) with the most losses each season averaged just over 20. Seventy percent of the time, one pitcher would be the unlucky leader in this category, though in 1924 and 1949 three hurlers shared the unwanted record. Their 17 losses also happened to be the second lowest number. (Sixteen "led" in 1946.)

In 1951, a record six American League hurlers tied for the "honor" by losing a record low 14 contests. They were Cleveland's Bob Lemon (17–14), White Soxer Billy Pierce (15–14), Philadelphia's Alex Kellner (a 20-game loser in 1950, 11–14), Tiger duo Paul "Dizzy" Trout (9–14) and Ted Gray (7–14), and

US park ranger **Dixie Tourangeau** *wrote this story on his day off while watching the five 2001 opening day games on ESPN and the Red Sox blow another Pedro win.*

poor Brownie Duane Pillette (6–14). Lemon's mound mates for the second-place Indians, Early Wynn (20–13) and Mike Garcia (20–13), nearly joined the crowded circle.

Each pitcher took a different route to his 14 losses. Below are some of the practical statistics to compare them by, in addition to the normal differences in the strengths of their respective team offenses and defenses. The "Years" column equals how many 50-inning major league seasons they pitched before 1951. Ages are calculated from start of season.

Player	Age	Yrs	Inn	GS	CG	Ks	ERA	1950	1952
Lemon-R	30	5	263	34	17	132	3.52	23–11	22–11
Pierce-L	24	3	240	28	18	113	3.03	12–16	15–12
Kellner-L	26	2	209	29	11	94	4.46	08–20	12–14
Gray-L	26	3	197	28	9	131	4.06	10–07	12–17
Trout-R	36	12	192·	22	7	89	4.04	13–05	10–13
Pillette-R	28	1	191	24	6	65	4.99	03–05	10–13

Some Particulars—*Cleveland 93–61.* Lemon was 5–5 in June and 9–9 by mid July when he won seven straight games. He finished by losing four of five and had only one start left after losing number 14. Chicago and New York each beat him three times; each AL squad beat Lemon at least once. The Hall of Famer lost 14 games three times in his career and 15 games in 1953.

Chicago 81–73. Pierce started off very well, 7–2 by early June. Then he went 2–7 for a 9–9 record as August began. Already having 14 losses by September

8, the youngster won his final three starts to avoid winning the Loser's Derby. Every team beat Pierce at least once, but the champ Yankees did it five times. He lost 15 twice (rookie 1949 and pennant 1959) and 16 in 1950.

Detroit 73–81. Veteran Trout was 2–2 before losing nine of 10 games through July 4. He didn't pitch much in July and lost one game in August. He then lost his final game on September 29 to Cleveland, placing himself in the Derby. Trout lost to all clubs except New York. Cleveland beat him four times. Trout lost 18 in 1942 and 15 in 1945.

Gray was 3–10 by July 13 and had lost number 14 by September 12. He rallied to defeat Washington and St. Louis to avoid that fifteenth loss. Though Philadelphia didn't beat Gray, the Red Sox did—five times. He lost 17 in 1952 and 15 more in 1953, his last full season.

Athletics 70–84. Kellner was 20–12 as a 1949 rookie but fell to 8–20 the next year—his 20 topped the league. He was 7–8 as August 1951 began, the month in which he lost five straight. Losing his fourteenth game on September 3 to New York put Kellner in a good position to take the Derby but he won three straight to end the campaign. Kellner lost five to New York, and at least once to the six other teams. He was 6–17 in 1954, the A's final year in Philadelphia.

St. Louis 52–102. Playing for the worst team by far, Pillette had 14 losses by August 25, but he managed to avoid the "special" fifteenth in his seven later appearances. In 1954 (10–14), he won the first game ever for the new Baltimore Oriole franchise, but in 1951 his consecutive mid-June complete-game wins over New York and Washington were his only highlights. He defeated Cleveland for his first 1951 win and never lost to them. Chicago beat him four times, New York and Detroit three times each.

Of the three clubs that did not have a pitcher on this small roster, the Yankees managed to take 19 of their 98 victories from the Derby squad, while Boston had 14 of 87 wins and the Senators 10 of 62.

AL facts

From 1952 to the end of the century, the highest number of season losses slowly decreased, dramatically, since 1982. The shortened strike year of 1981 is the only time that 13 losses was the high (2-win rookie Juan Berenguer of Kansas City and Toronto, 7-game Bluejay winner Luis Leal, and 4-win Jerry Koosman with Minnesota and Chicago. In the 1990s, the average highest loss number was 16.

Pedro Ramos of the Washington Senators-Minnesota Twins holds a "loser" record by being top dog four straight years (18-19-18-20, 1958-1961). Bobo Newsom also led the AL in defeats four times but they were far from consecutive. John "Happy" Townsend of Washington (5–26, 1904) and rookie Bob Groom (7–26, 1909) also for Washington, share the single-season high-loss mark, according to *Total Baseball*'s revamped stats for that era. Red Ruffing holds the post-1920 record with 25 losses for the 1928 Red Sox. He added a league high 22 in 1929 for an unchallenged two-season, twentieth-century mark of 47.

NL facts

Over in the National League, the smallest number of defeats to lead the league was 17 until 1958, when Pirate Ron Kline led with 16. The NL leader had 14 losses during the strike years of 1981 and 1994. In 1981, Met Pat Zachry was 7-14, and Padre Steve Mura was 5-14. In '94, Padre Andy Benes was 6-14.

The NL pitchers who tied in that strange year of 1951, were Ken Raffensberger (16–17) of Cincinnati who was 12–17 when September began; teammate Willie Ramsdell (9–17), who was 9–10 on August 3; and Cubbie Paul Minner (6–17), who was 6–11 in mid August with three shutouts—two over Ramsdell. Pittsburgh's workhorse Murry Dickson was 20–16.

In 1952, 1953, and 1954, Dickson led the NL in losses for Pittsburgh and then Philadelphia (19-20-20). Comparing their four-year totals, Ramos (49 wins) tied Dickson (54 wins) with 75 defeats. In 1905, Boston's Vic Willis set the modern National League record with 29 losses. Paul Derringer struggled through 27 for St. Louis (0–2) and Cincinnati (7–25) in 1933, giving us the post-Deadball mark.

Winning Pitcher: Luebbers

Starting pitchers' wins of less than five innings

Jim Storer

Octodber 3, 1999. Dateline—St. Louis.

This was a weird one. Only on the last day of the season could something as truly remarkable as this happen. And, of course, it had to involve the Cubs.

In a meaningless game that had no possible effect on the pennant races, the 67-94 Chicago Cubs visited the 74-86 St. Louis Cardinals, as the Cubs' Steve Trachsel (8-18) took to the hill against the Cards' Larry Luebbers (2-3).

The most amazing event that took place that day was (pick one):

A. Both Mark McGwire and Sammy Sosa homered in the same game.

B. McGwire's homer came against Trachsel, who also gave up McGwire's historic, record breaking sixty-second home run in 1998.

C. Rookie Rick Ankiel picked up his first, and perhaps his only, major league save.

D. None of the above.

The correct answer is "D." The game featured two rain delays and was called after the fifth inning, resulting in a rain-shortened 9-5 win for the Cardinals. Although scoring 14 runs in 4-1/2 innings is impressive enough, even more amazing is that Cardinals' starting pitcher Larry Luebbers was credited with the win for pitching four innings. The Cards' complete pitching line score is repeated below:

	IP	H	R	ER	BB	K	NP
Luebbers, W (3-3)	4	6	5	5	0	1	76
Ankiel S (1)	1	0	0	0	0	1	5

How could Luebbers have been credited with a win for pitching only four innings in a game in which he was the starting pitcher? This surely flies in the face of the immutable rule, learned by all fans in their youth, that the starter must go at least five innings to pick up the win. How many times have we watched a starting pitcher nurse a one-run lead, struggling with one or two out in the fifth inning, as his manager nervously fidgets in the dugout, hoping that he can avoid making that fateful call to the bullpen that will deny his starter a chance for the "W"?

On October 25, 2000, starting pitcher Denny Neagle was pulled with two out in the fifth inning of Game 4 of the 2000 "Subway Series," in favor of an aging David Cone, who had been tragically ineffective all year. Yankees' manager Joe Torre clearly dreaded pulling Neagle, but felt that strategic considerations compelled him to do so at that time. The team's success obviously had to be a higher priority to Torre than the possibility of Neagle's embellishing his career statistics with a World Series win.[1]

The answer to this apparent contradiction is to be found in Rule 10.19 of the Official Rules of Baseball.

Jim Storer *is an attorney and sabermetrician in "small market" Branford, Connecticut. He is a regular contributor to BRJ, and hopes to publish a book on baseball law and economics sometime before the next lockout.*

The part we all know is:

Winning and losing pitcher—10.19 (a) Credit the starting pitcher with a game won only if he has pitched at least five complete innings and his team not only is in the lead when he is replaced but remains in the lead the remainder of the game.

But the arcane and seldom used part of the rule follows immediately thereafter:

(b) The "must pitch five complete innings" rule in respect to the starting pitcher shall be in effect for all games of six or more innings. In a five-inning game, credit the starting pitcher with a game won only if he has pitched at least four complete innings and his team not only is in the lead when he is replaced but remains in the lead the remainder of the game.

So Luebbers qualified for the win because of the exception to the rule regarding a starting pitcher's needing to go five complete innings to qualify for a win: when the game itself is only five innings, the starter need go only four complete.[2]

This got me to wondering whether there were any other exceptions to the rule. There are. Subsection (g) of this rule provides that in "some non-championship games," such as the major league All-Star Game, a starter who pitches "a stated number of innings, usually two or three," may qualify for the win. This scoring rule is commonly used in exhibitions at various levels of play.

I had also heard rumblings that there was recently a time during which a starting pitcher could qualify for a win while pitching less than five innings in a regular season major league game. Yes and no. In recounting the end of the 1990 lockout, Kenneth M. Jennings noted that in the spring of 1990 the players and owners agreed to the following working condition: "Starting pitchers in the regular season's first two weeks could earn a victory by pitching only three or four innings instead of the previously required five,

unless the official scorer deemed they did not pitch effectively."[3]

However, the April 3, 1990, New York Times reported that "The [players and owners], however, did not resurrect the rule modification that would have enabled starting pitchers to receive credit for victories even if they pitched only three or four innings instead of the required five."[4] An examination of the box scores for games played during the first week of the 1990 season also indicates that in no instance was a starting pitcher credited with a win for pitching fewer than five innings in a game that went six or more innings.

Therefore, Rule 10.19 is alive and well. Starting pitchers had better be prepared to go five or more innings if they want to garner a win. Unless, of course, it's overcast and Larry Luebbers is on the mound....

Postscript—On June 1, 2001, in New York, Cleveland Indians' rookie lefthander C.C. Sabathia was credited with a win against the Yankees in a game that was called after 5-1/2 innings due to rain. Sabathia continued the tradition of starting pitchers' poor performances in their wins of less than five innings by allowing a run in each of the four innings he pitched, while yielding four hits and five walks.

Notes:

1. Things ended well for the Yankees as Cone retired the one batter he faced. Neagle fled from the Yankees to the Rockies via free agency two months later.

2. Only two other occasions since 1987 have starting pitchers been awarded wins in starts of less than five innings. On July 20, 1987, the Orioles' Mike Griffin gave up one run over four innings in a rain-shortened 4-1 win over the White Sox. On July 31, 1992, Richie Lewis, also of the Orioles, picked up a win while pitching 4-1/3 innings against the Red Sox. (Lewis was sent to the minors the next day.) The author wishes to thank David Pinto for his research in identifying these two games.

3. K.Jennings, *Balls and Strikes: Moribund Labor Relations in Professional Baseball* (Westport, Conn: Praeger, 1997), p. 15.

4. *New York Times*, April 3, 1990, p. B-13.

Remembering Carl Mays

Think you know this guy?

Kenneth D. Richard

Carl Mays is unfortunately remembered for two incidents. To some, he is remembered as the man who threw the pitch that felled Ray Chapman. To others, he is remembered as the man who lost a suspicious game during the 1921 World Series. He should be remembered for much more.

Mays's career accomplishments from 1915 through 1929 exceed those of all of his contemporaries except Walter Johnson and Grover Cleveland Alexander. He is the forgotten star of his era. Why?

Perhaps it is the albatross created by the Chapman accident. Perhaps it is the allegation first introduced by noted baseball writer Fred Lieb that Mays "threw" a game in the 1921 World Series. Perhaps it was his dour, morose personality. The true reason will never be known. The writers who saw him play and failed to extol his virtues are now gone. The batters who stepped gingerly up to the plate against him have met the same fate. In short, there is no one left to ask.

Let's do the best we can with the information available.

Call him "Sub"—Mays's famous sidearm/underhand motion was his recipe for success. He got so low on his pitches that his pitching hand sometimes dragged along the mound. This was not, however, his natural motion. When he started his pro career, he threw hard with the conventional overhand motion.

That changed in 1913. Mays was in spring training with the Portland club of the Northwest League. His first day of practice was uneventful. The next day, though, he came up lame. He thought a few days off rest would alleviate the throbbing pain, but it did not. In that era, teams had no room for sore-armed pitchers. Mays felt desperate and began to look for ways to compensate.

Finally, he found a way thanks to "Iron Man" Joe McGinnity, who that year was player-manager for Tacoma. McGinnity threw underhand and with ease. Mays decided to give the submarine motion a fling. When he did, he found he was able to whip the ball without pain. For the rest of the season, Mays practiced the new motion an hour a day. He gradually became more proficient and more comfortable with it. He also found that the lower he dropped his arm, the more "action" he got on his pitches. Along the way, he earned the nickname "Sub."

This funky motion undoubtedly provided Mays with an advantage. The underhanded, whip-like arm action gave his pitches a queer spin that allowed them to dip and dive on their flights to the batter. One of Mays's longtime catchers, Muddy Ruel, put it best when he said Mays's pitches took "remarkable shoots, jumps and twists." Mays mastered the submarine motion; he became an excellent control pitcher, though he hit many batters during his career.

Finding hope in Providence—The off-season between 1913 and 1914 was tumultuous for Mays. He

Kenneth D. Richard *is an attorney and tortured Red Sox fan who has yet to forgive traitor Harry Frazee for being the architect of the Yankee dynasty. Ken lives in Cumberland, Rhode Island.*

spent that winter in Portland, with Franklin Pierce Mays, a distant relative and a lifelong mentor. During the off-season, Mays was sold to the Detroit Tigers along with Harry Heilmann. Mays was not pleased with the thought of going to Detroit. Almost before he was able to voice his displeasure, he was released to Providence of the International League. His spirits plummeted, but his ruffled feathers were smoothed when the Providence club sent a contract paying him $300 per month. Paying a man more money in one month than he had ever seen at one time in his life has a way of curing many ills.

During his stay in Providence, Mays was the stopper of the staff, winning 24 games. He helped the Providence club to the 1914 International League pennant. At the conclusion of the season, he moved up to the Red Sox along with a teammate named Babe Ruth. Mays saw no action for the Red Sox during the remainder of the 1914 season.

The motion that earned Carl Mays the nickname "Sub."

The Boston experience—Mays's major league debut came on April 15, 1915, in a relief role in which he picked up the victory. His first start came a few days later against Walter Johnson. Mays lost, 1-0. Despite pitching brilliantly, he left that game in the sixth inning with a bruised foot caused by a slide into home. Returning to the lineup three weeks later, he appeared in 38 games, starting only six. He won six games, and, using modern calculations, collected a league leading seven saves.

The 1916 season started Mays's ascent to the top of the class of starting pitchers. He appeared in 44 games, more than half of which he started. He won 18

games in his split role for the pennant-winning Red Sox. His star continued to rise in 1917 and 1918, when he won 22 and 21 games respectively. Then came the crash of 1919.

Mays's temperament is partly to blame for his troubled 1919 season. He had a reputation as a hothead and a headhunter. Teammates disliked him because he refused to carouse or drink with them. He sulked when things did not go his way and raged at players who made errors behind him, alienating himself even further. Partly, of course, this stemmed from the professional athlete's intense desire to succeed.

Mays's hothead reputation was exceeded only by his reputation as a headhunter, for which he was despised by opponents.

Mays was beset by personal and professional problems throughout the 1919 season. Spring training started on a sour note with a contract squabble. Then, on March 26, he received notice that the house he built for his mother had been destroyed by fire, along with the personal belongings, which he had stored there. Mays had insured the house for only a fraction of its value; the fire ruined him financially. In need of money, he grudgingly signed on the Red Sox' terms.

Baseball offered no solace from this personal tragedy, as he suffered a series of demoralizing defeats. The Red Sox either scored no runs while he was pitching or allowed a slew of unearned runs. With each defeat, Mays became more sullen and more frustrated.

His temper boiled over on July 13 against the White Sox. Chicago scored four first inning runs on Red Sox fielding gaffes. At the end of the second inning, he Mays walked off the mound and shouted that he was not going to pitch for the Red Sox again. He stomped into the clubhouse, tore off his uniform, stormed out, and hopped the next train to Boston. Upon his arrival, he announced to a reporter that he was going fishing. His record was 5-11.

Mays's vacation lasted seventeen days. Red Sox owner Harry Frazee, in the midst of the 1919 version of the salary dump, wanted desperately to peddle Mays so that he could raise some much-needed cash. Five teams (the Yankees, White Sox, Senators, Indians and Tigers) were interested in the AWOL star.

American League president Ban Johnson directed the Red Sox to suspend Mays for his insubordination. Johnson was not about to allow a disgruntled player to essentially demand a trade or sale. Frazee refused. He wanted the money Mays's sale would bring in. Johnson won temporarily, as the interested clubs agreed to back off.

Finally, though, the aggressive Yankees, determined to build a winner, broke ranks. They worked out a deal directly with Mays, almost as if he were a free agent. Yankee co-owner "Cap" Huston then contacted Frazee and agreed upon terms. The Red Sox would receive $40,000, and two pitchers, Allan Russell and Bob McGraw.

Johnson found out about the trade when he read the headlines in the next day's paper. Enraged, he immediately suspended Mays, infuriating the Yankees and the Red Sox in the process.

The league split into two factions. The pro-Johnson group was made up of the Senators, Indians, Tigers, Browns and A's. The Yankees, the Red Sox, and the White Sox (whose owner, Charles Comiskey, hated Johnson for his own reasons), were allied on the other side. Johnson voided the Red Sox-Yankees deal, then called a league meeting to iron matters out.

The meeting only solidified hard feelings. The Yankees were determined to use their new pitcher in the pennant race, and they obtained a temporary injunction against the implementation of Johnson's ruling in each city in which Mays pitched for them. Mays went 9-3 with New York.

The Mays debacle, which spilled into the 1919-20 off-season, effectively ended Johnson's tyrannical rule over baseball. It reminded baseball executives that they had to observe limits to their power if they wanted to retain their control over players. The Mays acquisition helped propel the Yankees to their dynasty—and helped put an end to any hopes that the Red Sox might become the game's dominant club.

Ignominy in New York—Mays's 1920 season was filled with triumph and tragedy. He won 26 games and helped keep the Yankees in the pennant race. New York finished third, three games behind the Indians and only one game behind the second-place White Sox. Mays was the ace of the staff. His .703 winning percentage far exceeded the team winning percentage of .617.

But August 16 became a day that forever changed the baseball world's perception of Mays, and his perception of it. The Indians and the Yankees were in the middle of the hot pennant race when they squared off.

The Indians carried a 3-0 lead into the fifth inning. Ray Chapman, the Indians' regular shortstop, led off the fifth. Chapman was affable, well-liked, and highly regarded by teammates and opponents—the antithesis of Mays. Chapman worked the count to one ball and one strike. Catcher Muddy Ruel called for a fastball low in the strike zone. As Mays reached back to throw, he saw Chapman shift his back foot as if to prepare to lay down a push bunt. Mays did the usual—he changed the location of his pitch to high and tight to make it more difficult to bunt.

Chapman crowded the plate, much like many modern players. For some reason, he froze as the pitch bore down on him. The ball struck him squarely on the left temple, hitting him so hard that it made a crack similar to that of bat hitting ball. The blow caused a fatal double skull fracture.

After the game, Mays sat in front of his locker with his head in his hands, visibly shaken. When he learned that Chapman had died, he became depressed and withdrawn. He later stated that "it was the most regrettable incident of my career, and I would give anything if I could undo what has happened."

Because of his reputation as a headhunter, opponents and fans turned on Mays, calling for his expulsion from baseball. Old nemesis Ban Johnson joined the cry. Mays was never officially punished but, the strain of the incident took its toll. Mays pitched poorly in four of his next six starts, probably costing the Yankees second place and possibly the pennant.

Mays rebounded in 1921 to win 27 games and help lead the Yankees to their first pennant. Mays was far and away the ace of the staff, with a .750 winning percentage for a .641 Yankee club.

The storm clouds returned in 1922, when Mays was only 13-14. Nine of his losses occurred when the Yankees scored two runs or less. Nonetheless, manager Miller Huggins seethed over Mays's losing ways. Huggins's disenchantment was solidified when Mays lost Game 4 of the World Series. The manager's caldron of disenchantment boiled while the weather chilled. During the off-season, Huggins placed Mays on waivers to teach him a lesson. When other clubs tried to claim the pitcher, his name was withdrawn. Mays remained a Yankee, but in 1923 he collected more splinters than wins. He was rarely used, pitched in only 81 innings and won only five games all season. Fred Lieb described the Huggins-Mays feud in his book, *Baseball As I Have Known It*:

> In 1923 Huggins really made Mays suffer. While Carl claimed he was in fine physical condition and that his arm felt as strong as ever, he got almost no work, despite being one of the highest salaried pitchers on the club. Sometimes two or three weeks would go by, and then Huggins would let him finish a losing game.

In Martin Smelser's book *The Life That Ruth Built*, he described Huggins' conduct toward Mays in 1923 as a public shaming. Huggins would not permit Mays to pitch batting practice or even warm up in the bullpen. Catchers were ordered to refrain from catching him. The height of humiliation happened on July 17, when a rusty Mays started a game against the Indians and was allowed to absorb a 13-0 shellacking. The Indians pasted Mays for 20 hits and four walks. This "Huggins show" so disgusted shortstop Everett Scott and first baseman Wally Pipp that they walked off the field during a game. Huggins began telling anyone that would listen that Mays had lost some on the fast one.

Banished to Cincinnati—Huggins's dislike toward Mays knew no bounds. Mays was waived again after the 1923 season. Cincinnati gladly claimed him for $20,000. Huggins took one last jab at him with a letter to Reds president, Garry Herrmann. He acknowledged Mays as one of his best pitchers, saying he did not want Mays pitching against the Yankees (that is why he would only accept inter-league waivers on him). He said he did not want Mays because he was a tough man to handle, and that Herrmann should cut his salary in half because of this. Perhaps the best explanation for Huggins' conduct lies with his character. In *The Life That Ruth Built*, Smelser described Huggins as a brilliant talent evaluator, yet small-minded, mean, and subject to throwing tantrums.

Mays regained his focus for the 1924 season. He won 20 games for the fourth-place Reds, and won a $2,000 raise for 1925. Meanwhile, the Yankees lost the 1924 pennant to the Senators by two games. Mays might well have made the difference in the Bronx.

In 1925, Mays suffered all season with a sore arm and appeared in only 12 games.

Mays returned to health for most of the 1926 season. On September 14, with eight games to go, Mays collapsed during pregame warmup, prematurely ending his season. Earlier in the season, Pirate outfielder Kiki Cuyler hit a vicious line drive off Mays's shin. The blow to the leg had somehow become infected. Without their ace, the Reds were unable to overtake the Cardinals and lost the pennant by two games.

Injuries marred 1927, too. Mays suffered a double hernia and pitched sparingly. When he returned, he had lost the zip off his pitches and was through as a regular starter. He got into only 14 games for the Reds in 1928 (4-1), and though he appeared 37 times for the Giants in 1929 (7-2), 29 of those appearances were in relief.

World Series play—Mays participated in the Series of 1916, 1918, 1921, and 1922 (he rode the bench for the '23 Series). He compiled a mediocre 3-4 record, but he built a 2.20 ERA and permitted only 47 hits in 57 innings.

Mays's role in the 1921 World Series became controversial after the publication of Fred Lieb's history of the Yankees in 1947.

Mays started Game 4 on October 4, and breezed through the first seven innings without allowing a run. In the eighth, he seemed to tire, and lost command of his pitches. With the Yankees leading, 1-0, the Giants' Irish Meusel led off with a triple and scored when the next batter, Johnny Rawlings, singled him home. Frank Snyder laid down a sacrifice bunt that Mays tried to field, when he fell. Snyder was safe at first and Rawlings moved to second. Phil Douglas sacrificed the runners to second and third. George Burns followed with a double that scored Rawlings and Snyder. Mays then retired Bancroft and Frisch, but the Giants emerged from the inning with a 3-1 lead and eventually won the contest, 4-2.

Lieb blew the dust off this "suspicious" game a quarter century after it took place, and it has since haunted Mays's reputation almost as much as the Chapman accident. According to Lieb, a man (unidentified) approached the reporter a few hours after Game 4 and accused Mays of throwing the game. Lieb, accuser in tow, rushed to Commissioner Landis's hotel suite and reported the story to him. Landis hired a detective to investigate and to tail Mays for the remainder of the Series. At the conclusion of the Series, Landis told Lieb the private investigator was unable to corroborate any of the allegations and was unable to observe Mays engaging in suspicious conduct. Mays was cleared by the Commissioner's investigation, but Lieb's publication of this episode has forever sullied his reputation.

Career perspective—Mays was among the top pitchers of his era. He collected 207 wins while compiling a .622 winning percentage. The teams for which he played compiled a winning percentage of .578. Mays's career winning percentage translates into almost 20 more career wins than the average pitcher who pitched for these clubs.

During his tenure, the league batted .272 against the competition, but only .257 against him. The pitchers of this period allowed an average of 3.57 runs per nine innings. Mays's ERA over that period was 2.92.

Mays also consistently ranked in the top five of various pitching categories. His top five rankings are as follows:

1. Twice in saves (by modern calculations)
2. Six times in wins
3. Six times in winning percentage
4. Six times in complete games
5. Four times in fewest hits allowed per game
6. Three times in ERA
7. Twice in shutouts
8. Four times in innings pitched
9. Once in strikeouts
10. Twice in games pitched.

He was clearly among the elite pitchers of his era.

Mays played partly in the Deadball Era and partly during the live ball era. Excluding Walter Johnson and Grover Cleveland Alexander, who were in a class of their own, eight pitchers who spanned similar years are enshrined in the Hall of Fame. The "elite eight" are Stan Coveleski, Red Faber, Jesse Haines, Waite Hoyt, Rube Marquard, Herb Pennock, Eppa Rixey, and Burleigh Grimes. Mays compares favorably with each of these men, and in some cases exceeds their accomplishments.

The elite eight exceed Mays in total career wins, but they also played more seasons. His three career interruptions clearly affected Mays's win total.

On average, Mays had 13.8 wins per season. This figure exceeds Faber's (12.7), Haines's (11), Hoyt's (11.3), Marquard's (11.2), Pennock's (11), Rixey's (12.7). Only Coveleski (15.4) and Grimes (14.2) have higher averages.

Mays's career winning percentage is higher (significantly so in many cases) than that of each of the elite eight. It is three percent higher than Coveleski's .602. It is four percent higher than Pennock's .598, nine percent higher than Haines's .571, ten percent higher than Hoyt's .566 and Grimes's .560, 13 percent higher than Faber's .544, 17 percent higher than Marquard's .532, and 20 percent higher than Rixey's .515.

Mays's ERA far surpasses that of all but Coveleski, whose 2.89 career ERA is slightly better than Mays's. Marquard's 3.08 career ERA is six percent higher than Mays's. Rixey's 3.15 and Faber's 3.15 career ERAs are seven percent higher. Grimes's 3.53 is 17 percent higher. Pennock's 3.60 and Hoyt's 3.59 careers ERAs are 18 percent higher. Haines's 3.64 is a whopping 20 percent higher than Mays's.

Mays was one of the best pitchers of his era, a vital cog for two of the game's early dynasties. He played a role (albeit unwittingly) in shaping baseball's approach to labor and its very power structure. His on-field exploits are shadowed by a bad attitude, terrible tragedy, and what could fairly be called character assassination. But what a fascinating man. What a wonderful career. It is now time to begin the oral tradition—pull up a chair, son. Have you ever heard of Sub Mays? You haven't! Well, listen closely....

Sources:

McGarigle, Bob, *Baseball's Great Tragedy.*

Sowell, Mike, *The Pitch That Killed.*

Lieb, Fred, *Baseball As I Have Known It.*

Smelser, Martin, *The Life That Ruth Built.*

A Tale of Two Hornsbys

A sweetheart back home

Howard Green

If there had been a Pulitzer Prize for batting, Rogers Hornsby would have won several. In 1924, line drives flew off his bat to the tune of .424, best ever for a twentieth-century season. His career average of .358 is second only to Ty Cobb's, and he is invariably called, "greatest of right-handed hitters." He is also often called a number of less pleasant things.

Blunt and independent, Hornsby feuded with St. Louis' Sam Breadon, New York's Charles Stoneham, Boston's Emil Fuchs, Cincinnati's Gabe Paul, and the Bill Veecks—elder and younger—at Chicago and St. Louis. In 1926, with the Cards, became the only manager ever to be dismissed after a World Series championship. He was too blunt-speaking to remain.

In 1953, Puss Ervin, a Fort Worth *Press* columnist, invited me to sit with him and Hornsby at a Texas League game at LaGrave Field. Having heard so much of his rank rudeness, I was hesitant to say much and certainly not to ask baseball questions. However, Hornsby could not have been more cordial. In about the fifth inning, I summoned enough courage to inquire if he thought Stan Musial would hit .400. He replied, "He just might do it. He's damn sure good enough hitter.'"

Around home, Rogers Hornsby seems not to have displayed the prickly attitude that made him so tough for baseball executives to deal with. The late Claude McAden, co-owner and GM of the 1950 Gulf Coast League Galveston White Caps: "I met a different Hornsby to the one I had read about. In baseball he was a Hall of Famer and I, a nobody, but he treated me as an equal." Others had similar memories.

The late attorney Sol Greines, who as a boy captained a team that opposed one led by Hornsby: "Often we were opposing pitchers, he for the team composed of boys living on the east side of North Main against my west side bunch. Rogers never forgot where he came from."

Ed Smith, retired Tarrant County purchasing agent: "My dad and mother grew up with Hornsby and liked him. When my mom died, he flew down from Chicago for the funeral."

The late John Reeves, for twenty years a front office fixture for the Fort Worth Texas League Cats: "Hornsby could handle a team on the playing field better than any manager we ever had. Also, he never smoked or drank—in that respect, a fine example for people of any age."

The late Milton Price, respected minor league executive and assistant to TL president J. Alvin Gardner: "Mr. Gardner thought so highly of Hornsby that he tried to buy the Phillies from Gary Nugent in 1941 and give Hornsby the dual role of manager and general manger. We got outbid."

With the press, Flem Hall remembered Hornsby as a straight shooter: "He never embroidered the facts. I don't think Rogers ever lied to anybody. His personal

---

Howard Green, *the youngest league president in Organized Baseball history, is a longtime SABR stalwart who lives in Fort Worth, Texas.*

habits were circumspect."

The late Walter Morris was a legend in his own time, president and organizer of numerous leagues. At the time Hornsby was growing up, Morris, assisted by Paul LaGrave, was operating the Fort Worth Cats. He had this to say: "As sure as the sun came up, this skinny kid was at the park every day, shagging flies and asking questions. There never was a kid so determined to be a ballplayer. In my many meetings with Hornsby over a lifetime of years, I never saw that 'blunt manner.' I liked him as a boy and as a real man."

Umpire Len Roberts, who would become a National Leaguer, worked the Texas League in 1950 during Hornsby's successful Beaumont season: "Rogers Hornsby was a true gentleman on the field—he never questioned a decision. I don't think there was a dishonest bone in his body."

In addition to Fort Worth and Beaumont, Hornsby also managed Oklahoma City in the Texas League. Owner Jimmy Humphries recalled: "I thoroughly enjoyed Rogers, and he was one of the best, if not the best, manager I ever had. We both enjoyed the ponies."

Turbulent moments often prevailed during the exciting life of Rogers Hornsby, but back home in Texas he left a more positive image than he did in the big league cities of the north and east. But he was, indeed, his own man, and he had the brash confidence of the supremely gifted. This is the fellow, after all, who reputedly said: "I never saw a pitcher I didn't feel sorry for."

Brad Huff

Let Me Count the Ways

High-scoring games may have unique line scores

Ron Visco

In the 1915 World Series between the Boston Red Sox and the Philadelphia Phillies, the second, third, and fourth games all ended in identical scores of 2-1. Remarkably, the Red Sox won each of these games (the Phillies won the first game 3-1). Nonetheless, each of these games was unique.

The final score does not tell us in what innings the runs scored or whether the home or visiting team won. These questions are answered by examining the line score, the inning-by-inning account of the game. For example, here is the line score for the third game:

```
Philadelphia    0 0 1   0 0 0   0 0 0
Boston          0 0 0   1 0 0   0 0 1
```

Examining the line scores for this and the other 1915 games raises the question: Given a 2-1 score, how many line scores could there be? How many ways could those three runs be distributed among the nine innings? We disregard extra-inning games, because then the number (in theory) becomes unlimited.

The team scoring one run may do so in any of its nine half-innings, so we'll say there are nine "ways" to score one run. For the team scoring two runs, there are 45 ways to do so: there are 45 distinct distributions of two runs over nine half-innings. To see this, first count the ways to score two runs assuming that

the first run scores in the first inning: the second run may score in any of nine innings (the first inning on): nine ways under that condition. If the first run scores in the second inning, the second run may score in any of eight innings (the second inning on): eight more ways. And so on, to the case where the first run scores in the ninth; then the second run must also score in the ninth, and that adds one way. So the total ways to score two runs in nine innings is $9 + 8 + 7 + 6 + 5 + 4 + 3 + 2 + 1 = 45$.

The team that scores two runs may be the visiting team or the home team, and the corresponding reverse case for the team scoring one run. The line score from the second game of the 1915 World Series will illustrate:

```
Boston          1 0 0   0 0 0   0 0 1
Philadelphia    0 0 0   0 1 0   0 0 0
```

Imagine Boston as the home team, which would "flip-flop" the line score and create a second way to have a 2-1 game with the same half-inning tallies for each team. Putting it together, the number of ways to get a 2-1 game is $9 \times 45 \times 2 = 810$.

The fifth game of the 1915 series was another dramatic contest, ending 5-4 in Boston's favor. There are dramatically more ways to get a 5-4 score than a 2-1 score. We can use the method above, but other statistical techniques work, too. Let's simply summarize the

Ron Visco *lives in Cooperstown New York, does consulting, and works in the Education Department at the Baseball Hall of Fame. His Email address is: rvisco@stny.rr.com.*

ways for one team to score a given number of runs (up to nine) in a nine inning game.

Runs	Ways
0	1
1	9
2	45
3	165
4	495
5	1,287
6	3,003
7	6,435
8	12,870
9	24,310

Then (with a minor exception noted) we may calculate the number of ways to get a given score: multiply the number of ways given for the run totals in question (say, under 5 and 4), and then double that product (for the home-visitor factor). In the case of the 5-4 fifth game in 1915, take the product of 1,287 and 495, then double that: you get 1,274,132. That's right, there are well over a million ways to get a 5-4 score: over a million different line scores ending in a 5-4 game. The fifth game of the 1915 World Series was one of them.

Two points of clarification should be made. First, if the home team has the lead entering the ninth and therefore does not bat, it has the same effect on counting ways as if zero runs had scored; the calculations are not changed. Second, there does have to be a slight adjustment (which we will not do here) if the score differential is greater than four runs. Consider the example where the final score is 8-2 in favor of the home team. Then we know from the rules of baseball that the home team did not bat in the bottom of the ninth inning; the game would have ended before

that. So we cannot multiply the 12,870 ways (given under 8 runs in the chart) by the 45 ways (under 2 runs) by two. That would overestimate the total ways, since some would be impossible, although that number would be small relative to the total. Note that the visiting team can win 8-2. Of course, 6-2 (for instance) is always possible (under modern rules), since the game could end on a grand slam in the bottom of the ninth.

Let's consider the most complex case offered by our chart above: a 9-8 game. Such a game was played in the great 1947 World Series between the Dodgers and Yankees. There are 24,310 x 12,870 x 2 ways to reach such a score: 625,739,400 ways.

This number of possibilities is almost unimaginable. Think of it this way: Suppose a team of ten (crazy) people works at writing down possible line scores for 9-8 games (without duplication) at the rate of one every thirty seconds. The team is relieved when necessary so that the task continues around the clock, ten people working constantly. It would still take about sixty years to record all the possible 9-8 outcomes. So if you or I were not familiar with the third game of the 1947 World Series, yet tried to guess when the runs were scored, it's unlikely we could do so in our lifetimes.

Certainly, line scores for 1-0 games have been duplicated. Most, though possibly not all, line scores for 2-1 games have occurred more than once. But what about a 5-4 contest? Or any game in which, say, nine or more runs have been scored? Have two such games ever resulted in identical line scores? The author would invite readers to report any such identical outcomes. The results presented here suggest that the vast majority of games with a considerable number of runs will have line scores unique in the history of major league baseball.

From a Researcher's Notebook

BRJ's longest-running feature

Al Kermisch

Taylor Shaffer, brother of the "Orator," shortchanged on playing record

Taylor Shaffer, younger brother of George "Orator" Shaffer, has a short listing in the baseball encyclopedias: Born, July, 1870; Philadelphia Athletics, American Association, 1890. However, I find that Taylor was born in 1864, was 5-foot-7, weighed 155 pounds, and played in the 1884 Union Association with Altoona, Kansas City, and Baltimore.

The encyclopedias say it is a Frank Shaffer who should be connected to those facts. A note I found in the Missouri *Republican* of May 14, 1884, helped clear up the situation. "George Shaffer's brother has joined the Altoona nine. He is said to be as graceful and efficient as the St. Louis right fielder but not quite as hard a batter. The Altoonas have released Cleary Cross and he will return to the Lucas Amateurs. They have also released Shaffer, a Cincinnati player." Clearly, there were two players named Shaffer with Altoona in 1884. The first was released when Taylor was signed.

When the Altoona club disbanded on May 31, its players were transferred to Kansas City. Taylor was released on August 23, and joined Baltimore in early

September. On September 5, the Baltimore *American* stated: "Taylor Shaffer, brother of George, played right field for the Baltimore Unions." Taylor played three games, got only one hit, and was released.

Babe Ruth and Dizzy Dean pitched complete game victories on same day in 1930

On September 28, 1930, the last day of the season, thirty-five-year-old home run king Babe Ruth and twenty-year-old rookie Dizzy Dean, making his major league debut, pitched complete game victories. Dean was brought up from Houston, Texas League, and pitched a three-hitter in a 3-1 Cardinal victory over the Pirates. On that day Ruth had 565 career home runs, and the day before had hit two homers, one a grand slam, off George Earnshaw of the Athletics, in a 10-8 Yankee victory in Philadelphia.

Ruth's 9-3 victory over the Red Sox in Boston was the first time he had pitched in a major league game since October 1, 1921 when he pitched four innings of the second game of a doubleheader against the Athletics. With the Yankees leading, 6-0, he promptly gave up six runs to allow the A's to tie the score. He finally got the win, as the Yankees scored in the eleventh for a 7-6 victory. Ruth's 1930 triumph over the Red Sox was his first complete game in eleven years, since beating Washington for Boston at Fenway park on September 1, 1919.

Al Kermisch *began researching baseball in 1935.*

Earl Weaver carried third base bag from field in 1963

When Pittsburgh manager Lloyd McClendon, after an argument with an umpire this past season, picked up third base and carried it into the dugout, it reminded me of the time that Earl Weaver pulled the stunt when he was managing Elmira, Eastern League, in 1963. In a game at Charleston, West Virginia, on August 25, won by Elmira, 5-4, Weaver was thumbed out of the game by Umpire Fred Branford in the fifth inning, but he stayed on the Elmira bench and in the sixth inning went to third base to continue coaching.

Branford reminded Weaver that he had been put out of the game. Weaver sat down on third base, refusing to leave until the umpire pulled out his watch and threatened to forfeit the game to Charleston. Weaver finally stalked off, taking third base with him. He was fined $100, and Eastern League president Rankin Johnson warned him that the next time he was ordered out of a game he would automatically be suspended.

Bucky Harris and Walter Johnson ignored "unwritten rules" on no-hit games

When Ben Davis of San Diego bunted to break up Curt Schilling's bid for a perfect game last May 28, Arizona manager Bob Brenly criticized Davis for bunting. When Brenly had time to reflect on his actions he realized that he was off base and that San Diego still had a chance to win, but the event sparked comments about "unwritten rules" that supposedly come into play in the late innings of no-hit and perfect games.

Hall of Fame manager Bucky Harris and Hall of Fame pitcher Walter Johnson had no truck with "unwritten rules." In the second game of a doubleheader in Washington on September 19, 1925, Ted Lyons of the White Sox held the Senators hitless for 8-2/3 innings. Despite the fact that the White Sox held a commanding 17-0 advantage, Harris sent veteran Bobby Veach up to pinch hit. Veach asked the manager what he wanted him to do. "You're going up there to hit, aren't you?" replied Harris. Veach stepped to the plate and hit a sharp single to right field, breaking up the no-hitter.

Fast forward to August 5, 1932. Johnson was now managing his old club, which was being beaten, 13-0, by Tommy Bridges, who needed one more out for a perfect game. Johnson took a leaf out of his old manager's book and sent Sheriff Harris, a very good pinch hitter, up to hit for pitcher Bobby Burke. The crowd of 7,000 booed lustily. The Sheriff blooped Bridges' first pitch over second base for a single. Sam Rice, the next batter, grounded out to first baseman Harry Davis and Bridges had to be content with a one-hit shutout.

Johnson said later that he was sorry that Bridges lost his perfect game, but for himself he would not want to be credited with a perfect game if he did not earn it. Sheriff Harris said: "I'm getting paid to hit and he's getting paid to pitch. He never gave me any breaks at the plate. Why should I give him any?"

Time to delete Harry Schafer's fielding records from record book

In *Baseball Research Journal* Number 9, 1980, I pointed out that two fielding records credited to Harry Schafer, Boston National League right fielder, on September 26, 1877, could not be substantiated. Schafer's alleged records were listed in *The Spalding Baseball Record* for 1919, and have been passed on without anyone taking the trouble to check on it. The records in question were for four assists and eleven chances (seven putouts, four assists) in a nine-inning game for right fielders.

I now have more proof that the records were not legitimate. Not only did Schafer not have four assists and seven putouts in that game but the entire Boston outfield had neither a putout nor an assist that day. A "Special Telegram" to the Cincinnati *Commercial*, dated September 26, 1877, stated that "none of the Boston outfield had a chance for a catch." The box score as published in the Boston *Globe* listed the three Boston outfielders—Andy Leonard, left field; Jim O'Rourke, center field; and Schafer, right field, without a putout or assist. It is time to delete Harry Schafer's name from *The Sporting News Record Book*.

Johnny Vander Meer's breakthrough in 1938 not foretold by previous record

When Johnny Vander Meer stunned the baseball world by becoming the first pitcher in major league history to pitch successive no-hitters, my thoughts went back to September 6, 1937, when I was covering International League games in Baltimore. On that day, Syracuse was in town for a Labor Day double-header with the Orioles. Baltimore won both games and the hard-throwing but erratic Vander Meer was the losing pitcher in both games.

In the first game, the Orioles rallied for four runs in the ninth, as Vander Meer gave up the winning run, allowing two hits in one-third of an inning. He started the seven-inning nightcap and again was the loser, 4-0. He gave up only four hits but also walked four batters and was touched for home runs by Ab Wright and Roy Schalk.

Johnny had started the 1937 season with Cincinnati, but after posting a 3-5 record in ten games he was sent to Syracuse where he registered a 5-11 record in seventeen games. In five years in the minors before 1938, Vander Meer had an unspectacular 53-46 record. He still commanded attention on the strength of his 1936 season with Durham in the Class B Piedmont League. Although he did not join the club until June 1, he won 19 games while losing only six. With his blazing fastball, he struck out 295 batters in 214 innings, and *The Sporting News* named him Minor League Player of the Year. The award surprised the baseball experts but after the back-to-back no-hitters the staff of *The Sporting News* certainly deserved to take a bow.

Cleveland's thrilling victory after a 12-run deficit recalled 1925 game

The thrilling come-from-behind, 15-14, victory over Seattle on August 5 was a joy to all baseball enthusiasts around the globe. It was the first comeback from twelve runs behind since the Philadelphia Athletics rallied to win, 17-15, over Cleveland on June 15, 1925.

Six future Hall of Famers were members of the two clubs. The Indians had two: manager-outfielder Tris Speaker and shortstop Joe Sewell. The Athletics had four: outfielder Al Simmons and three rookies—pitcher Lefty Grove, catcher Mickey Cochrane and catcher-pinch hitter Jimmy Foxx. All but Grove took part in the game. Foxx, who was seventeen years old, played in only ten games, nine as a pinch hitter, but he had six hits in nine times at bat.

Following is the play-by-play of Philadelphia's sensational eighth inning:

Chick Galloway drew a walk. Tom Glass flied to Cliff Lee. Max Bishop walked. Jimmy Dykes tripled to the scoreboard, scoring Galloway and Bishop. Bill Lamar's single over second scored Dykes. Byron Speece replaced Walter (Jake) Miller on the mound.

Al Simmons bounced a hit over Bob Knode's head. Frank Welsh singled to right, scoring Lamar. Charlie Berry's single to left field scored Simmons. Carl Yowell replaced Speece on the hill.

Jim Poole walked, loading the bases. Galloway singled to left center, scoring Welsh and Berry. Sammy Hale batted for Glass. Yowell was replaced by George Uhle.

Hale's single took a bad hop over Joe Sewell's head and Poole scored. Hale stole second base. Bishop singled over second. Dykes forced Bishop, Sewell to Fred Spurgeon. Walter French ran for Dykes. Lamar walked. Simmons hit a home run over the roof of the left field grandstand, scoring French and Lamar ahead of him. Welsh flied to Lee. Thirteen runs, nine hits, no errors.

Ripken's mom believed he would make Hall

Early in the career of Cal Ripken, Jr., I was sitting with a friend watching the Orioles take fielding practice before the spring training game that night at Miami Stadium. We were sitting in the Oriole section next to the dugout. The only person nearby was a lady two rows below us. My friend and I were talking about Hall of Fame inductions. Suddenly the lady turned around, pointed to the shortstop position, and said, "And he will be there one day, too." I nudged my friend and whispered: "Did you hear that?" He whispered back: "Don't let it throw you. That's his mother."

I eventually got to know Mrs. Ripken, and was impressed by her baseball knowledge. I remember asking her if she thought son Billy would make the majors. "Yes," she answered. "If you check his record you will notice that he hasn't played too many games, and when he gets more games under his belt I think he will make it." Vi Ripken was right again. A slick fielding second baseman, Billy teamed with his brother for many years. Primarily a second baseman, Billy was also adept at shortstop and third base and finished his twelve-year major league career with a .987 fielding average.

Like This Book? Order More of SABR's Stock

Baseball Research Journal

The **Baseball Research Journal,** the annual publication of the society, features some of the best member research. Articles range from statistical to biographical sketches, plus nearly every other topic in baseball.

*	1975 (112 pp)	
____	1976 (128 pp)	$4.00
*	1977 (144 pp)	
____	1978 (160 pp)	$4.00
____	1979 (160 pp)	$5.00
____	1980 (180 pp)	$5.00
*	1981 (180 pp)	
*	1982 (184 pp)	
*	1983 (188 pp)	

larger format

____	1984 (88 pp)	
____	1985 (88 pp)	$6.00
____	1986 (88 pp)	$6.00
____	1987 (88 pp)	$6.00
____	1988 (88 pp)	$7.00
*	1989 (88 pp)	$8.00
____	1990 (88 pp)	$8.00
____	1991 (88 pp)	$8.00
____	1992 (96 pp)	$7.95
____	1993 (112 pp)	$9.95
____	1994 (112 pp)	$9.95
____	1995 (144 pp)	$9.95
____	1996 (154 pp)	$9.95
____	1997 (144 pp)	$9.95
____	1998 (116 pp)	$9.95
____	1999 (144 pp)	$12.00
____	2000 (144 pp)	$12.00

SABR's Books on the 19th C

Nineteenth Century Stars
____ 1988 (144 pp) $10.00
Bios of America's First Heroes (Non-Hall of Famers)

Baseball's First Stars
____ 1996 (183 pp) $14.95
More Bios, including the Hall of Famers

Base Ball: How to Become a Player
by John Montgomery Ward *(reprint of 1888)*
____ 1993 (149 pp) $9.95

* - out of print

The National Pastime

The National Pastime features articles by members more general in nature, although some volumes are arranged around a theme, as noted below.

*	#1 Fall, 1982 (88 pp)	
*	#2 Fall, 1983 (88 pp)	
____	#3 Spring 1984 (88 pp)	
	19th Century Pictorial	$7.00
____	#4 Spring 1985 (88 pp)	$6.00
____	#5 Winter, 1985 (88 pp)	$6.00
*	#6 Spring, 1986 (88 pp)	
	Dead Ball Era Pictorial	
____	#7 Winter, 1987 (88 pp)	$6.00
*	#8 Spring, 1988 (80 pp)	
*	#9 1989 (88 pp)	
____	#10 Fall, 1990 (88 pp)	$8.00
____	#11 Fall, 1991 (88 pp)	$7.95
____	#12 Summer, 1992 (96 pp)	
	The International Pastime	$7.95
____	#13 Summer, 1993 (96 pp)	$7.95
____	#14 Summer, 1994 (112 pp)	$9.95
____	#15 Spring, 1995 (156 pp)	$9.95
____	#16 Spring, 1996 (144 pp.)	$9.95
____	#17 Spring, 1997 (144 pp.)	$9.95
*	#18 Spring, 1998 (144 pp)	
____	#19 Summer, 1999 (116 pp.)	$12.00
____	#20 Summer, 2000 (132 pp.)	$12.00
____	#21 Summer, 2001 (126 pp.)	$12.00

SABR Review of Books

____	Volume 1, 1986	$6.00
____	Volume 2, 1987	$6.00
____	Volume 3, 1988	$7.00
____	Volume 4, 1989	$7.00
*	Volume 5, 1990	

Baseball Historical Review
____ 1981; Best of the 1972-74 BRJs $6.00

Baseball for the Fun of It
A pictorial looking at the joy of baseball
____ 1997 (92 pp) $14.95

Cooperstown Corner
Columns From The Sporting News *by Lee Allen*
____ 1990 (181 pp) $10.00

Home Runs in the Old Ballparks
____ 1995 $9.95
Listings of top 5 HR hitters in parks no longer in use.

Biographies by SABR

Lefty Grove: An American Original
____ 200 (315 pp) $12.95
Biography of Hall of Fame Pitcher Lefty Grove written by former Sports Illustrated write, Jim Kaplar

Uncle Robbie
____ 1999 (200 pp) $12.95
Biography of Hall of Fame Manager Wilbert Robinson by Jack Kavanagh and Norman Macht

Addie Joss: King of the Pitchers
____ 1998 (141 pp) $14.95
Biography of Hall of Fame Pitcher Addie Joss by Scott Longert

★★★★

The Negro Leagues Book
____ 1994 (382 pp, hardcover) $49.95
____ 1994 (382 pp, limited edit.) $149.95
(Leather bound, slipcase, autographed)

Minor League History Journal
*	Volume 1	
	Volume 2 (54 pages)	$6.00
	Volume 3 (72 pages)	$7.00

Run, Rabbit, Run
Tales of Walter "Rabbit" Maranville
____ 1991 (96 pp) $9.95

Batting
____ 2001 (227 pp) $14.95
The reprinted edition of F.C. Lane's 1925 classic is a compilation of tips and comments from 200 of the best hitters of the early 20th Century.

Memories of a Ballplayer: Bill Werber and Baseball in the 1930s
____ 2001 (250 pp) $14.95
Third base man Bill Werber is the last man alive who traveled with the '27 Yankees. Werber's memories of the players, umpires, managers, and fans of the 1930s take us back to an era long gone.

How to Do Baseball Research
____ 2000 (163 pp) $12.95
A primer on how one goes about researching baseball with ideas, information, advice and techniques that will serve any researcher well

---

Name: _____

Address: _____

City, State, ZIP: _____

Daytime Phone (in case of questions): _____

Send your order to:
University of Nebraska Press, 233 North 8th Street, Lincoln, NE 68588-0255.
Call 1-800-755-1105 weekdays from 8am to 5pm CT
Order on-line at: http://nebraskapress.unl.edu
10/22/01

Book Total	$_____
Shipping charges are $4.00 for the first book and 50 cents for each additional book.	$_____
NE residents, add sales tax	$_____
TOTAL	$_____

Master Card & Visa Accepted

Card # _____

Exp Date _____